THE ELIZABETHAN
UNDERWORLD

Gãmini Salgãdo

SUTTON PUBLISHING

First published in the United Kingdom in 1977 by
J.M. Dent & Sons Ltd

First published in this edition in 1992 by
Alan Sutton Publishing Ltd, an imprint of Sutton Publishing Ltd
Phoenix Mill · Thrupp · Stroud · Gloucestershire · GL5 2BU

First published in paperback in this edition in 1995

Reprinted 1997

British Library Cataloguing in Publication Data

Salgãdo, Gãmini
 The Elizabethan Underworld.
 1. Crime and criminals – England – London
 – History – 16th century
 I. Title
 364'.9421   HV6950.L7

ISBN 0-7509-0976-5

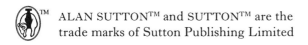 ALAN SUTTON™ and SUTTON™ are the
trade marks of Sutton Publishing Limited

Typeset in 10/13 Imprint.
Typesetting and origination by
Sutton Publishing Limited.
Printed in Great Britain by
WBC Ltd, Bridgend.

Contents

Illustrations

Preface

Like any other period, the Elizabethan age was one of spectacular contrasts. In literature, it produced England's greatest drama as well as some of the most tedious expository writing in the language, in painting the exquisite miniatures of Hilliard and Oliver and wall-paintings of exceptional crudity, in architecture buildings of great elegance together with others of aggressive vulgarity. In social life too these contrasts abound. At one end of the social scale the nobleman was surrounded by grace, luxury and ceremonious dignity. At Cowdray Castle in Sussex in 1595, for example, the daily dinner of Anthony, Viscount Montague was superintended by six ushers and the dishes were solemnly escorted by gentlemen-in-waiting while the household staff stood by in respectful silence; the Clerk of the Kitchen had orders not to allow the scullion to insult the Viscount's joint of meat by turning his back on it while it was roasting. At the bottom of the social ladder there were men, women and children who were glad to pick out a crust of bread from a pile of household refuse. When begging no longer served, many of these turned to thievery and cheating. Such folk far outnumbered the nobility and the gentry and their impact on the national life was great, not because of any decisions made by them but because they made the great of the land, as well as ordinary people, realize that vagabondage had become a feature of social life, a problem that needed to be dealt with.

Though beggars and vagrants had been familiar figures in Europe since the Middle Ages and before, their presence was beginning to be an acute and increasingly urgent problem in England as well as in Europe from the beginning of the sixteenth century. William Harrison in his *Description of England* written in the 1570s observed that 'it is not yet threescore years since this trade [i.e. vagrancy] began: how it hath prospered since that time it is easy to judge, for they are now supposed, of one sex and another, to amount unto above ten thousand persons, as I have reported.' Harrison may have been exaggerating, as he himself seems to be aware; in any case there were no reliable methods of assembling statistics of this kind though a document of 1569 tells us that in that year 13,000 rogues and masterless men were found throughout the kingdom as a result of 'privy watches and searches' ordered by the Privy Council and carried out by parish constables.

As we shall see, it took a long time before the sentiments of fear and hostility aroused by Elizabethan rogues and vagrants softened into constructive compassion. In the meantime they roamed the land in ever increasing numbers, sorely straining the resources of law enforcement which, especially outside London, were feeble enough at best. In addition to appearing in the official records of many civic courts and in similar documents, thieves and vagabonds enlivened much Elizabethan drama with their speech, manners and habits of life, and they inspired some of the most colourful prose of the period. The idiom of writers such as Nashe, Dekker and above all Greene has all the resourceful ingenuity and cheerful indiscipline which were the hallmark of the vagrant's way of life. Most of those who took to the roads were probably driven by dire hardship but once on the highway they showed remarkable resilience in adapting themselves to an existence which was nearly always only a short step away from destitution. In this book I have tried to convey the colour and energy of the underworld, to show how in response to the dire social conditions of the time these thieves, whores, cripples and tricksters developed their own society and hierarchy, their own intricate and elaborate strategies which enabled them to take advantage at every turn of the society from which they had been exiled.

Acknowledgements

My debts include one to Andrea Stadhard for typing the various drafts with a zeal and devotion over and above the call of secretarial duty, to my former colleagues, especially Michael Hawkins and Malcolm Kitch, and my present colleague Ivan Roots for saving me from much gross error (the irreducible minimum which has survived is of course my own responsibility).

Together with the publishers I would like to express my thanks to the following for the right to reproduce copyright material: The Folger Shakespeare Library, Washington (p. 16); His Grace the Archbishop of Canterbury and the Trustees of Lambeth Palace Library (p. 84); British Library (pp. 10, 29, 57, 112, 135, 146, 175); Bodleian Library, Oxford (pp. 2, 4, 8, 12, 18, 23, 38, 43, 47, 50, 68, 81, 97, 99, 122, 124, 126, 137, 151, 155, 158, 160, 163, 179, 194, 200); The Henry E. Huntington Library, California (pp. 25, 76, 88); Ashmolean Museum, Oxford (p. 107); Mary Evans Picture Library (p. 191); Exeter City Library (p. 93); The Master and Fellows, Magdalene College, Cambridge (p. 133).

THE BELMAN
OF LONDON.

Bringing to light the moſt notorious
villanies that are now practiſed
in the K I N G D O M E.

Profitable for Gentlemen, Lawyers, Merchants, Citizens, Farmers,
Maſters of Houſholds, and all ſortes of ſeruants, to marke,
and delightfull for all men to Reade.

Lege, Perlege, Relege.

Printed at London for N A T H A N I E L B V T T E R. 1 6 0 8.

A woodcut from the title-page of *The Bellman of London*. The bellman patrolled the streets calling
the time and guarding citizens against fire and robbery: 'Remember the clocks/Look well to your
locks'

CHAPTER ONE

London–Flower of Cities All

Elizabethen London was livelier, noisier, smellier, probably more dangerous and certainly more colourful than the city we know today. It occupied roughly the area that is now taken up by the City of London. It was the largest city in Europe, ten times as big as its nearest English rivals, Bristol and Norwich; the great boom town of the period. Cradled by the Thames to the south, it was still a walled city on its other sides, though to the north and west it was already spreading beyond the old city walls. At nightfall, when Bow Bell sounded, the huge doors of the city gates were shut and the bellman set out to patrol the streets, calling the hour and guarding the citizens against fire and robbery:

> Remember the clocks,
> Look well to your locks,
> Fire and your light,
> And God give you good night
> For now the bell ringeth.

Aldersgate, Cripplegate, Moorgate, Bishopsgate and Aldgate marked the northern limits of London, while the grim bulk of the Tower guarded the eastern wall. North of Aldgate, where Liverpool Street underground station now stands, was the hospital of St Mary of Bethlehem, the Bedlam to which Londoners took a stroll to entertain themselves with the antics and anguish of madmen. The prisons of Ludgate and Newgate stood at the western entrances and through the bars of Ludgate prisoners begged passers-by for alms.

London's river was its busiest thoroughfare, spanned by a single bridge which was one of the city's glories. Its twenty arches supported a narrow covered way that ran the whole length of the bridge, while the handsome timber framed houses that lined it, the dwellings of wealthy merchants and tradesmen, were much admired by foreign visitors. Another feature of London Bridge which these visitors remarked on were the poles over the gatehouse tower which were adorned by the heads of executed traitors; as many as thirty or thirty-five heads stood rotting at a time while

London Bridge, the only bridge to span the river Thames during Elizabethan times, was one of the city's glories. Lined with the handsome timber framed houses of wealthy merchants and tradesmen, the gatehouse tower was adorned with the heads of executed criminals the wheeling scavenger kites picked greedily at their mouldering flesh. Criminals were also chained to the river bank.

The arches of London Bridge were so narrow that the force of the water made shooting the bridge a risky enterprise, especially at high tide. All but the hardiest spirits preferred to break their river journey at the bridge and take the boat again on the other side. The east-west journey cost about sixpence while it cost a penny to cross from the city to the Surrey bank, to visit the playhouses, the bear-baiting rings or the brothels. Cries of 'Eastward ho!' or 'Westward ho!' rang out along the river and the watermen, a thriving and vociferous community, were not slow to express their feelings if they were insufficiently tipped. The Thames was not only London's busiest thoroughfare but undoubtedly also its cleanest. On the stretch of river bank called the Strand stood the great houses of the nobility, most of them the town houses of bishops before the dissolution of the monasteries. Somerset House, Arundel House, Leicester House—each had its pleasant garden, its terrace and its stairs down to the river.

The broadest of London's streets was Cheapside, which boasted the houses and shops of the goldsmiths 'all in one frame, uniformly builded, four storeys high, beautified towards the street with the goldsmiths' arms', in the words of London's loving chronicler, John Stow. Along the centre of the street, from St Paul's to the Carfax, was an open market with stalls selling all manner of goods from London and the surrounding villages—bread from Stratford, turnips from Hackney, cheese cakes from Holloway, pudding pies from Pimlico, besides more exotic items of merchandise, such as live peacocks and apes. Every important public procession passed through Cheapside and shoddily produced goods were traditionally burnt in public there.

The average Elizabethan certainly needed a strong stomach to cope with the many smells that assailed him every time he went out. Indoors, at least in the great houses, the floors were kept clean with freshly strewn rushes and the air was perfumed with pomanders. Even humbler dwellings would not usually suffer from anything stronger than the smell of stale cooking and smoke. But outside, it was a different matter. Apart from Cheapside and the Strand, London had no real streets to speak of, only narrow tracks which in wet weather were no more than channels of churned-up mud, and in all weathers stank with the slime of generations of filth and garbage daily renewed by the discharge from doors and windows. Only when the plague ravaged the city was anything done about the piles of refuse that stood outside every front door. Each man was then required to burn his own rubbish at least three times a week. For the rest, though in 1563 the Mayor and Council sternly ordered that 'the filthy dunghill lying in the highway near unto Finsbury Court be removed and carried away', the civic authorities were generally content to leave garbage disposal to the kites overhead; the citizen must tread the streets as warily as he could.

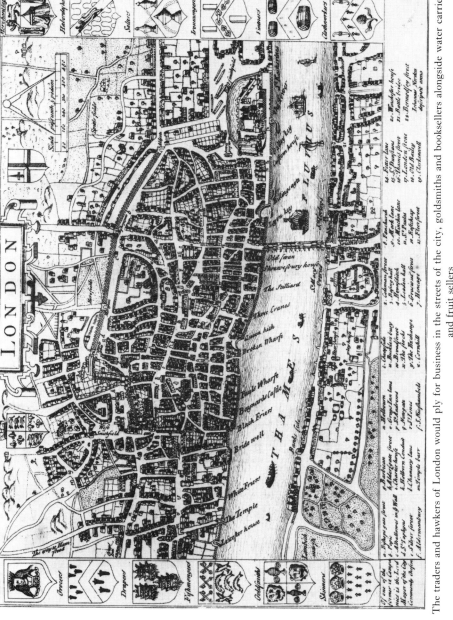

The traders and hawkers of London would ply for business in the streets of the city, goldsmiths and booksellers alongside water carriers and fruit sellers

LONDON–FLOWER OF CITIES ALL

It was just as well for him that London could boast so many gardens and open green spaces. Though the city more than doubled its population during the reign of Elizabeth, the countryside was never very far. Charing Cross was a rural island between the interdependent cities of London and Westminster, fresh water was piped to London conduits from the country near Paddington, there was a real heath at Hampstead. Islington and Highgate were real villages, and the Oxford road, a muddy track leading to Tyburn, began at the village of St Giles, now St Giles Circus. The Londoner could walk along Moorfields, watching the washerwomen lay out their washing, or go hawking where the British Museum stands today, or shoot wild ducks at Islington Ponds. By Thames side near Holborn, Gerrard the herbalist collected his specimens; wild foxgloves grew in Piccadilly ditches. London, the flower of cities all, was compounded of many fragrances.

It was also a city full of sounds and sweet airs. The Elizabethans seem to have been much less inhibited about giving vocal expression to their needs and feelings than their present-day descendants. The river was loud with the cries of the watermen and their clients and on the Surrey side the ballad sellers declaimed with gusto from their wares. Street brawls were common here, especially those involving apprentices whose rallying cry of 'Clubs!' was dreaded by the sober citizenry. It is no coincidence that the district of Southwark, noted for its playhouses, bear and bull rings and 'stews' [brothels] had no less than five prisons—the Clink, the Compter, the King's Bench, the Marshalsea and the White Lyon. 'They care little for foreigners', the Duke of Würtemberg noted in 1592, 'but scoff and laugh at them; and moreover one dare not oppose them, else the street-boys and apprentices collect together in immense crowds and strike to the right and left unmercifully without regard to person; and because they are the strongest, one is obliged to put up with the insult as well as the injury'.

Elsewhere in the city the more peaceable sounds of craft and commerce filled the air. The booksellers stood outside their stalls in Paul's Yard tempting their customers with news of the latest publications, the puppeteers in Fleet Street announced their latest 'motions' above the din of lathes and hammers busily turning out barrels and candlesticks, pots and pans. By eight in the morning the colliers were abroad with their sacks of coal and the chimney sweeps called out 'Sweep chimney sweep mistress, with a hey derry sweep from the bottom to the top, sweep chimney sweep'. They competed for the attention of customers with orange sellers and oyster sellers, hawkers of cures for corns, chilblains and sciatica, fresh water carriers with their yokes and buckets, sellers of fruit, herbs and pies and a hundred others. Something of the noise and bustle of London life is caught in these lines of Ben Jonson, a Londoner born and bred:

5

[I will fetch thee a leap]
From the top of Paul's steeple to the standard in Cheap
And lead thee a dance through the streets without fail
Like a needle of Spain, with a thread at my tail.
We will survey the suburbs, and make forth our sallies
Down Petticoat Lane, and up the Smock-alleys,
To Shoreditch, Whitechapel, and so to St Kather'n's,
To drink with the Dutch there, and take forth their patterns.
From thence we will put in at Custom-house quay there,
And see how the factors and prentices play there,
False with their masters; and geld many a full pack,
To spend it in pies at the Dagger, and Woolsack.

Nay, boy, I will bring thee to the bawds, and the roysters
At Billingsgate, feasting with claret-wine and oysters;
From thence shoot the Bridge, child, to the Cranes i'th'Vintry,
And see there the gimblets [fops] how they make their entry!
Or, if thou hadst rather, to the Strand down to fall,
'Gainst the lawyers come dabbled from Westminster hall,
And mark how they cling, with their clients together,
Like ivy to oak, so velvet to leather.

(The Devil is an Ass, I i. 55–75.)

London, then, was a place of vivid contrasts. There was the contrast between the largest and most crowded city in Europe and the little havens of rural peace within and around it. There was the contrast between the broad and spacious thoroughfares such as Cheapside and the Strand and the miry runnels of mud that served the rest of the city. There was the contrast between the palatial mansions of the nobility along the Strand or the splendid black and white frame houses in Goldsmiths Row and the wretched hovels that were already beginning to scar the city like an eczema. Above all there was the contrast between those who, whether rich or poor, felt more or less secure within the hierarchical society of the time and those who felt themselves exiled from it—discharged soldiers, masterless men, beggars, thieves, whores, vagrants, cripples and tricksters. Not, of course, that these were peculiar to London, but within the city their style of life, their idiom and even their outward appearance were distinctively different from those of their counterparts in the rest of the country. For one thing London offered far greater opportunities for beggary and fraud than the rest of England, and the chances of apprehension were smaller, for the London underworld appears to have had its own security system and intelligence network which were probably more than a match for the rudimentary and quasi-amateur police force which was all the city could boast. Thus Laurence Pickering, whom Greene calls the King of Cutpurses and brother-in-law to no less a personage than Bull the Tyburn hangman, organized weekly meetings of the thieving fraternity at his house in Kent Street where, amidst the general merrymaking, serious items of news were exchanged regarding likely 'prospects' as well as the activities of the law-enforcing bodies. The underworld also had its own special quarters in London where a criminal on the run could find refuge from the hue and cry. One such district was Alsatia, the area between Whitefriars and Carmelite Street, with the Thames as its southern boundary and Fleet Street to the north. Another was Southwark, noted as we have seen, for its stews, as well as other 'safe' southern suburbs such as Newington Butts. The brick kilns of Islington and the Savoy were well-known underworld haunts, as were Whitefriars, Whetstone Park, Ram Alley and St Martins; yet others went by such names as the Bermudas, Damnation Alley and Devil's Gap.

The denizens of such localities emerged by day and by night to practise their wiles on the decent and law-abiding citizens of London, on country 'gulls' and on foreign vistors. They encountered their prospective prey in Paul's Walk, in taverns and 'ordinaries' [eating houses], in bowling alleys, baiting rings and theatres, in brothels and gambling dens. If they were caught in their villainy the punishment was likely to be severe—the least they could expect was to be burned through the gristle of the ear, branded or whipped till their backs ran blood. Their ingenuity was proportionate to the risks they ran, so much so that a whole literature sprang up whose declared purpose was to expose the 'black arts' of London's underworld so that the unwary might take warning. Pamphlet after pamphlet poured from the Elizabethan press warning countryman and Londoner alike of what lay in store for him if he failed to be prudent and vigilant. Whether they saved anyone from loss or disaster it is impossible to say. What is certain is that they present, in scenes of unmatched vividness and colour, the seamy side of life in Elizabeth's London. It is from them that the scenes, characters and incidents that make up this book are largely taken, though we shall also meet the vast and ragged army that roamed the woods and fields of England. The most prolific producer of 'conycatching' pamphlets, Robert Greene, always insisted on the didactic purpose of his writings:

Seeing then such inconvenience grows from the caterpillars of the commonwealth, and that a multitude of the monsters here about London, particularly and generally abroad in England, to the great overthrow of many simple men that are inveigled by their flatteries, I thought good not only to discover their villainies in a dialogue, but also to manifest by an example how prejudicial their life is to the state of the land, that such as are warned by an instance, may learn and look before they leap.

THE

Groundworke of Conny-catching,

the manner of their Pedlers-French, and the meanes
to vnderstand the same, with the cunning slights
of the Counterfeit Cranke.

Therein are handled the practises of the *Visiter*, the fetches
of the Shifter and Rufflar, the deceits of their Doxes, the deuises
of Priggers, the names of the base loytering Losels, and
the meanes of euery Blacke-Art mans shifts, with
the reproofe of all their diuellish
practises.

Done by a Iustice of Peace of great authoritie, who hath
had the examining of diuers of them.

Printed at London by Iohn Danter for William Barley, and are to
be sold at his shop at the vpper end of Gratious streete,
ouer against Leaden-hall, 1592.

Woodcut from the title-page of *The Groundworke of Conycatching*, one of the pamphlets warning
the countryman and Londoner of what lay in store if they were not prudent and vigilant

Whatever we may think of the sincerity of Greene and others like him in their declared intention, they brought to vivid life a part of Elizabethan society which more polite writers either ignored or caricatured.

In some ways St Paul's was the very heart of the city. It was not of course the magnificent domed structure which Wren created, but an older, less elegant but probably just as impressive edifice. In a skyline dominated by spires, Old St Paul's, built during the twelfth and thirteenth centuries, originally rose 520 feet from the ground, though in Elizabeth's reign the steeple was destroyed by lightning. It drew the eye by its size and solidity and within its precincts the teeming life of London could be found in microcosm. It stood at the western end of Cheapside and the churchyard covered twelve-and-a-half acres, with houses and shops crowding the precinct walls. At Paul's Cross, in the centre of the churchyard, important state proclamations were made, as on 20 August 1588 when the news of the Spanish Armada's defeat had been given to rejoicing Londoners. In 1561, a provincial bishop found nothing but faults in every part of the great edifice, or rather in the uses to which it was put: 'The south alley for popery and usury, the north for simony, and the horse fair in the midst for all kinds of bargains, meetings, brawlings, murders, conspiracies, and the font for ordinary payment of money, as well known to all men as the beggar knows his bush'. Elizabethan St Paul's was as much a den of thieves as a house of prayer, for within it there gathered every day not only respectable citizens such as merchants, lawyers and their clients, but a various and colourful collection of crooks, con-men and assorted criminals. 'Paul's Walk' [the middle aisle of the cathedral] wrote John Earle 'is the land's epitome, or you may call it the lesser isle of Great Britain. It is more than this the whole world's map, which you may here discern in its perfectest motion, jostling and turning. It is a heap of stones and men, with a vast confusion of languages, and were the steeple not sanctified, nothing liker Babel'. Servants seeking employment eagerly scanned the notices of vacancies posted up on the 'Si quis Door', so called because such notices usually began with the Latin words *si quis* ('if anyone'). Some of those who crowded round these notices would no doubt be seeking opportunities for burglary rather than employment. Gallants would toss their cloaks carelessly over their shoulders to reveal expensive satin linings while would-be gallants wore theirs more circumspectly to hide frayed elbows.

Among the latter would be cutpurses and pickpockets on the lookout for pickings, while more sophisticated tricksters hoped to gain their reward by elaborate confidence tricks practised on gullible country folk. Often they worked in groups or pairs, one acting as decoy. Even the most down-at-heel crook expected at the very least to cadge his way into a meal here and if he failed even in that would walk up and down by Duke Humphrey's tomb (actually the monument to Sir John

The nave of St Paul's, 'Paul's walk is the land's epitome or you may call it the lesser isle of Great Britain'. Here one could witness the meeting of the respectable and disreputable in Elizabethan society

Beauchamp—Humphrey, Duke of Gloucester is buried at St Albans)—'dining with Duke Humphrey' as it was called—while his more fortunate brethren refreshed themselves at the tavern or ordinary. The world thronged Paul's Walk and one could daily witness there the meeting of the respectable and the disreputable in Elizabethan society—'foot by foot and elbow by elbow shall you see walking the knight, the gull, the gallant, the upstart, the gentleman, the clown, the captain, the apple-squire, the lawyer, the usurer, the citizen, the bankrupt, the scholar, the beggar, the doctor, the idiot, the ruffian, the cheater, the Puritan, the cut-throat'.

In the churchyard outside, men-about-town patronized the shop which sold the fashionable new weed, tobacco, while others listened to a fiery sermon preached from Paul's Cross or browsed among the many bookstalls, sampling the latest satirical pamphlet, ballad or play text. But sometimes the churchyard offered a grimmer and more compelling spectacle. Henry Machyn noted in his diary that on the morning of 10 January 1560, a new pair of gallows was set up at the west door of the cathedral, and, between nine and ten in the morning, two men were hanged; they were left there till four in the afternoon, when the bodies were cut down and taken to St Gregory's churchyard where they were stripped naked by the hangman and tumbled into a common grave. Though the best-known permanent gallows was at Tyburn (near a pleasant brook popular with anglers) Paul's yard was only one of many places in London where temporary scaffolds were set up for executions. Every law day between twenty and thirty condemned men were hanged. In 1606, when the Jesuit Henry Garnet was hanged in Paul's yard, King James expressly ordered that the authorities made sure he was dead before the body was quartered, contrary to the usual practice with executed traitors; an efficient hangman was expected to cut down the body while it was still alive, open the victim's belly, pull out his entrails and show them to him before his eyes closed in death. And yet it appears that quite often the hangman was not a professional but a butcher seconded for the task. John Stow, the antiquary, tells us that he once saw a man hanged outside his own front door.

Anyone in a hurry could avoid walking all round the churchyard by slipping through in one door of St Paul's and out the other. But most of those who entered the aisles of Paul's stayed a while, for business or pleasure. Since every section of society was represented there, it was important for a person to identify his position not only by dress and deportment but by where he walked. Dekker in his *Gull's Horn-Book* (1609) solemnly advises the would-be gallant to avoid the *siquis* door: 'Now for your venturing into the walk, be circumspect and wary what pillar you come in at and take heed in any case, as you love the reputation of your honour, that you avoid the servingman's log and approach not within five fathom of that pillar but bend your course directly to the middle line, that the whole body of the church may appear to be yours.' Likewise, the gallant would be ill-advised to linger too long in the vicinity of Humphrey's tomb which stood in one of the aisles, for fear of being taken for one who 'dines with Duke Humphrey'.

St Paul's was thus a tourist landmark, fashion centre, information and employment exchange and shopping arcade rolled into one. (Divine services were also held there of course, and we know that sermons were preached at Paul's Cross in the churchyard outside.) This made it an ideal centre for underworld activities,

St Paul's Cathedral was a tourist landmark, fashion centre, information and employment exchange
and shopping arcade rolled into one

both those that were performed *in situ* and those that were only put in train there for future execution. The easist prey would of course be the young farmer up from the country for the law term. His dress and gait would set him apart at once, to say nothing of the wide-eyed wonderment with which he gazed at the thronged aisles and the great clock with the figure of the man in the moon. 'In St Paul's, especially in the term-time', writes Greene,

> between ten and eleven, then is their hour and there they walk, and perhaps, if there be great press, strike a stroke in the middle walk, that is upon some plain man that stands gazing about, having never seen the church before; but their chiefest time is at divine service, when men devoutly given do go up to hear either a sermon, or else the harmony of the choir and the organs. There the nip and the foist, as devoutly as if he were some zealous person, standeth soberly, with his eyes elevated to heaven, when his hand is either on the purse or in the pocket, surveying every corner of it for coin.

In St Paul's itself, the countryman was a ready prey for the 'nip' and the 'foist'. One of the simplest ways of relieving him of his money was to fall in a faint before him and cut his purse when he came to help. More difficult 'prospects' required more elaborate methods, often involving collaborative efforts among the cutpurses. Greene tells the story of a foist who heard a farmer boasting to a friend (who had himself just had his purse cut at Westminster Hall) that no nip or foist was agile enough to take *his* purse, which he had about him constantly and which contained £40 in gold. This was too much for the listening foist who determined that the farmer should pay dearly for his boast. (Bartholomew Cokes in Jonson's play *Bartholomew Fair*, likewise, asserts loudly, in the presence of Ezekiel Edgeworth who has already robbed him once, that no one would pick his pocket again.)

The foist returned to his den and reported the matter to his colleagues who all offered to help him in his project. During the next few days several of them tried to wrest the purse from the farmer, but all to no purpose. Finally they decided on a more indirect way of going about it. One of them went to the Counter, the notorious debtor's prison, and, having ascertained the farmer's name and dwelling, entered an action against him for trespass. The advantage of such a move was that the person named could be held in prison till the case came up. Having done this the foist paid two sergeants to arrest the farmer when so instructed. Meanwhile another group of foists followed the farmer from his lodgings to St Paul's, whither the original complainant had brought the arresting officers. As the farmer entered the West door, the sergeants, acting on orders, stepped forward to arrest him. Dumbfounded, the countryman enquired at whose suit he was being arrested. 'At whose suit soever it be' said one of the rogues coming forward, 'you are wronged, honest man, for he hath arrested you here in a place of privilege, where the sheriffs nor the officers have nothing to do with you, and therefore you are unwise if you obey him.' Whether the sheriff's writ did in fact run within the cathedral precincts is not clear. At any rate in the ensuing dispute one of the men drew his sword, another dragged the farmer away from the sergeant, who promptly shouted 'Clubs!' In the ensuing fray one of the foists had no difficulty in picking the farmer's purse and they all disappeared. At last the arresting officers took the farmer to a tavern to talk things over. While they were there, a note came from the man who had laid the original charge requesting the farmer's immediate release as it had been a case of mistaken identity. The sergeants said he was free to go as soon as he had paid them, which the unfortunate farmer was only too happy to do, except that he no longer had any money on him. In the end, his friend, the original victim, had to bail him out.

It was not always greenhorns from the country who fell victim to the wiles of the light-fingered crew at St Paul's. Once a group of cutpurses, having spent a profitless morning in the aisles, were resolved to go off to the playhouse or the bowling alleys in search of prey when one of them roundly declared: 'I have vowed not to depart, but something or other I'll have before I go. My mind gives me that this place yet will yield us all our suppers this night.' One of his companions decided to stay with him and they walked awhile, on the lookout for a likely victim. Eventually a country client came in at the north door accompanied by a lawyer whose open gown disclosed a bulging purple velvet purse at his girdle. The two cutpurses separated and stalked their prospective prey for some time, but their best efforts yielded them nothing, for the lawyer walked in the most open part of the church and kept good guard on his purse. The resolute thief was at his wit's end when he spied his 'trug' [whore] coming up. 'Away' he said to his companion, 'go look you for some other purchase; this wench and I are sufficient for this.' Between them the nip and the trug hatched a plan to get their hands on the lawyer's fat purple purse.

It happened that the woman knew the identity of the lawyer, having helped to 'cozen' him on an earlier occasion, though he did not know her. She walked up and down, taking money out of her own purse, and evidently trying to catch the lawyer's eye. The latter, sniffing profit, quickly dismissed his client, whereupon the woman told him she had been sent by Master So-and-so to obtain the lawyer's advice on a certain matter; the lawyer had no reason to suspect that anything was amiss, especially as he was handed a generous consultation fee. While he was listening to the details of the alleged case, the nip came up from behind and clapped his hands over the lawyer's eyes, playfully crying 'Guess who?', giving the whore ample time to make off with the velvet purse. The nip then took his hands away, full of apologies for having mistaken the lawyer for a friend of his and invited him to partake of some wine by way of amends. The lawyer declined and it was only when, at supper time that evening, he reached for his purse to send for a bottle of sack, that he discovered the loss of his purse with 'seven pound in gold, beside thirty shillings and odd white money'.

The art of the nip and the foist was often combined, as we see, with that of the confidence trickster. Such combination was essential when the booty in view was not a purse but some costly article of apparel, such as a cloak or a chain. There is a fascinating story of a widower intending to remarry who came up to London to buy fine stuffs and jewels for his prospective bride, including a fine gold chain costing £57. Pleased with his purchase, he walked a turn or two in Paul's with the chain about his neck, dismissing his servant on some errand or other. The foists now had their chance. One of them followed the servant, calling him by random names till either he hit on the right one or the servant answered him anyway. 'Are you not the servant of Master So-and-so, my very good friend?' enquired the foist. 'No, sir' replied the servant and obligingly told him his master's real name. 'Ah, to be sure' said the foist, 'Master So-and-so of —— country, is he not?' 'No indeed, sir' came the answer, 'my master hails from ——shire, a mile from the town of ——, near the manor of Sir Thus-and-thus.' (Before we charge the servant with excessive simple-mindedness we should remember that information such as this would be common property for miles round in the country and could hardly be turned to advantage there.) 'Well away' said the foist 'there's a pretty coincidence. I am a blood cousin of Sir Thus-and-thus myself.' He then passed on the information to his accomplice who used it to strike up an acquaintance with the wealthy widower. In the course of the conversation, he persuaded the latter not to display his costly chain so openly, citing several sad cases of gentlemen who had their chains snatched from their very necks. Suitably impressed, the gentleman wrapped the chain up in a handkerchief and put it in his sleeve, boasting: 'If the cony-catcher get it here, let him not spare it.' The 'cony-catchers' were now ready to do just that.

At length they took their leave of each other but the con-man kept an eye on the gentleman from behind a pillar. When he saw that he was about to go, he hurried on ahead and waited just outside the door, while the others followed the widower. As the widower was stepping out the cony-catcher stepped in, his hat shading his face, and stooped to pick up a key he had dropped. For the moment the gentleman could move neither forwards nor backwards.

At this instant one of those behind the victim pretended to recognize the man who had dropped the key as an old enemy and drew his sword shouting 'Do I meet the villain? Nay, he shall not 'scape me now!' The key-dropper looked up and was recognized by the country gentleman as his helpful acquaintance. The gentleman tried to intervene, and was tripped up by the man behind. When he picked himself up, he was poorer by a chain and a handkerchief. His efforts to make the peace

15

John Selman, a notorious cutpurse, who was arrested on Christmas Day, 1611, for cutting the purse
of a servant of Lord Harrington's in the chapel in Whitehall and in the King's presence.
He was executed a year later

between the combatants were naturally of no avail and they all disappeared muttering darkly that honour must be satisfied and that meant a duel to the death. 'Near to St Dunstan's church, the gentleman remembered himself, and feeling his pocket so light, had suddenly more grief at his heart than ever happened to him or any man again. Back he comes to see if he could espy any of them, but they were far enough from him.'

Just as fascinating as the *modus operandi* of the nip and the foist were the various 'lines' they spun to hook their prey. For the libidinously inclined, they were equipped with the Elizabethan equivalent of dirty postcards, a set of French engravings illustrating Aretino's erotic sonnets. They could also tell where the best whores were, according to a person's taste. If avarice was a man's ruling passion, they would have infallible formulae for making gold out of goose-grease. If travel interested him, they were as familiar with all Europe as they were with Paul's Walk itself. They would even offer to accompany one abroad and, if we are to believe Greene, there were young masters up from the country who were happy to pay for the company of such experienced travellers, though he warned that there was an even chance of them absconding with one's money, leaving one stranded in foreign parts.

They had love powders to charm a beloved and potions of poison to make short work of a man's enemies:

> he can frame a ring with such a quaint device, that if a wench put it on her finger, she shall not choose but follow you up and down the streets . . . . He'll teach you . . . to stand on top of Paul's with a burning-glass in your hand, and cast the sun with such a force on a man's face that walks under, that it shall strike him stark dead more violently than lightning.

Among the more sinister wares offered, there was even an early prototype of the mechanical letter-bomb: 'a letter full of needles, which shall be laid after such a mathematical order, that when he opens it to whom it is sent, they shall all spring up and fly into his body as forcibly as if they had been blown with gunpowder'.

One of the remarkable features of the Elizabethan underworld was the high proportion of gentlemen crooks which the profession attracted, especially in London. In a society whose consciousness of differences of dress was so acute that it extended to legislation as to which persons could or could not wear which types of clothing, a good deal of deception depended on being taken for a man of quality when you were not one. This in turn involved not only wearing certain clothes as if to the manner born, but being familiar with the gestures and the style of conversation associated with such clothes. Naturally those who were best able to do this were people who had actually had first-hand experience of it. And there were,

The title-page of *An Arrant Thief* illustrates how the thieves of Elizabethan London were not only beggars and vagrants. A high proportion of the crooks were in dress, manner and style of conversation indistinguishable from the gentlemen of the day

18

in and around the Court, a good many persons who fell into this category. These were the sons of respectable tradesmen or yeoman farmers who, by virtue of education, address, graft or good fortune, had managed to secure some sort of clerical or secretarial appointment with some influential courtier. The distinction between being a servant of state and being a statesman's servant hardly existed at this time on this level. But the court, as so much of the poetry, drama and pamphlet literature of the time attests, was a slippery and treacherous place, where the great man of today could become yesterday's man tomorrow. And the gust that blew him out of office usually swept his minions into the streets of the city too. Here with nothing but their clothes and their educational background to assist them, they turned to the lucrative but hazardous task of cony-catching, or confidence trickery. Thus the swindler who inveigles the narrator to take part in a crooked game of dice in Gilbert Walker's (?) A *Manifest Detection of Dice-Play* (*c*. 1552) passes himself off as an experienced courtier and first gains his victim's attention by the magnificence of his apparel:

> Haply as I roamed me in the church of Paul's now twenty days ago . . . there walked up and down by me in the body of the church a gentleman, fair dressed in silk, gold and jewels, with three or four servants in gay liveries all broidered with sundry colours, attending upon him. I advised [i.e. observed] him well, as one that pleased me much for his proper personage, and more for the wearing of his gear.

Conversely, the cony-catchers spotted their likeliest victims in the form of country farmers and yeomen come to town, perhaps on business, perhaps to consult a lawyer at Westminster Hall, as Robert Greene explains in A *Notable Discovery of Cozenage* (1592):

> The cony-catchers, apparelled like honest civil gentlemen or good fellows, with a smooth face, as if butter would not melt in their mouths, after dinner when the clients are come from Westminster Hall and are at leisure to walk up and down Paul's, Fleet Street, Holborn, the Strand, and such common-haunted places, where these cozening companions attend only to spy out a prey; who, as soon as they see a plain country fellow, well and cleanly apparelled, either in a coat of homespun russet, or of frieze, as the time requires, and a side-pouch at his side – 'There is a cony' saith one.

Apparel often proclaimed a man to his detriment in Elizabethan London.

St Paul's, then, offered the 'cozeners' the opportunity to spy out their prey and the nips and foists the chance to ply their trade. From there, the activities of the vast and various army of cony-catchers radiated outwards towards taverns and ordinaries, playhouses, gambling dens and bowling alleys, and the stews. The goings-on in the last-named are the subject of a separate chapter, but let us here follow the 'sharper' and his victim, the gull, into these other places of entertainment and cozenage. Most of those who went into a gambling hall, bowling alley and, of course, a playhouse did so voluntarily, so there was no problem involved in getting them there. Where, however, the ordinary and the tavern were concerned, the first stage of the operation was to persuade the 'cony' to walk into the cony-catchers' haunt. The simplest way of doing this was for the cony-catcher to greet the intended victim in the street with the pretence that they were both from the same part of the country and had many acquaintances in common: 'Sir, God save you, you are welcome to London! How doth all our good friends in the country? [i.e. county] I hope they be all in health?' With a little ingenuity, enough information could be painlessly extracted from the cony to convince him that he was being saluted by a fellow-countryman. If on the strength of this he accepted the con-man's invitation to step into the nearest tavern and share a pot of ale, he was as good as caught. If the invitation was declined, the cony-catcher simply passed on all the information he had acquired to an accomplice who would try to accost the countryman in the street later on and strike up an even more plausible acquaintance.

If even this method did not work, the cony-catcher sometimes resorted to the old coin-dropping gambit. He dropped a coin where the gull was bound to see it. As soon as he had picked it up, the cony-catcher's accomplice, coming up from behind and pretending to have seen the coin at the same moment, demanded a half-share. If the gull agreed, he was invited to spend it on drink; if he declined, the sharper offered to buy the drink out of his share. If this offer was refused the sharper had to take his half-share and depart and the cony-catchers would have lost half of their investment. But they had not finished with the cony yet.

If the swindlers knew which county their prey came from, one of them would ask him if he would be good enough to take a letter to an acquaintance there, offering the countryman twelvepence for his trouble. The latter willingly agreed, but it turned out that the letter was not quite finished yet. So then they would call in at an ordinary to finish the letter and have a drink.

So much for ways of inducing the fly to come into the parlour. Once there he was fair game for the nip and the foist as well as for the 'punk' [whore] and the 'pimp', and also of course for the numerous expert cheats at dice and cards. Sometimes, however, the object of the trickery could be rather unusual. Two young men were once entertaining the customers at an inn on lute and virginals. During a break in their playing a well-dressed gallant came up, complimented them on their playing and hinted that he might be able to help them to permanent musical employment

Woodcut of a tavern scene. Taverns and ordinaries were the haunt of the nip and foist, the whore and pimp, as well as expert cheats at dice and cards

in a great house. Perhaps, when they had finished playing, they would care to drink some wine with him at a neighbouring hostelry and discuss the matter further?

The young musicians were delighted. They went to the tavern and the gallant ordered a pint of white wine and one of claret which was duly brought in, with two silver goblets (one for each wine, as was the custom when healths were being pledged among friends). After the white wine had been drunk, the gallant took a sip of the claret, said it needed a dash of sugar and rosewater, and went out to fetch it from the back, tossing his cloak carelessly down on the table. That was the last the musicians saw of him or the goblet. They were left to pay for that and for the wine; the cloak he had left behind was tawdry stuff, not worth two shillings. 'Take heed how you drink wine with any such companions.'

There were different grades of ordinary and tavern into which the cony was lured by the cony-catchers, ranging from the fashionably expensive to the squalid. 'At your twelvepenny ordinary' writes Thomas Dekker, 'you may give any Justice of Peace or young knight, if he sit but one degree towards the equinoctial of the salt-cellar, leave to pay for the wine.' These were the exclusive eating houses where men of fashion, or those who pretended to be, took their meals and settled down afterwards to dice or cards. Halfway down the scale came the citizens' ordinary:

21

to which your London usurer, your stale bachelor and your thrifty attorney do resort: the price threepence: the rooms as full of company as a jail, and indeed divided into several wards, like the beds of an hospital. The compliment between these is not so much, their words few: for the belly hath no ears; every man's eye here is upon the other man's trencher [wooden eating dish] to note whether his fellow lurch [get more than his share] or no.

Finally there was the lowest class of ordinary, where the business of eating and drinking was largely incidental to other more dubious occupations. George Whetstone gives a vivid picture of these in *A Touchstone for the Time* (1584):

Now remaineth the discovery of the third sort of these haunts, which are placed in alleys, gardens, and other obscure corners out of the common walks of the magistrate. The daily guests of these privy houses are masterless men, needy shifters, thieves, cutpurses, unthrifty servants, both serving men and prentices. Here a man may pick out mates for all purposes, save such as are good . . . the most of these idle persons have neither lands nor credit, nor will live by an honest occupation: forsooth they have yet hands to filch, heads to deceive, and friends to receive: and by these helps, shift meetly badly well.

As has been noted, dice-play and cards were the principal means by which young gentlemen were induced to part with their money, both at ordinaries and taverns and at gaming houses proper. Cheating or Cheating Law was originally a term specifically applied to the art of using false dice and of skilfully substituting one set of dice for another. There were no less than fourteen different kinds of false dice, with such exotic names as 'A bale of barred cinque-deuces', 'a bale of langrets contrary to the vantage' and 'a bale of gourds with as many high men as low men for passage'. All of these dice were designed to diminish or eliminate the element of randomness in their behaviour without this fact being apparent to the intended victim. Thus some dice were made with some faces slightly longer than others so that certain faces fell more often or more rarely. 'Fullams' were dice loaded with lead or quicksilver, 'bristles' had a short hair set in to one side to prevent that face from lying upwards and 'gourds' were dice hollowed out on one side. 'High men' and 'low men' were dice so-called because of their tendency to turn up high numbers or low ones. The standard compendium on this subject, repeatedly filched from by other Elizabethan and Jacobean popular pamphleteers, is Gilbert Walker's *A Manifest Detection of Dice-Play*.

The art of winning at dice-play, even with the dice loaded in one's favour, was not a simple or easily acquired one. It consisted, essentially, of the sleight of hand required to substitute dice, the quick-wittedness to know which combinations of

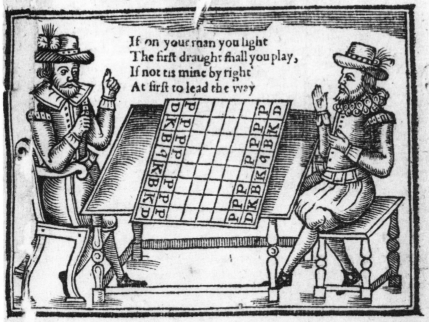

The famous game
of Chesse-play,

Truely difcouered, and all doubts refolued;
So that by reading this fmall Booke thou
fhalt profit more then by the playing
a thoufand

An Exercife full of deligh   rinces, or any
perfon of what q   e foener.

Newly publifhed   A.S. Gent.

If on your man you light
The firft draught fhall you play,
If not tis mine by right
At firft to lead the way

Printed at London for *Roger Iackson*, and are to be
fould at his fhop neere Fleetftreet-Conduit. 1614.

Another fashionable distraction in taverns and gaming houses was the game of Chesse-play. No doubt the sleight of hand and quick-wittedness used in games of dice and cards applied equally here

numbers were likely to be produced by which dice, and the strong-mindedness to resist winning too often (an accomplice was invaluable here). 'Is it a small time, think you?' asks Sir John Harington in *A Treatise on Plays* (*c.* 1597) 'that one of these cunning gamesters spends in practising to slur a die surely, to stop a card cleanly, to lay a pack cunningly? I have heard some (and those no novices in these mysteries) affirm, that the deviser of the set at the new cut (that did cut so many ere the edge was fully discovered,) could not spend so little as a month's earnest study, beating his brains ere he could contrive it,—if it could be done without the help of the devil.' According to Walker, there were flourishing workshops for the manufacture of false dice in at least two prisons, the King's Bench and the Marshalsea, though 'Bird of Holborn is the finest workman, acquaint yourself with him.'

Dice and cards were played not only in private houses, taverns and ordinaries but also in specially licensed gaming houses. The official attitude to this, as to prostitution, was characteristically two-faced. From the beginning of Elizabeth's reign, dice-play and gambling were forbidden by law, along with tennis, bowls and half-a-dozen other sports and pastimes. Instead, the manly and socially useful sport of archery was commended to the patriotic and law-abiding Englishman. Unfortunately, as London's chronicler John Stow sadly records more than once in his *Survey*, archery yards were everywhere being scrapped to make room for dicing houses and bowling alleys. The reason was not far to seek. Gambling was a habit deeply ingrained among Elizabethan Englishmen. Indeed the statute prohibiting it was so constantly broken that in 1576 the Queen granted a patent to Thomas Cornwallis, Groom-Porter (the official responsible for arranging gambling games for the royal household at Christmas time), which recognized 'the inclination of men to be given and bent to the aforesaid pastimes and play, and that secretly or openly they do commonly play, and that no penalty of the laws or statutes aforesaid hath heretofore restrained them'. Henceforth the patent for licensing gambling houses was a lucrative perquisite of the Groom-Porter's office, while official permission to run a gaming house was almost a licence to coin money.

Needless to say, these licensed gambling dens were the favourite haunt of sharpers in search of prey because the latter were already assembled there, ready to be fleeced. Repeated attempts were made to prevent the use of false dice and crooked play, but apparently without success. The making of false dice and cards was reprehensible in the Groom-Porter's eyes not only on general moral grounds but also he held the monopoly for the supply of genuine bales of dice and decks of cards. But not even a stiff penalty (three shillings and fourpence for each offence) stopped the making and selling of false dice.

Anyone who has any experience of the seamy side of the 'entertainment' world in a large city will recognize the shifts and stratagems of Elizabethan dice-cheats. Neither the practitioners nor the victims have changed, except outwardly. Gilbert

Noethrift

Noethrift's a gamester that with cardes and dice
rasts whats his oune, yet's full of Auarice
Of rounds he mackes noe small a ccount he dare
Hazard his soule vpon a dye thats' square,

'Noethrift' the dice-player. Gambling was a habit deeply ingrained among Elizabethan Englishmen

Walker's pious conclusion remains as ineffectually platitudinous today as when it was written more than four hundred years ago: 'The feat of losing is easily learned, and, as I told you in the beginning that the cheaters beat and busy their brains only about fraud and subtlety, so can it not be chosen but give themselves over all to that purpose, and must every day forge out one new point of knavery or other to deceive the simple withal.'

In *A Notable Discovery of Cozenage*, Greene specifically reserves the term 'cony-catching' for cheating at cards, although elsewhere he uses it for confidence trickery generally and the phase probably goes back, in the form 'cunny catching', to swindles involving prostitutes. The paraphernalia used in this form of cheating had all the imagination, energy, sense of timing and understanding of character that we find in the Elizabethan drama itself. In his *Table of Words of Art, used in the effecting these base villainies, wherein is discovered the nature of every term, being proper to none but the professors thereof* Greene introduces the *dramatis personae*. First, there is 'the party that taketh up the cony' called the 'setter'. His activities have already been recounted. The person who begins the actual game is called the 'verser', the accomplice who strays in from the outside and is either persuaded or asks to join in is the 'barnacle', and the booty to be won the 'purchase'. Many Elizabethan card games were extremely simple, often involving only two or three players and opportunities for cheating were abundant. The use of false decks, pricked or nicked cards, cards with a slightly raised edge and the like was common, though the skilful card-sharp often scorned such aids and relied more on the quickness of his hand and his reading of his intended victim's character (but a mirror strategically placed to reflect the other man's cards was always useful). One of the simplest and commonest card games, which Greene called Mumchance-at-cards (and is sometimes called 'Baby-cutting' today) consists simply of the players each calling a card, whereupon the pack is dealt out, the winner being the player whose card turns up first. An elegant swindle based on this which exploits the gull's cupidity as well as his stupidity was that in which one of the swindlers pretended to enlist the gull's support in order to swindle the other. The setter asks the gull to call a card for him against the barnacle and deals so that the cony catches sight of a card which comes near the top of the pack. This works several times, with the cony now staking his own money and the barnacle, though apparently losing, doubling the stakes each time. But at the decisive moment, when the kitty was full to overflowing, something would go wrong, the card named by the cony would not turn up first and all would be lost. Often the trick was played by three men, one of whom turned up apparently drunk at the tavern door and impatient to play at cards. 'If you play among strangers' warns Reginald Scot in his *Discovery of Witchcraft* (1584) 'beware of him that seems simple or drunken; for under their habit the most special cozeners are presented, and while you think by their simplicity and imperfections to beguile them . . . you yourself will be most of all overtaken'.

An entire branch of cozenage, rather fancifully called 'Vincent's Law' by Greene, centred on the bowling alleys, which were the scene of general gambling and disorder. Like gambling houses, the bowling alleys were highly profitable sources of income both for their owners and for the Groom-Porter who licensed them. The sober Puritan's objection to them was vigorously expressed by Stephen Gosson in his *School of Abuse* (1579): 'Common bowling alleys' he exclaimed 'are privy moths that eat up the credit of many idle citizens, whose gains at home are not able to weigh down their losses abroad [i.e. outdoors], whose shops are so far from maintaining their play, that their wives and children cry out for bread, and go to bed supperless oft in the year.' Most of the swindling at bowling alleys was based on collaboration between the players, or 'bawkers', and those who laid bets on the game, the 'gripes'. The players would conduct the game in such a way that to the gull (or 'vincent') looking on, the superior skill of one player was immediately apparent. Then along came a couple of solid-looking citizens who sportingly offered to bet on the game. After that it was simply a matter of timing, encouraging the vincent to stake more by letting him win one or two small sums and setting him up for the kill at the right moment. The many references to bowling by Shakespeare and other Elizabethan dramatists give some idea of the popularity of the sport. An example of the opportunities for cheating open to the expert bowler can be seen in the ironic 'Last Will and Testament of Laurence Lucifer' which is a part of Thomas Middleton's *Black Book* (1604):

> *Item*, I give and bequeath to you old Bias, alias Humphrey Hollowbank, true cheating bowler and lurcher, the one half of all bets, cunning hooks, subtleties and cross-lays that are ventured upon the landing of your bowl, and the safe arriving at the haven of the mistress [i.e. the jade or smaller bowl which was aimed at], if it chance to pass all the dangerous rocks and rubs of the alley, and be not choked in the sound, like a merchant's ship, before it comes half-way home, which is none of your fault, you'll say and swear, although in your own turned conscience you know that you threw it about three yards short out of hand, upon every set purpose.

If the vincent could actually be persuaded to play a game, the professionals always won in the end, either because of their superior skill or because of such strategems as those described by Greene: 'if they fear to have the worse, or suspect the other's play to be better than theirs, then they have a trick in watering of the alley, to give such a moisture to the bank, that he that offers to strike a bowl with a shore [i.e. a curving throw], shall never hit it whilst he lives, because the moisture of the bank

27

hinders the proportion of his aiming.' Many an honest Elizabethan would have been sadly familiar with the experience embodied in the words that Shakespeare's Coriolanus utters symbolically:

> Nay, sometimes
> Like to a bowl upon a subtle ground,
> I have tumbled past the throw.

Cockfighting and bear- and bull-baiting were other popular pastimes which offered scope to the enterprising swindler mainly through 'rigged' wagers.

Apart from taverns, gambling dens, brothels and bowling alleys, the playhouse was the other great venue for the activities of the thief and the cheat. Like Paul's Walk, the playhouse offered opportunities for the cutting of purses and the laying of plots which were to be hatched later at the stews or elsewhere, though, according to Dekker, the private rooms adjacent to the stage were frequently used for activities other than watching the play. In the *Gull's Horn-Book* he writes of 'the Lord's room, which is now but the stage's suburbs . . . those boxes, by the iniquity of custom, conspiracy of waiting-women and gentlemen-ushers that there sweat together, and the covetousness of sharers, are contemptibly thrust into the rear and much new satin is there damned by being smothered to death in darkness'. Unlike its modern equivalent, the Elizabethan playhouse was the scene of bustle and disorder both on and off the stage. Active and vocal participation rather than watchful silence was the usual reaction of the audience to a play that caught their interest. During one that did not, the audience diverted themselves with a variety of activities ranging from dicing and card-playing (sometimes on the stage itself) to swearing, spitting, munching apples, cracking nuts and making passes at the women.

And, of course, cutting purses. A good play served, as far as the nip and the foist were concerned, much the same purpose as a ballad-singer in drawing a crowd together and distracting its attention while pockets were picked. Sometimes the diversion created could be to the disadvantage of the professional. A novice nip, newly arrived in London, went one afternoon to the Red Bull in Bishopsgate, an inn converted to a playhouse. Having fixed on a likely prey he cut his purse, but on going into the stable yard to examine his spoils he discovered that the purse contained only a few white tokens like those sometimes used in gambling, and a broken threepence. Disappointed the young nip returned to the playhouse and recognized a newly arrived couple as one of the best professional pickpockets in town and his female accomplice. He resolved to observe their methods closely and profit from them. He sat next to them when the play started and in a short while saw that the expert nip had cut his first purse, though for the life of him the novice

Das bereits (Tab. XXXIV.) erwähnte Fechthaus zu Nürnberg war auch der Schauplatz der noch in einigen grossen Städten Deutschlands üblichen Hetze. Hier wurden wilde Bären und Stiere durch allerley Mittel und Werkzeuge, welche unsre Tafel zum Theil vorstellt, zum äussersten Grimm gereitzt, und hernach mit grossen und starken Hunden gehetzt. Die Metzger waren es vorzüglich, die an dieser Hetze ihren Antheil nahmen, und ihre Hunde dazu gebrauchten, doch hatten auch andere verwegene Leute, welche mit agiren und ihre Hunde daben versuchen wollten, zuweilen Zutritt. Es fiel aber dieses Vergnügen nicht nur öfters für die Hunde und anhetzenden Personen sehr mißlich aus, und sie wurden getödtet oder beschädigt, sondern es wurden auch zuweilen die Zuschauer dadurch in Schrecken und Angst gesetzt. —— Ehre für Nürnberg, daß diese unsinnige Ergötzlichkeit, die der Menschheit Schande macht, abgestellt ist.

A seventeenth-century woodcut of bull-baiting which was, together with bear-baiting and cockfighting, a popular pastime offering scope to the enterprising swindler

29

could not see how he had done it. The nip with the purse nudged his accomplice in order to pass over the booty but she paid no heed 'being somewhat mindful of the play because a merriment was then on the stage'. Her inattention was to be dearly paid for. Her partner twitched her cloak to draw her attention, but it was not her cloak that he had got hold of but the young nip's. Obligingly the latter put out his hand and received the purse which contained 'thirty seven shillings and odd money'. The grateful novice then himself twitched the woman's cloak who now reached her hand to him, thinking it was her accomplice; for her pains the novice nip passed her the purse he had cut, complete with tokens and broken threepence.

No account of the playhouse and the underworld should leave out the life and nefarious activities of Mary Frith, alias Mary Markham, alias Moll Cutpurse, alias the Roaring Girl. The latter is the title of a play by Middleton and Dekker, performed in about 1607, in which they give a highly idealized picture of a real-life cutpurse, whore, bawd and fence who had several other claims to notoriety. She was, to begin with, one of the pioneers of female emancipation in dress and manners, preferring doublet and breeches as her customary attire and being addicted to swearing and smoking a pipe. In another play where she appears, Nathan Field's *Amends for Ladies* (1612), she is castigated in no uncertain terms by the heroine Grace Seldom:

> Hence lewd impudent
> I know not what to term thee, man or woman,
> For nature shaming to acknowledge thee
> For either, hath produced thee to the world
> Without a sex; some say thou art a woman
> Others a man, and many thou art both
> Woman and man, but I think rather neither
> Of man and horse, as the old centaurs were feigned.

The roaring girl's connection with the theatre does not consist simply in being a character in two plays and being alluded to in several others. There is some reason to believe that she actually appeared on stage herself, in which case she has a claim to be regarded as the first professional actress in England. In 1605 the *Consistory of London Correction Book* records that Mary Frith confessed to having appeared in man's attire (an interesting variation on usual Elizabethan stage practice) at the Fortune, uttering lascivious speeches and singing bawdy songs while playing the lute. Neither of the plays mentioned above are reliable guides to Moll's actual life. Our chief source of information for this is an anonymous pamphlet *The Life and Death of Mrs Mary Frith commonly called Moll Cutpurse* published in 1612. She was born in or about the 1570s in Aldersgate Street, the daughter of a shoemaker,

Moll Cutpurse, 'a notorious baggage that used to go in man's apparel, and challenged the field of diverse gallants'

and died of dropsy in Fleet Street in 1650 when she was well into her seventies. Into her three score years and ten she continued to pack an impressive variety of activities, all of them lucrative and most of them unlawful. During the English Civil War when she was in her forties or fifties she waylaid General Fairfax, shot him in the arm, killed two of his servant's horses and robbed him of his gold. She was pursued by the parliamentary officers quartered in Hounslow, caught at Turnham Green and taken to Newgate. There she was sentenced to hang but bribed her way out, apparently at a cost of £2,000. It is not surprising that she should have chosen a career not normally open to female talent at the time:

> a very torn-rig or rumpscuttle she was, and delighted and sported only in boys' play and pastime, not minding or companying with the girls: many a bang and blow this hoyting procured her, but she was not so to be tamed or taken off from her rude inclinations; she could not endure their sedentary life of sewing or stitching; a sampler was as grievous as a winding-sheet; her needle, bodkin, and thimble she could not think on quietly, wishing them changed into sword and dagger for a bout at cudgels.

Whether appearing in the public playhouse or not, a sense of the theatrical seems to have been second nature to her. Early in 1612, she was sentenced to do penance at Paul's Cross for one of the numerous offences with which her career was chequered. John Chamberlain, a shrewd observer of the Elizabethan scene, recalls the occasion in a letter to his patron Dudley Carleton: 'The last Sunday, Moll Cutpurse, a notorious baggage that used to go in man's apparel, and challenged the field of diverse gallants, was brought to the same place [Paul's Cross], where she wept bitterly, and seemed very penitent; but it is since doubted she was maudlin drunk, being discovered to have tippled of three-quarters of sack before she came to her penance.' A girl after Falstaff's own heart, evidently. Drunk or sober, though, Moll could hold her audience. The preacher of the admonitory sermon on Moll that Sunday was one Radcliffe of Brasenose whose heart was evidently not in his words, since he was something given to venery himself. At any rate Moll gradually took his congregation away from him with her stirring stories of misdemeanours and her heart-warming declarations of repentance and future reformation.

These pious promises were not, however, realized. Less than ten years later, we find Moll named in a complaint of wrongful arrest and imprisonment in the Star Chamber, which was where members of the Privy Council dealt with cases that did not come within the jurisdiction of the ordinary courts. From her own evidence on this occasion, it is clear that she was a figure of considerable influence in the underworld, as people would come to her to try and recover stolen property—a fact which the authors of *The Roaring Girl* used in the portrait of the heroine. 'Heart,' says Moll to a cutpurse in the play, 'there's a knight to whom I'm bound for many favours lost his purse at the last new play i'the Swan, seven angels in't,' and adds, with scarcely veiled menace, 'make it good, you're best; do you see? no more'. Perhaps she had special responsibility for the underworld activities of the playhouse.

Whatever may have been the case with petty criminals on the road, it is clear that the London underworld was highly organized—far more efficiently organized, indeed, than the forces of law and order. Division of labour, demarcation of area, prompt disposal of goods and the systematic training of recruits were as much a part of the underworld as they were of the wealthiest and most respectable livery guild. Moll Cutpurse was actively involved in all these, particularly in receiving stolen goods and in running a school for thieves. The kind of training received by young hopefuls in such an establishment is strikingly reminiscent of that provided by Fagin in *Oliver Twist*, as we can see from a letter to Lord Treasurer Cecil written by William Fleetwood, Recorder of the City of London and scourge of the bawds, vagrants and cutpurses. The letter dates from the year 1585, about the time that Moll Cutpurse was born. It tells the story of one Wotton, once a merchant in a prosperous way of business who, falling on hard times, was driven to keep an alehouse near Billingsgate. When this was closed by the authorities for some misdemeanour, Wotton took to running his school for thieves in the same house. 'He procured all the cutpurses about the city to repair to his said house' writes Fleetwood and goes on to describe the training provided by these professionals:

There was a school house set up to learn young boys to cut purses. There were hung up two devices, the one was a pocket, the other was a purse. The pocket had in it certain counters and was hung about with hawks' bells, and over the top did hang a little sacring bell; and he that could take out a counter without any noise was allowed to be a Public Foister; and he that could take a piece of silver out of the purse without the noise of any of the bells, he was adjudged a Judicial Nipper.

Fleetwood then explains what these terms mean and adds that among the inspiring mottoes adoring Wotton's academy were the following: *Si spie, sporte. Si non spie, tunc steale* and *Si spie, si non spie, lift, shave and spare not* (to lift was to rob a shop or a private chamber and to shave was to steal a cloak, sword, silver spoon or similar smallish article).

What Greene calls the Black Art or the picking of locks did not afford much scope for enterprise or ingenuity. With the right tools it was an easy job to pick locks. But Lifting and its variant of Curbing were another matter. The objects

The Black Art or the picking of locks—
one of the many skills learned in the
underworld

most commonly sought by the 'lift' were those most easily disposed of afterwards—
plate, jewellery and cloth. The lift came into the shop dressed like a country
gentleman, but was careful not to have a cloak about him, so that the tradesman
could see he had no opportunity to conceal any goods about his person. His crony,
the 'marker', who also entered with him had, however, a capacious and specially
designed cloak. The lifter asked to see various bolts of cloth and, when a sufficient
number were scattered about the shop, sent the shopkeeper to fetch some article,
which required a few minutes. This was the signal for the marker to pack as much
as he could into his cloak. At a signal from him, the third party in the operation,
the 'santar', who had been waiting outside walked past the open window of the
shop, apparently in a great hurry. The marker asked him to stop for a minute as he
had a message to be delivered to Master so-and-so. When the shopkeeper returned,
the marker was in earnest conversation with the santar at the open window where
'he delivers him whatsoever the lift hath conveyed unto him'. Even if the theft was
discovered while the lift and the marker were in the shop, their outraged
protestations of innocence carried the day as no stolen goods (or 'garbage' in the
thieves' idiom) were found on or about them.

The 'curber' or 'hooker' got his name from the long curb or hook which he
carried about him (folded to look like a walking staff) and used to hook articles of
clothing from open windows. The 'diver' was one who, instead of using a curb,

employed a small and limber lad to wriggle through the window. The curber, too, had an assistant, called the 'warp', who not only acted as lookout but also received the stolen articles one by one from the curber. Night was the natural time for the curber's activities and striking up an acquaintance with a serving maid was an invaluable way of getting a window left open or learning the exact layout of the rooms in the house. Not every curber was as neatly caught on his own hook as the one mentioned by Greene who was unfortunate enough to try hooking clothes from the porter's lodge of a great house while the porter was wide awake. The porter sent the yeoman of the wine cellar to summon the watch while he let the hooker try to filch various items of clothing. But each time the porter took the article off the hook as it was about to pass out of the window. The exasperated hooker tried sharpening his tools, but to no avail. 'The devil is abroad tonight' he muttered, 'I have such hard fortune.' 'Nay' whispered the yeoman of the wine cellar in his ear 'there is three abroad, and we are come to fetch you and your hooks to hell.'

This kind of thievery naturally presupposed the existence of a system of disposal for the booty. This was provided either by bawds such as Moll Cutpurse for whom acting as a fence was one of many underworld activities or by brokers (or 'broggers') who often carried on a legitimate line of business but were always ready, day or night, not only to buy up stolen goods but to help the lift and the curber in many other ways, such as by providing timely information, alibis or even occasionally accomplices. Any goods which were dangerous to sell in England, because they could easily be identified by the person from whom they were stolen, were sold to Frenchmen or Dutchmen who smuggled them out of the country. At the beginning of the seventeenth century, the Lord Mayor and Aldermen of London were so concerned about the activities of these dishonest brokers that they addressed a letter to Sir Edward Coke, The Queen's Attorney General, commending to him a bill then before Parliament 'for the reformation of abuses practised by brokers in and about the city'. From this it appears that a favourite dodge was to operate in the 'liberties' or areas of London where by historical precedent the Lord Mayor had no legal authority.

The broker moved in the twilight area that extended from downright criminality to shady dealing and sharp practice. We shall conclude our picture of the London underworld by touching briefly on those who, though they kept on the right side of the law most of the time, indulged in activities whose spirit and nature were very much akin to those of the acknowledged underworld. These spanned the whole range of society, from courtiers who used their monopolies and patents in decidedly questionable ways to colliers who repacked coal in long, narrow sacks to make them look larger than they were, with coal at the top and dust inside. First among these was the 'forestaller' or 'engrosser' who reckoned on making a killing either by buying up all of a particular commodity or by dissuading someone from selling at a particular time. These were indictable offences but far less easy to prove than to commit. Closely allied to the forestaller was the 'regrater' who specialized in buying up all the corn, wine or fish at a market in order to sell it at a higher price in the same or a nearby market. Then there was the 'projector' who selflessly wanted to help people make their fortune by investing their money in a project that just could not fail. Some examples of such projects are given by Meercraft in Jonson's *The Devil is an Ass*—dressing dog skins, making wine out of raisins, reclaiming all the submerged land in England and so forth. As for the double-, triple- and quadruple-dealings of lawyers, it would require a whole volume to do them justice. Perhaps the aptest comment on the bond between the underworld and the respectable world of commerce and the professions is that of Gilbert Walker in *A Manifest Detection*:

> Think you the noblemen could do as they do, if in this hard world they should maintain so great a port only upon their rent? Think you the lawyers could be such purchasers [i.e. of land] if their pleas were short, and all their judgments justice and conscience? Suppose ye that offices would be so dearly bought, and the buyers so soon enriched, if they counted not pillage an honest point of purchase? Could merchants, without lies, false marking their wares, and selling them by a crooked light to deceive the chapman in the thread or colour, grow so soon rich and to a baron's possessions, and make all their posterity gentlemen?

As far as the underworld and its ways were concerned, therefore, London offered both a microcosm of the country as a whole and also, somewhat paradoxically, a unique situation. Many sharp practices found in a refined form in the taverns and ordinaries of the metropolis could be matched, in cruder versions, at any country alehouse or fair. On the other hand the manifold activities and the comparatively dense population of the city provided opportunities to the criminal and confidence man on a variety and scale not available elsewhere in the country. Nowhere is this truer than in the sphere of prostitution and allied activities which are the subject of the next chapter.

CHAPTER TWO

The Suburbs of Sin

In Shakespeare's *Julius Caesar* there is a poignant scene where Brutus' wife Portia kneels before her husband begging him to tell her what is troubling his mind. 'Within the bond of marriage' she beseeches him

> Is it excepted, I should know no secrets
> That appertain to you? Am I yourself
> But as it were in sort, or limitation?
> To keep with you at meals, comfort your bed,
> And talk to you sometimes? Dwell I but in the suburbs
> Of your good pleasure? If it be no more,
> Portia is Brutus' harlot, not his wife.

Portia's allusion to 'the suburbs of your good pleasure' is more than a mildly figurative indication of remoteness from her husband's thoughts. To Shakespeare's contemporaries the suburbs of London, particularly that across the river at Southwark, signified, as they had done for centuries, the haunts of pleasure and vice—well organized, well protected and highly profitable—where the sober citizenry as well as their less sober brethren could amuse themselves with playgoing, bear-baiting and whoring before they crossed the water back to the comfort of their walled and gated city.

The association of Southwark with pleasures of various kinds probably goes back to the time when the first Roman legions encamped there in AD 54. When Henry II promulgated his 'Ordinances touching upon the government of the stews in Southwark' in 1161, a large part of Southwark had already been under the control of the Bishop of Winchester for over half a century. That an area which consisted mainly of brothels should have been episcopal property will surprise no one who knows anything about the activities of early prelates or about the equivocal attitude of the Church towards the sin of lust and lechery (not mentioned as such, incidentally, in the Bible). Lechery was certainly a sin, especially if clerics were guilty of it, but prostitution was another matter. 'Suppress prostitution' wrote St

37

A Common Whore

With all thefe graces grac'd,
Shee's very honeft, beauti-
full and chafte.

Writtten By IOHN TAYLOR

Printed at London for *Henry Goffon.* 1635.

John Taylor the Water Poet wrote of the 'Common Whore', that after being banished by Henry VIII, they were replaced by 'a damned crew of private whores'–wives who offered their favours to others simply for the excitement of tasting forbidden fruit

Augustine 'and capricious lusts will overthrow society', while Aquinas was even more explicit: 'Prostitution in the towns is like the cesspool in the palace; take away the cesspool and the palace will become an unclean and evil-smelling place.' It was doubtless in order to prevent such civic catastrophe that the rules laid down by the brothel-keeping bishops and enforceable in a session of the Episcopal Court required, among other things, that stewholders were not to prevent the freedom of movement of single women, nor detain any woman who wished to give up whoring, nor have any married women or nuns on the establishment's strength. Although whores were permitted to sit at the door of the stew, they could not solicit in any way nor 'chide or throw stones' at passers-by.

The attitude of the city fathers towards their unruly neighbour across the Thames was almost as double-faced as the Church's attitude towards prostitution. On the one hand Southwark was the cesspool which drained the city, offering rich pickings to the substantial burghers to whom the Bishop of Winchester farmed it out. On the other hand, the writ of the city did not for a long time run in Southwark with the result that any wanted man had only to cross London bridge or take a boat across the river in order to find a refuge. This uneasy state of affairs continued for several centuries during which repeated attempts were made to control or even shut down the brothels (the latter was ordered in 1546, by, of all people, Henry VIII). Southwark was intermittently raided throughout this period, on the orders of the monarch or bishop and always yielded a large quota of undesirables, often more than the other twenty-five wards put together. But the effort to abolish the stews entirely was no more successful than the similar experiment tried out in Vienna by Duke Angelo in Shakespeare's *Measure for Measure*, and for the same reason suggested by the bawd Pompey Bum in that play: 'Does your worship mean to geld and splay all the youth of the city?' he asks, and on receiving 'No' for answer comments succinctly: 'Truly, sir, in my poor opinion, they will to't then.' He might have added that there was too much money to be made in the stew as well; both Philip Henslowe, the best-known impresario of the Elizabethan theatre, and his son-in-law Edward Alleyn, the most celebrated actor of the day, found brothel-owning as profitable as the theatre. Indeed, as we shall soon see, the connection between the two institutions was more than one of geographical contiguity. When Dryden, late in the seventeenth century, wrote:

> The playhouse is their place of traffic, where
> Nightly they sit to sell their rotten ware

he was alluding to a state of affairs that had already been widely commented on both in the Elizabethan period and earlier.

It was not till 1550 that the borough of Southwark became part of London, a

Frontispiece showing a well-known brothel. 'In the fields and suburbs of the cities they have gardens . . . walled round about very high, with their arbours and bowers fit for the purpose'

privilege for which the civic authorities had to pay Edward VI a thousand marks. The new ward was known as Bridge Ward Without and the first alderman sworn at Whitsuntide. At last the stews truly belonged to London.

The antiquary John Stow explains that Stew Lane near Queenhithe derived its name from 'a stew or hot house there kept'. Originally a stew was a sweating or steam-bath, a legacy from the Roman conquest. The association between such baths and bawdy houses was already common in Rome and was doubtless reinforced by the practice of sweating as a cure for venereal disease. Bankside was Stews' Bank by the time of Henry VIII and stews became a general term for brothels in Elizabethan England.

Until Henry VIII's ban came into force, all brothels had to be painted white and to carry a distinctive sign. One of the most celebrated signs was called The Cardinal's Hat, possibly not because of any particular ecclesiastical connection but because of association in colour and shape with the tip of the male sexual organ. Henry's decree lasted only as long as his life which came to a syphilitic end the following year. In the reign of his son, Edward VI, the brothels were opened again, complete with whitewash and signs, and they continued more or less unmolested under the reign of Mary Tudor, though bawds and strumpets (as well as religious dissidents) continued to be put in stocks and cages. At least this was an improvement on the branding of whores, a piece of legislation which had been introduced for the first time during Henry VIII's reign. (It is ironical that at the same time the great Cardinal Wolsey reportedly had an inscription over one of the doors at Hampton Court which read: 'The rooms of the whores of my Lord Cardinal' while the King himself was said to have had a similar legend over one of the doors of his own palace.) From the first year of Mary's reign, too, comes one of the infrequent instances when a man was punished by being paraded through the streets in a cart for bawdry. Parson Chekyn of St Nicholas in Old Fish Street suffered this indignity for offering the sexual services of his wife 'which he said he had married'.

During the long reign of Queen Elizabeth both the patronage and the punishment of bawds and strumpets continued unabated. The Queen's own cousin Lord Hunsdon had farmed out various holdings in Paris Gardens, a well-known part of Southwark, to Francis Langley owner of the Swan Theatre and others. Prostitution was still a legal offence but it evidently flourished and it was sometimes far from inexpensive, even in terms of money alone. A broadsheet entitled *A Mirror for Magistrates of Cities* published in 1584 tells us that a young man might have to part with 'forty shillings or better' in 'some blind [i.e. obscure] brothel house about the suburbs' for the privilege of 'a pottle or two of wine, the embracement of a painted strumpet and the French welcome [pox]'. If the purveyors of these delights, the whores themselves, were convicted, they faced a variety of punishments, ending with the house of correction at Bridewell. To begin with, the guilty woman was likely to have her head shaven and be carted about the streets with a paper on her forehead announcing her shame and accompanied by the clatter of barbers' basins beaten in mockery. (Barbers had a useful side-line in hiring out vessels on such occasions. In medieval times whores were taken through the town to the accompaniment of music from minstrels, a curious variant, perhaps, on the pagan custom of honouring the gods with music at fertility rituals.)

Hardened offenders were tied to the 'cart's arse' and dragged through the streets, while some were fortunate enough to ride on horseback, like the one Henry Machyn saw on 8 December 1559. Sometimes the poor woman would be whipped at the cart's tail as well as at Bridewell. The whipping at the house of correction was a very formal affair conducted in the presence of the board of governors, though as we imagine the scene we may be reminded of the wild outpourings of Shakespeare's mad king, Lear:

> Thou rascal beadle, hold thy bloody hand!
> Why dost thou lash that whore? Strip thine own back;
> Thou hotly lust'st to use her in that kind
> For which thou whip'st her.

There are many references in the literature of the time to beadles and watchmen being bribed to turn a blind eye to the brothels, one of the bribes being the offer of free sampling. When, in spite of all precautions, those who ran the brothels were caught, their punishment was roughly comparable to that given to the whores themselves, though *unguentem aureum* was an efficacious remedy in softening or avoiding it. It did not, however, help John Holybring, Gent. of Middlesex, in June 1575; he was adjudged 'of evil life, pimp, adulterer, fornicator', for keeping a common brothel in St Giles and was sentenced to be carted from there to Newgate.

Neither punishment nor prohibition had any noticeable effect on the activities of these 'Winchester geese' as the women were called, in acknowledgement of the Bishop's association. In Robert Greene's *A Disputation between a He-Conycatcher and a She-Conycatcher* 'whether a whore or a thief is most prejudicial' (1592) a whore gives a brief account of her activities:

> I removed my lodging and gat me into one of those houses of good hospitality whereunto persons resort, commonly called a trugging-house, or to be plain, a whore-house, where I gave myself to entertain all companions, sitting or standing at the door like a stale, to allow or draw in wanton passengers, refusing none that would with his purse purchase me to be his, to satisfy the disordinate desire of his filthy lust.

In Dekker's *Lanthorn and Candlelight* (1608) a visitor from Hell takes a first look at the suburbs: 'And what saw he there? . . . He saw the doors of notorious carted bawds like Hell gates stand night and day wide open, with a pair of harlots in taffeta gowns, like two painted posts, garnishing out those doors, being better to the house than a double sign.'

The association between the metropolis underworld of thieves, whores, murderers and bawds and the kingdom of hell went back beyond Elizabethan times to the medieval morality drama, and even to the sermon. Most of the Elizabethan pamphleteers and dramatists—Greene, Nashe and Dekker among them—drew on a well-established convention wherein the underworld was the image of hell and vice versa. For Dekker in particular, the whore was the representative figure of the underworld. His solid bourgeois imagination was outraged at the thought of the spiritual and material corruption wrought on the body politic by her activities. In *The Honest Whore* Hippolito delivers a long diatribe on the prostitute which has the effect of converting Bellafront from her evil trade. In the course of it he says:

> for your body
> Is like the common shore, that still receives
> All the town's filth. The sin of many men
> Is within you; and thus much I suppose,
> That if all your committers stood in rank,
> They'd make a lane in which your shame might dwell
> And with their spaces reach from hence to hell.

For Dekker, the question which Greene's thief and whore discuss with almost

Thomas Dekker likened the suburbs and their brothels to 'Hell gates', the whore being the representative figure of the underworld

amiable irony is dark and weighty and can admit of only one answer; the whore is a far more grievous burden to the commonwealth than the thief, for

> there has been known
> As many by one harlot maimed and dismembered
> As would ha' stuffed an hospital.

The threat of venereal disease was of course the visible and ever-present sign of God's retribution on those who made use of the prostitute's abominable services. Venereal disease had been known, though not diagnosed as such, as far back as records went, and even syphilis had probably reached England by the beginning of the fourteenth century, well before Columbus' voyage to the New World, of which it is generally believed to have been an unwelcome by-product.

The prevalence of venereal disease in those times was widespread (several monarchs suffered from it), which is hardly surprising when we consider not only the primitive condition of medicine but the vastly more primitive notions of personal hygiene and public sanitation that went with it. Urine and excrement were regularly emptied into the unpaved streets along with other domestic refuse, while defecation in public places was commonplace; the many 'Rose Alleys' in old English towns nearly always had less to do with fragrant flowers than with the habit of 'plucking a rose'—an Elizabethan euphemism for making water. As for washing and bathing these were very much the exception rather than the rule; there is little doubt that most Elizabethans were dirty and smelly.

The only regular prophylactic against venereal disease was the washing of genitals in vinegar or white wine and 'hard pissing'. In the superior brothels it was usual to have two chamber pots, one for the whore and one which she held for her client to use. In a late seventeenth-century pamphlet called *The Wandering Whore* the writer describes himself as 'pissing . . . till I made it whurra and roar like the tide at London Bridge to the endangering the breaking of my very twatling-strings with straining backwards, for I know no better way or remedy more safe than pissing presently [i.e. immediately] to prevent the French pox, gonnorhoea, the perilous infirmity of burning or getting with child.' As we would imagine, the threat of sexual disease and its ravages casts its monstrous shadow across most of the drama of the time. It underpins Timon's curses against the harlots Phrynia and Timandra in Shakespeare's play:

> Consumptions sow
> In hollow bones of men; strike their sharp shins,
> And mar men's spurring. Crack the lawyer's voice,
> That he may never more false title plead,

Nor sound his quillets shrilly: hear the flamen,
That scolds against the quality of flesh
And not believes himself: down with the nose,
Down with it flat; take the bridge quite away
Of him that, his particular to foresee,
Smells from the general weal: make curl'd-pate ruffians bald;
And let the unscarr'd braggarts of the war
Derive some pain from you: plague all;
That your activity may defeat and quell
The source of all erection.

The usual symptoms of venereal disease—aching bones, decayed noses, baldness—
are explicitly invoked by Timon here. In the ravings of Lear there is a more
universal and even more powerful denunciation of woman's sexual parts as the
source of corruption and destruction:

Down from the waist they are centaurs,
Though women all above:
But to the girdle do the gods inherit,
Beneath is all the fiends';
There's hell, there's darkness, there's the sulphurous pit,
Burning, scalding, stench, consumption; fie, fie, fie!
Pah, pah! Give me an ounce of civet, good apothecary, to sweeten my
    imagination.

In the comic mode, however, Freevill defends the whore's trade and its attendant
risks to the client in these terms in John Marston's city comedy *The Dutch
Courtesan* (1605):

But employ your money upon women, and a thousand to nothing some one of
them will bestow that on you which shall stick by you as long as you live. They
are no ungrateful persons; they will give quit for quo: do ye protest, they'll
swear; do you give them the French crown, they'll give you the French ——
O justus, justa, justum!

Between these two extremes almost every shade of reaction to the dreaded malady
is to be found throughout contemporary drama. The attitude of preachers and
pamphleteers was, predictably, much simpler and more straightforward; the pox
was God's swift and painful punishment for the horrible sin of lechery, a foretaste
on earth of the torments of hell. Philip Stubbes, the Puritan author of *The*

45

Anatomy of Abuses (1583) was wholly convinced that 'there is no greater sin before the face of God than whoredom' and gives us a comprehensive list of its dread consequences:

> for besides that it brings everlasting damnation to all that live therein to the end without repentance, it also bringeth these inconveniences, with many more: *videlicet*, it dimmeth the sight, it impaireth the hearing, it infirmeth the sinews, it weakeneth the joints, it exhausteth the marrow, consumeth the moisture and supplement of the body, it rivelleth the face, appalleth the countenance, it dulleth the spirits, it hurteth the memory, it weakeneth the whole body, it bringeth it into a consumption, it bringeth ulcerations, scab, scurf, blain, botch, pocks, and biles; it maketh hoar hairs and bald pates; it induceth old age, and, in fine, bringeth death before nature urge it, malady enforce it, or age require it.

Even this compendious catalogue of catastrophe is insufficient to satisfy Stubbes' religious revulsion. For one thing, it has plainly failed to turn young people away from the horrible sin, for 'it is so little feared in Ailgna [i.e. Anglia], that, until everyone hath two or three bastards apiece, they esteem him no man (for they call a man's deed); insomuch as every boy of twelve, sixteen or twenty years of age, will make no conscience of it to have two or three, peradventure half a dozen several women with child at once.' Stubbes advocates a very short way indeed with whoremongers:

> I would wish that the man or woman, who are certainly known, without all scruple or doubt, to have committed the horrible fact of whoredom, adultery, incest, or fornication, either should drink a full draught of Moses' cup, that is, taste present death (as God's word doth command, and good policy allow); or else, if that be thought too severe, . . . then would God they might be cauterized and seared with a hot iron on the cheek, forehead or some other part of their body that might be seen, to the end the honest and chaste Christians might be discerned from the adulterous children of Satan.

Fortunately, except for a brief period from 1513 onwards, the savagery urged by Stubbes was not found in England. The usual punishment for adultery was to make the guilty party stand outside a church in a white sheet, holding a white wand, before the service for three consecutive Sundays, which, according to Stubbes, 'doth rather animate and embolden them to the act than fear them from it'. Still, he consoles himself grimly that those who considered that the pleasures of whoredom outweighed its hazards had other penalties in store for them: 'they who

'The Batchelor's Triumph', from the Roxburghe ballads. Prostitutes were often found in taverns as well as their own brothels. They frequently joined with the tricksters and thieves to dupe an unsuspecting prey

think it such sweet meat here, shall find the sauce sour and styptic enough in hell'. By way of foretaste of such penalties, Stubbes repeats a popular story of a seventy-year-old haberdasher called Brustar (or Rasturb as Stubbes insists on calling him) who was burned to death together with a woman he had bailed out from Bridewell while they 'were playing the vile Sodomites together in his chamber', though we are not told how the writer came by this last detail since, on Stubbes' own admission, Brustar was fully clothed when he was found dead.

Although Southwark, and the Bankside in particular, was the principal brothel district of London, there were of course other areas within the city which were also the recognized habitation of prostitutes. Turnbull Street was one such area and Milford Lane in the Whitefriars district another. Shakespeare's Falstaff refers to the first and a couplet by Henry Savile to the other:

> In Milford Lane, near to St Clement's steeple
> There lived a nymph, kind to all Christian people.

One of the seventeenth-century Roxburghe ballads introduces us to other areas of London where the seeker after pleasure may find what he is looking for:

In Whitecross Street and Golden Lane
Do strapping lasses dwell,
And so there do in every street
'Twixt that and Clerkenwell.
At Cowcross and at Smithfield
I have much pleasure found,
Where wenches like to fairies
Did often trace the ground.

Finally, in *Pierce Penniless His Supplication to the Devil* (1595) Thomas Nashe refers to 'our unclean sisters in Shoreditch and the Spittle [Spitalfields], Southwark and Westminster' whom he piously commends to the devil.

We see therefore that statutes, cartings and whippings notwithstanding, the pleasure business flourished vigorously in Elizabethan London. As mentioned earlier, the playhouse was a favourite prelude to the brothel, either as a place of assignation or as an appetizer for later pleasures. In *Skialetheia* (1598) we read of a citizen:

Who coming from the Curtain, sneaketh in
To some odd garden, noted house of sin

and ten years later, as another poem, *The Court of Conscience*, tells us, things had not changed:

Towards the Curtain then you must be gone,
The garden-alleys paled on either side;
If it be too narrow walking, there you slide.

The Curtain was one of the earliest of the London theatres. Within three years of its opening in 1576, Stephen Gosson was publicly accusing the playhouse of being no more than an ante-room for the brothel. In his *The School of Abuse* (1579) he writes:

For they that lack customers all the week, either because their haunt is unknown, or the constables and officers of their parish watch them so narrowly that they dare not quetch [i.e. stir], to celebrate the Sabbath flock to theatres, and there keep a general market of bawdry. Not that any filthiness in deed is committed within the compass of that ground, as was done in Rome, but that every wanton and his paramour, every man and his mistress, every John and his Joan, every knave and his queen, are there first acquainted and cheapen [i.e bargain for] the merchandise in that place, which they pay for elsewhere as they can agree.

Gosson may exaggerate slightly, but there is little doubt that he was generally right. The connection between theatres and whore-houses ran all the way from prostitutes and clients to their managers and owners. Most theatre owners— Henslowe, Alleyn, Longley, Aaron Holland and others—were brothel owners too. Alleyn's wife, who was Henslowe's stepdaughter, was carted along with some others in 1593, though it may have been for failing to shut down a brothel during the plague rather than for being a whore or bawd herself. At any rate, in Alleyn's letter which is our source for this information, he expresses regret that she had been 'made to ride in a cart by my Lord Mayor's officer'.

The gardens and garden-alleys were not always part of the professional establishments. There is a well-documented tradition at this time of enthusiastic amateurs offering serious competition to the professional prostitutes. The latter would have been mainly women of the poorer classes, especially the wives and daughters of the dispossessed rural poor who found their way to London and took the line of least resistance in order to obtain a reasonably comfortable livelihood. The wives of solid citizens, on the other hand, offered their favours to others than their husbands presumably not so much for money (though this was not unknown) but for the excitement of tasting forbidden fruit. The point is neatly put by John Taylor the Water Poet:

> The stews in England bore a beastly sway
> Till the eighth Henry banished them away.
> And since the common whores were quite put down
> A damnéd crew of private whores are grown.

An insider's view of the same phenomenon is offered by Punk Alice, 'mistress o' the game', as she berates Judge Overdo's wife in Jonson's *Bartholomew Fair*:

> A mischief on you, they are such as you that undo us and take our trade from us, with your tuft-taffeta haunches! . . . The poor common whores can ha' no traffic for the privy rich ones; your caps and hoods of velvet call away our customers, and lick the fact from us.

And much of the mischief was done, apparently, in the garden-alleys earlier referred to, and the pleasure houses erected therein. According to the indefatigable Stubbes 'some of these places are little better than the stews and brothel houses were in times past'. Corsica, in Massinger's play *The Bondman*, boasts 'I have a

Frontispiece of *The Wits*. The theatres and brothels of London were closely linked, most owners of the former also owning the latter. Some theatres, it was claimed, acted as a front, or even an ante-room, for brothels

coach and a banqueting-house in my orchard, where many a man of honour has not scorned to spend an afternoon'. Stubbes is even more forthright:

> In the fields and suburbs of the cities they have gardens, either paled or walled round about very high, with their arbours and bowers fit for the purpose. And lest they might be espied in these open places, they have their banqueting-houses with galleries, turrets, and what not else therein sumptuously erected: Wherein they may (and doubtless do) many of them play the filthy persons. And for that their gardens are locked, some of them have three or four keys apiece, whereof one they keep for themselves, the other their paramours have to go in before them, lest happily they should be perceived, for then were all their sport dashed. Then to these gardens they repair when they list, with a basket and a boy, where they, meeting their sweethearts, receive their wished desires. These gardens are excellent places, and for the purpose; for if they can speak with their dearlings nowhere else, yet there they may be sure to meet them, and to receive the guerdon of their pains: they know best what I mean.

These resorts of pleasure were used by the light-heeled or bored citizen's wife as well as by the superior type of courtesan. There are several cases on record like that of the haberdasher Middleton who in 1550 was arraigned along with his wife for letting both her and their daughter, as well as a ten-year-old serving maid, have carnal relations with one Nicholas Ballard, gentleman. In the previous year Bishop Latimer in a sermon had thundered against parts of London where the law was helpless against lechery: 'and there men do bring their whores, yea, other men's wives, and there is no reformation of it.' Captain Knockem in *Bartholomew Fair*, alluding to the then fashionable habit of having one's own coach, says: 'Every pettifogger's wife has 'em; for first he buys a coach that he may marry, and then he marries that he may be made cuckold in't; for if their wives ride not to their cuckolding, they do them no credit.' For the woman's point of view we may turn to the fourth gossip in Samuel Rowland's *Crew of Kind Gossip* (1609):

> There are kind gentlemen, some two or three,
> And they indeed my loving kinsmen be,
> Which will not see me want, I know it, I:
> Two of them at my house in term-time lie,
> And comfort me with jests and odd device,
> When as my husband's out-a-nights at dice.
> For if I were without a merry friend,
> I could not live a twelve month to an end.

The picture that emerges, therefore, is one of comprehensive sexual intrigue, both professional and otherwise, spanning all classes of society from the courts and great houses to the stews and the streets. Outwardly the velvet-hooded matron may have looked respectably different from the 'frail sisterhood' with their nearly bared breasts, painted nipples and satin-and-taffeta finery, but they were sisters under the skin, if the moralists and the popular pamphleteers are to be believed; and their opinion is corroborated by many court records.

A brief outline of some of the tricks of the professional harlot's trade may fittingly conclude this survey of the stews. In addition to the disputation between the whore and the pickpocket as to which does the most harm to the Commonwealth, Robert Greene also produced an authoritative account, in *A Notable Discovery of Cozenage* (1592), of the wiles of whores and their keepers. He divided his analysis into two parts: the 'Sacking Law' and the 'Crossbiting Law'. The distinction was often hard to draw, but broadly speaking sacking referred to the business of straightforward prostitution and crossbiting to the various forms of swindling, threat and blackmail commonly associated with it. Greene introduces quasi-technical terms for the parties involved in both sacking and crossbiting. Thus we have the 'apple-squire' or male bawd, the 'crossbiters' and the 'simpler', being the villains and the victims respectively, and the 'commodity' or 'traffic', the whore herself. The crossbiters are pithily characterized:

> there are resident in London and the suburbs certain men attired like gentlemen, brave fellows, but basely minded, who, living in want, as their last refuge, fall unto this crossbiting law, and to maintain themselves either marry some stale whore, or else forsooth keep one as their friend . . . . These, when their other trades fail . . . then, to maintain the main chance, they use the benefit of their wives or friends to the cross-biting of such as lust after their filthy enormities.

Interestingly enough, it is difficult to say exactly whether Greene was thinking of amateurs or professionals, though the reference to 'some stale whore' seems to indicate the latter.

The commonest crossbiting trick, and one still practised today, was the outraged husband gambit, where the crossbiter stormed in to catch the whore and the simpler *in flagrante delicto* and demanded that his marital honour be exorbitantly satisfied. 'This is but an easy cozenage' Greene concludes, but apparently no less effective for that. Another common trick was for the whore to pick the gull's purse in a tavern, pass it at a convenient moment to the waiting crossbiter and, when the loss was discovered, offer herself willingly if reproachfully to be searched.

A more imaginative variation of the crossbiter's art was where the crossbiter

Bare-bosomed women at table. 'First we feign ourselves hungry, for the benefit of the house, although our bellies were never so full. . . . And let him be sure every dish is well sauced, for he shall pay for a pippin-pie that cost in the market fourpence, at one of the trugging houses eighteenpence'

pretended to be an apparitor or servant of the Court of Arches, the ecclesiastical court in which cases of adultery were tried. Having ascertained the identity of a citizen who had frequented a woman not his wife or even got her with child, he would inform the man that a charge had been laid against him, whereupon 'the party, afraid to have his credit cracked with the worshipful of the City and the rest of his neighbours, and grieving highly his wife should hear of it, straight takes composition with his cozenor for some twenty marks'. Where the woman in the case was herself respectably married, there was additional income to be obtained by threatening her with proceedings as well.

It hardly needs to be said that the Elizabethan version of the clip-joint was a thriving and lucrative institution. Nan, the whore in Greene's *Disputation*, is refreshingly candid as she recounts the entertainment offered a prospective client once he has been persuaded to enter the door of a brothel or 'pick-hatch' (so called because of the hatch-door set with metal spikes to discourage sudden intruders such as officers of the law):

But if he come into a house, then let our trade alone to verse upon him, for first we feign ourselves hungry, for the benefit of the house, although our bellies were never so full, and no doubt the good pander or bawd she comes forth like a sober matron, and sets store of cakes on the table, and then I shall fall aboard them, and though I can eat little, yet I make havoc of all. And let him be sure every dish is well sauced, for he shall pay for a pippin-pie that cost in the market fourpence, at one of the trugging houses eighteenpence.

Part of the profits were doubtless used on overheads, for there is ample evidence as to the splendour and elegance of English courtesans dressed for duty. Here is Greene in *A Notable Discovery*: 'Oh, might the justices send out spials in the night! They should see how these streetwalkers will jet in rich-guarded gowns, quaint periwigs, ruffs of the largest size, quarter-and-half-deep, gloried richly with blue starch, their cheeks dyed with surfling water—thus are they tricked up, and either walk like stales up and down the streets, or stand like the devil's *si quis* at a tavern or ale-house.' It is difficult to say whether the vigour that informs Greene's outburst is due to moral indignation or civic pride.

Attention naturally focuses on the stews of London because they were the most notorious of the day and because the few other English towns of the time were merely pale imitations of London as far as the suburbs and their activities were concerned. But it is worth casting a brief glance at the itinerant whore or 'bawdy basket', whose chief function was to go from house to house selling pins and other trifles and spying out possible sites for burglary by her male accomplice. But the bawdy basket was not averse to augmenting her earnings by prostitution when the opportunity offered. The opportunities for crossbiting were necessarily limited in her case, though the incident recounted later (p. 132) by Harman, of how a bawdy basket and an 'upright man' extorted money from a lame beggar, will give some idea of the scope of their activities which were generally small-time and run-of-the-mill, relying more on the brute strength of their male accomplices than on any native wit or imagination.

These qualities are well illustrated by Greene's story of how one particular whore duped a foist or pickpocket. The foist had lately arrived from the country and was known to be doing a thriving trade in and around Westminster Hall where many country folk and others came to see lawyers. He had £20 sewn into his doublet so that, try as they might, none of the city pickpockets could rob him of it. But the young whore undertook to do it and succeeded in the following manner. She struck up an acquaintance with the foist who took her to supper in a tavern and after the meal was eager for further intimacies. Suspecting that she was a professional, he enquired how much she charged; 'she held it scorn she said, to set a salary price on her body'. The foist thereupon put 10s in his pocket (though his doublet still contained the £20) and they returned to the whore-house and 'went straight to bed by leave of Dame Bawd'. At about midnight came a rap on the door and a group of men entered, apparently a search party sent out by Justice So-and-so (and here they named a Justice known for his severity towards pickpockets) to search for a Jesuit and other suspected persons. The foist, seeking to escape, took the whore's advice and locked himself, naked as he was, in a closet. When the watch came into the room they refused to believe the woman when she said she had been sleeping alone, for there plainly on the bed were the imprints of two bodies. They also discovered the doublet and hose. The whore wept and begged for mercy telling the men it was her husband. The watch quite properly disbelieved this, pointing out that if this was so, there would have been no need to have denied it in the first place. When the bawd was questioned, she admitted that she had let the room to a man and a woman but denied all further knowledge of the couple, saying they had claimed to be married. The watch was now convinced that some notorious villain was hiding in the closet and made as if to break it open. But the bawd entreated them not to do so, giving them her word that she would produced the man in the morning. This did not satisfy the watch who seized the doublet and hose and also took the whore away with them, promising to come for the man in the morning. When they had left, Dame Bawd let the foist out of the closet and insisted on holding him till the morning. The foist begged her to give him a blanket to wrap himself in till he got back home. Reluctantly she let herself be persuaded to loan him a blanket in return for the surety of the foist's gold ring. It only remains to be added that the 'watch' were of course accomplices of the whore and the bawd and acting according to the plan previously hatched by the former.

Neither denunciation by moralists, nor social reforms, nor periodic raids by the authorities, nor the dreaded scourge of the pox made any real impression on Elizabethan brothels, in Bankside or elsewhere. Then, as now, they flourished on the very doorstep of the booming and respectable city because they answered a widely felt social need and because a lot of people in high places stood to make a lot of money from them. The elaborate nature and ingenuity of the devices adopted by whores to entice their victims may be explained partly as a love of complicated intrigue for its own sake and partly as a by-product of being in a highly competitive business. Though some of the tricks are, as we have noted, still in use in clip-joints all over the world, most of them have a splendid extravagance which is part of what we mean by the epithet Elizabethan.

CHAPTER THREE

The Fun of the Fair

The scale of Elizabethan life was much smaller than ours. Not only were there fewer people and smaller towns, but the routine of daily life did not usually involve mingling with large groups. The biggest regular gathering in which an ordinary man or woman was likely to take part was the weekly church congregation, but in most parishes this would rarely exceed a hundred souls. Outside London the Elizabethan's only experience of large crowds would be at harvest festivals and May games, great weddings, markets and fairs. Of these the last were the most common and usually the biggest.

Today, almost everywhere in England the life of the fairground has shrivelled to a couple of big wheels, a candy floss vendor and assorted mechanical and other devices for taking money expeditiously. It needs a real effort to imagine a time when a fair was the centre of social and commercial life—a combination of employment exchange, market-place, amusement arcade, sports arena, theatre, music hall, restaurant and casino—to mention only some of the more reputable entertainments and activities available. In *Far From The Madding Crowd* Thomas Hardy painted a bright and lively picture of a hiring fair of the sort that survived well into the nineteenth century. To such fairs in Elizabethan times would flock all those who were tired of tramping the roads in constant fear of parish searches and gaols, offering their services in return for a bed of straw, a suit of clothes and their daily bread and ale. Often they received no pay at all, but the security of being attached to a master meant a great deal in a society where, unless one belonged somewhere, life could be 'poor, nasty, brutish, and short'.

One way of proving that one 'belonged' was, as we have seen, to carry a passport or warrant but, if a person did not have a genuine passport, he could obtain the next best thing, at a price, from the many pedlars who frequented fairs and carried on a thriving trade in forged papers. In the spring of 1590 Arthur More appeared before the Justices in Essex on suspicion of being a vagrant. His original story was that he had come into Essex from Norfolk a week earlier, having arrived in Dover in March after military service in the Low Countries. He was accompanied by one John Grene and their joint licence, apparently delivered in the Netherlands, was

A forged passport. Passports were very important in a society where unless one 'belonged' somewhere life was very hard. As a result, there was a thriving trade in forged passports, especially at fairs

drawn up by the clerk of the Captain's band and signed and sealed by a Captain Herington. Close examination, however, revealed that the passport had been made at Saffron Walden by John Crofts, a discharged soldier, and the seal added by Kit Miller, a pedlar who was a familiar figure at fairs, in his canvas breeches and Spanish leather jerkin slashed at the sides. Miller had made other passports for both More and Grene, whose real name turned out to be Thomas Hastings. Both men had met the pedlar at Chelmsford fair where, in addition to forging passports, Miller lent money to vagrants, to be repaid with interest out of the proceeds from their thefts at the fair and elsewhere. Miller's charge for a passsport was twelvepence. If this was beyond a client's means, there was a crippled tailor, Thomas Elms, in nearby Dedham, who could do one complete with seals at the bargain price of twopence. Elms's handiwork, however, was not quite good enough to keep him out of trouble when he forged a passport for Robert Buck, sawyer; he was convicted and imprisoned for two days in the village cage, wearing around his head a paper with the inscription: 'For counterfeiting of passports.'

Civic authorities were usually opposed to fairs because they attracted vagrants and often led to breaches of the peace. On the other hand, they brought in money to the owner of the land on which the fair was held, usually the lord of the manor. Disputes arising from accusations of horse-stealing were a common cause of brawling, as occurred in 1556 at St James' Fair at Thremhall Green, on the main London–Cambridge road near Bishops Stortford. The fair was held annually on St James's day (25 July), despite the opposition of the local authorities, as the land belonged to Lord Rich's manor of Hatfield. This same Lord Rich, as we shall see presently, also owned, among much else, the land on which was held each year the most ancient and famous fair in England.

Breaches of the peace at fairs were not always caused by vagrants, thieves or drunks. Sometimes the fair was a convenient area for the continuation of quarrels that had arisen earlier between local residents. At Hedingham fair (also held on St James's day) in 1569, Edward Glassock, gentleman, of Castle Hedingham attacked Robert Cockrell, a husbandman of Great Maplestead, with a sword and buckler. Some weeks earlier, while Cockrell was driving his cart, Glassock had apparently beaten him over the shoulder with a cudgel, saying 'Take thee that!' Cockrell had defended himself with his whip but the gentleman had lain in wait for him near his house armed with a long pike and Cockrell would have been killed if he had not taken shelter under his horse. At Hedingham fair murder would have been done but for people who forcibly parted the combatants. One of these public-spirited townsfolk, George Stroud, had the misfortune to be turned on by both Cockrell and Glassock. He managed to beat down their weapons and parted them three times, only to be arrested and put in the stocks by the constable who arrived on the scene. We can well understand the feeling behind the petition which speaks of this concluding episode as 'contrary to equity and justice'; it is frustrating not to know what happened to the principals in the dispute.

Fairs were held mainly during the summer and early autumn, though there were exceptions such as Newport Cold Fair which was held in November and was well known as a centre for horse-dealing and horse-stealing. Some fairs were more or less universally recognized as thieves' carnivals. The largest of these was Holyrood fair held at Durrest near Tewkesbury in Gloucestershire. Here, according to a knowledgeable contemporary, a thieves' market was held each night at which anything could be bought, from a stallion to a pair of 'stampers' [shoes]. At dawn the stolen goods disappeared and less suspect mechandise was put on display. The sturdiest rogue was chosen lord of the fair and proceedings concluded with a pitched battle involving all concerned. A similar event was a feature of the fair at Braintree, held each September and providing a display centre for the twin clothing towns of Braintree and Bocking. Festivities included a fight between the youth of the two towns. Perhaps it was local loyalty that led a thief at this fair in

1566 to make off with five bolts of cloth from a *London* man's booth.

The two largest fairs in England were those at Stourbridge, near Cambridge, and St Bartholomew's, at Smithfield. Both were protected by royal charters which were centuries old by the time of Elizabeth I. Bartholomew Fair was older by about a hundred years and is much more fully documented, both with actual records and through Ben Jonson's sprawling, zestful, larger-than-life dramatization of it. As we make our way through Bartholomew Fair with Jonson and others as our guide, we can capture something of the feel and flavour of all Elizabethan fairs where for a day or more the underworld mingled with the more respectable orders of society. For the most part we shall stay within the spacious and colourful limits of the great London fair but we shall pause occasionally to note some interesting points of difference between this and other fairs throughout the country.

One difference was that Bartholomew Fair, like the one at Stourbridge but unlike most other Elizabethan fairs, was a national rather than a regional occasion. The vendors, reputable and otherwise, seem to have been native Londoners but those who came to buy and/or be swindled hailed from all over England. At smaller fairs this situation would have been almost exactly reversed, for the clientele came from the locality while those who offered their wares came from afar.

Another distinctive feature arising directly from this is that Bartholomew Fair was the only real city fair in Elizabethan England. Although Elizabethan London was still close to the countryside, and visitors to Bartholomew Fair (which was held outside the north-western part of the city walls) would come across the green fields of Hoxton and Islington, the atmosphere of the fair, as it comes through to us not only in Jonson's incomparable play but in more prosaic accounts of the time, is that of London and its teeming life. Here, sixteen years before Jonson, is the opening ceremony of the fair as described by a German visitor, Paul Hentzner:

It is worthy of observation that every year, upon St Bartholomew's Day (August 24) when the fair is held, it is usual for the mayor, attended by the twelve principal aldermen, to walk in a neighbouring field, dressed in his scarlet gown, and about his neck a golden chain, to which is hung a golden fleece, and, besides, that particular ornament which distinguishes the most noble order of the Garter. When the mayor goes out of the precincts of the city, a sceptre and sword and a cap are borne before him, and he is followed by the principal aldermen in scarlet gowns with gold chains, himself and they on horseback. Upon their arrival at a place appointed for that purpose, where a tent is pitched, the mob begins to wrestle before them, two at a time; the conquerors receive rewards from the magistrates. After this is over, a parcel of live rabbits are turned loose among the crowd, which are pursued by a number of boys, who endeavour to catch them, with all the noise they can make.

Barthelemew Fair. Lud Du Guernier inv. et Sculp 1739.

A fairground gull being relieved of his purse. The cutpurse tickles his victim in the ear with a feather and when he takes his hand out of his pocket to scratch his ear, the rogue cuts his purse

THE FUN OF THE FAIR

It is sad but representative of the life of the fair that on this very occasion one of Herr Hentzner's party, Dr Tobias Salander, had his purse containing nine crowns filched 'by an Englishman who always kept very close to him, that the doctor did not perceive it'.

At the beginning of the twelfth century the monk Rahere founded St Bartholomew's hospital. It may have been stories of miraculous cures performed there which led to the popularity of the adjacent priory as a place of pilgrimage. Whatever the reason, it was not long before the annual fair was a lucrative source of income for the monks of St Bartholomew's. It was held on the eve, the day and the morrow of the saint's feast and until the dissolution of the monasteries all tolls from the traders went to the priory. Originally the commercial rather than the entertainment side of the fair was the more important. Cloth and wool were the main commodities offered for sale at first, with leather and pewter added later. During the early years of the fair booths were erected not only all over the graveyard but within the church itself; but as the fair grew larger and its entertainment more varied, the interior of the church ceased to be used for any part of it.

When the monastery was suppressed in 1539 the fair remained, but all rights in it, together with the monastery itself, were sold to Sir Richard Rich, whose descendants owned it in Jonson's time and for long after. The third Lord Rich (who married Sidney's Stella) covered the open fairground with as many buildings as he could squeeze into it, to swell his profits from leasing them at fair time, while his son ensured that the lease on every building on the site contained a clause whereby part of it was reserved by him for re-letting during Bartholomew Fair. From the time of the suppression of the monastery there was a constant tussle between the city authorities and the owners of the site for control of the fair and its revenue. In Elizabethan times, as we can gather from Hentzner's account, the mayor and aldermen presided over the opening ceremony. The formal opening was done by the Lord Mayor who, seated on horseback in his purple gown, read a proclamation at the great gate by the west façade of St Bartholomew's church which was the principal entrance to the fair. The proclamation began thus:

The Right Honourable Lord Mayor of the City of London, and his right worshipful brethren the aldermen of the said city, streightly charge and command, on the behalf of our sovereign lady the Queen, that all manner of persons of whatsoever estate, degree, or condition they be, having recourse to this fair, keep the peace of our said sovereign lady the Queen.

It then went on to direct that there should be no breaches of the peace, on pain of imprisonment and fine, and to specify that all food and drink offered for sale should be wholesome and of true measure. No activities were permitted within the fairground on a Sunday and arrests were to be made only by civic officials. Any complaints were to be directed to the stewards of the fair. Bartholomew Fair, like all others throughout Europe, had its own court where complaints relating to the purely commercial activities of the fair were heard. This was called the Court of Pie-Powder, a name variously derived from *pied poudre,* the 'dusty feet' of the travellers who came to the fair, or *pied puldreaux*, the latter word being the old French for 'pedlar'. According to the eminent Elizabethan lawyer Sir Edward Coke, justice was done at Pie-Powder Court as speedily as dust can fall from the foot. It needed to be, for the Court sat only at fair time and could give judgment only on things that happened at the fair within the duration of that particular fair. Even a thief who robbed at the fair was safe from the justice of Pie-Powder if he was caught outside the boundaries of the fair (though of course he would then be liable to appear before a severer court). Most of the offences which came before the Court of Pie-Powder related to trading without licences or with forged licences, not having the freedom of the city and giving false measure. Guildsmen from the Merchant Taylors, for instance, attended the fair and used to measure cloth with a silver yardstick; in 1566 one Pullen was committed to prison for using an unlawful yard.

From the words and actions of Justice Overdo, magistrate of Pie-Powder Court in Jonson's play, we see that the authorities had 'intelligencers' who went about in plain clothes to ensure that fair play was done: 'Many are the yearly enormities of this fair' declares Justice Overdo 'in whose courts of Pie Powders I have had the honour, during the three days sometimes to sit as judge. But this is the special day for the detection of these enormities. I am resolute to spare spy money hereafter, and make mine own discoveries.' Whereupon he wanders in disguise through the fair displaying more zeal than efficiency and discovering among other enormities that Joan Trash the gingerbread woman sells wares compounded of 'stale bread, rotten eggs, musty ginger and dead honey'. He already knows that the booth of Ursula the Pig Woman is a brothel by day and a den of thieves by night, but the discovery that the civil young gentleman Ezekiel Edgeworth whom he takes under his wing is a practised cutpurse comes as something of a shock. There was a real-life precedent for Justice Overdo's surveillance in disguise. It comes from a letter written by the Lord Mayor, Sir Thomas Hayes, to the Lord Chamberlain in the same year as Jonson's play, indeed in the month before the fair. In it Sir Thomas recounts how, having heard of lewd houses in the suburbs through his spies, he personally visited them in disguise and punished the offenders by carting, whipping and banishment from the city.

Drawn from the life, too, is Nightingale the ballad seller who assists young Ezekiel in his craft by gathering a crowd with his singing and then intimating through a system of pre-arranged signals who has the fattest purses. 'And i' your singing' Edgeworth tells his accomplice 'you must use your hawk's eye nimbly, and fly the purse to a mark still, where 'tis worn, and o' which side; that you may gi' me the sign with your beak, or hang your head that way i' the tune.' Needless to say, the ballad with which Nightingale entertains his audience is none other than *A Caveat Against Cutpurses* and begins:

> My masters and friends and good people draw near,
> And look to your purses, for that I do say,
> And though little money in them you do bear,
> It cost more to get, than to lose in a day.

And each verse concludes with the solemn refrain:

> Youth, youth, thou hadst better been starved by the nurse,
> Than live to be hanged for cutting a purse.

It takes barely three verses for Edgeworth to relieve Bartholomew Cokes, the typical fairground gull, of the purse which he has been clutching so tightly. Jonson's stage direction tells all as to how Ezekiel accomplishes this: *Edgeworth gets up to Cokes and tickles him in the ear with a straw twice to draw his hand out of his pocket.*

In 1614, the year in which Jonson's play was written, the muddy ground of Smithfield was paved, channels cut to clear rain water and a strong railing for the comfort of pedestrians constructed at a total cost of £1,600. By this time the cloth and horse trade, the two main commercial activities, were giving pride of place to the booths and stalls which offered refreshment and entertainment to visitors. We have already seen two of these in passing, Joan Trash's gingerbread stall where you could buy gingerbread dolls known as Bartholomew babies (if you weren't too particular about what went into their making), and the booth roofed over by an arbour of green boughs in which Ursula the Pig Woman offered for sale the speciality of the fairground, roast Bartholomew pig. 'HERE BE THE BEST PIGS/AND SHE DOES ROAST THEM AS WELL AS EVER SHE DID. The pig's head speaks it' runs the legend over Ursula's booth. No sign would of course advertise the fact that her booth was also a centre for receiving stolen goods, nor would one be necessary to proclaim that it was a brothel. A drink of ale and a pipe of tobacco could be obtained at Madame Ursula's though the waiter had instructions to froth the beer well while serving and remove half-drunk mugs whenever possible, while the tobacco was mixed with dried coltsfoot to make it go further. A counter measure recommended by Thomas Nashe to drinkers to guard against 'frothing' beer was to rub the inside of the can with the skin of a herring. However, neither Nashe nor any other writer I have come across has any constructive advice on what to do about coltsfoot in your pipe.

But Bartholomew pig is Ursula's pride and joy and she retails it with all the astuteness of a vendor who knows she has a seller's market: 'Look who's there, sirrah. Five shillings a pig is my price at least; if it be a sow-pig, sixpence more; if she be a great-bellied wife, sixpence more for that.' The notion that pregnant women craved Bartholomew pig is fairly well attested in both fact and fiction, as the following extract from the Register of Burials for All Hallows Church, Honey Lane shows: 'August 26, 1600. Nicholas Ems with his wife being lately come out of the Low Country being in Bartholomew Fair, she longed for the gullet of a pig and had it not, was delivered of a maid child being stillborn 26 of August and was buried immediately in the churchyard; she was delivered in Cheapside at Master Alderman's door.' So universal was the appeal of Bartholomew pig that Jonson's Rabbi Zeal-of-the-Land Busy contrives to reconcile the eating of it with his general Puritan condemnation of the fair and its activity: 'In the way of comfort to the weak I will go and eat. I will eat exceedingly, and prophesy. There may be a good use made of it, too, now I think on't; by the public eating of swine's flesh, to profess our hate and loathing of Judaism, whereof the Brethren stand taxed. I will therefore eat, yea, I will eat exceedingly.' But, as the Rabbi himself insists later, 'Only pig was not comprehended in my admonition: the rest were'. We shall meet him again as he roars his expansive imprecations on 'this Fair, this wicked and foul Fair—and fitter may it be called a Foul than a Fair—to protest against the abuses of it, the foul abuses of it' by which the company of Saints are 'troubled, very much troubled, exceedingly troubled'.

We may get some idea of how the cloth trade had declined since the early days of the fair by noting that the only person connected with it in Jonson's comedy is the drunken North Country clothier 'who does change cloth for ale at the fair here'. Horse-trading, however, is more fully represented in the person of 'Captain' Daniel 'Jordan' Knockem the 'courser'. We learn that a courser dealt in horses already in use while a horse-dealer only sold horses trained by him. Ribbons tied to the horses' manes and tails signified that they were for sale. When Ursula scalds her leg, Knockem offers a treatment for it which is evidently based on a prescription for covering up sore spots on horses: 'Patience Urse, take a good heart, 'tis but a blister as big as a windgall. I'll take it away with the white of an egg, a little honey, and hog's grease. Ha' they pasterns well rolled, and thou shalt pace again by tomorrow.'

Concealing defects in animals offered for sale was an exact and exacting Elizabethan art. The tricks of coursers at London's permanent horse and cattle market in neighbouring West Smithfield are described in fascinating detail by

Thomas Dekker in *Lanthorn and Candlelight*. According to Dekker, Smithfield was only the largest and most notorious of 'those markets of unwholesome horseflesh' which were found throughout the land in every 'blind country fair'. He compares the horse-courser's interest in his wares to the whoremonger's interest in whores; as long as the outside looks fair neither cares what diseases are harboured within. On this basis the horse-courser prefers to acquire for resale horses with sought-after colouring and marks, such as the milk-white, the dapple-grey and the coal-black with white heels or a white star on the forehead. But Dekker warns that such well-coloured animals are rarely sold unless they have some defect in them; let the prospective buyer be warned. Having purchased his horse at as low price as he can, the horse-courser (or 'jingler') proceeds to prepare the animal for resale in a variety of ways ranging from resprays to replacement or modification of various parts. Here in Dekker's own words is the courser's cure for glanders, a disease which gives horses a running nose:

> In the very morning when he is to be rifled away amongst the gamesters in Smithfield, before he thrust his head out of his master's stable, the horse-courser tickles his nose, not with a pipe of tobacco, but with a good quantity of the best [s]neezing powder that can be gotten; which with a quill being blown up into the nostrils to make it work the better, he stands poking there up and down with two long feathers plucked from the wing of a goose, they being dipped in the juice of garlic, or in any strong oil, and thrust up to the very top of his head, so far as possibly they can reach, to make the poor dumb beast avoid [i.e. bring out] the filth from his nostrils; which he will do in great abundance. This being done, he comes to him with a new medicine for a sick horse, and mingling the juice of bruised garlic, sharp biting mustard, and strong ale together, into both the nostrils with a horn is poured a good quantity of this filthy broth; which by the hand being held in by stopping the nostrils close together, at length with a little [s]neezing more, his nose will be cleaner than his master's the horse-courser, and the filth be so artificially stopped that for eight or ten hours a jade will hold up his head with the proudest gelding that gallops scornfully by him, and never have need of whipping.

But Dekker also explains how to avoid being taken in by this kind of horse-trick; grip the suspect animal 'hard about the weasand-pipe, close toward the roof of the tongue till it coughs'. If, when you release your hold, the horse's chaps 'begin to walk as if he were chewing down a horse-loaf' have no truck with the horse-courser at all, 'for his jade is as full of infirmity as the master of villainy'.

Some of the most frequent devices had to do with concealing a horse's age. One way to do this was to burn black marks on an animal's outermost upper and lower teeth with a small round heated iron, such marks being characteristic of a young animal. If the beast was so ancient that these teeth were missing, the answer was to prick its lips with a pin or nail so that it could not open its mouth properly. 'But' Dekker continues, 'a reasonable-sighted eye, without the help of spectacles, may easily discover this juggling, because it is gross and common'.

To conceal the fact that a horse has foundered and can hardly stand on his four legs, the horse-courser kept tickling it with a straw so that it would not stand still and thereby make its weakness evident.

A favourite gambit in disposing of a lame horse was to remove the shoe from the lame leg in order to make it appear that its absence was the only cause of the horse's halting; if necessary, witnesses could be found who were prepared to swear that this was indeed the case. If a defect in a horse's legs could not be hidden by any other means, the horse-courser would ride it up and down in the thickest and dirtiest mire he could find till the caked mud 'like a ruffled boot drawn up an ill-favoured gouty leg' hid the beast's infirmity from the prospective buyer.

To make a slow and heavy-footed horse appear swift and alert, the horse-courser would beat it on the buttocks with a cudgel repeatedly for several days till the animal was so sore that the slightest touch on the back made it run away instantly. The courser then took it to the fair and, when the hopeful customer mounted the animal for a test ride, tapped it on the back and 'away flies Bucephalus as if young Alexander were upon his back'. The same technique was used to make a horse keep its tail between his legs instead of thrashing about with it, a sign according to Dekker of a beast with spirit.

Captain Knockem it not only a horse-courser but 'a roarer, swearer, knight of the knife, child of the horn-thumb'. In short, under the guise of a fashionable bully boy about town he carries on a lucrative part-time trade as a cutpurse, like his business associate, Ezekiel Edgeworth. He is 'a child of the horn-thumb' because like many true professionals he has a small sliver of sharpened horn attached to his thumb, to make the task of cutting purses simple and unobtrusive. If his real-life counterpart were unlucky enough to be caught by the marshals who went about the fair, the very least he could expect would be to be put in the fairground stocks or whipped at the post (though in Jonson's Saturnalian comedy it is the figures of authority, Justice Overdo and Rabbi Busy, who wind up in the stocks).

A ballad dating from the same year as the play gives a predictable but timely warning about the characters we are likely to encounter at the fair:

> Room for company
> Here come good fellows,
> Room for company

> In Bartholomew Fair.
> Cutpurses and cheaters,
> And bawdy-house door keepers,
> Room for company
> In Bartholomew Fair,
> Punks, ay, and panders
> And cashiered commanders
> Room for company
> Ill may they fare.

Most of these personages figure in Jonson's play as we have seen. But the fair was not without other more legitimate attractions. Among these were a host of 'monsters' such as are still a feature of country fairs in remote parts of the world. These included dancing dogs, a black wolf and hare that played the tabor, a goose with three legs and a bull with five legs (and two pizzles, if we are to believe Jonson's Humphrey Waspe). Perhaps the most famous among this group was a trained ape who would leap over a chain when he heard the name of an English prince but would like sullenly still at the name of the Pope or the King of Spain. The eloquence of the ape's keeper and the strength of Protestant national feeling among the spectators doubtless made up for the apparent monotony of the performance.

Equally popular entertainment but of a more elaborate kind was provided by 'motions' or puppet shows managed in Jonson's comedy by Lanthorn Leatherhead, who also runs a stall selling 'rattles, drums, halberts, horses [i.e. 'hobby-horses'] babies o' the best, fiddles of the finest'. The particular motion which Leatherhead proudly presents to a crowd of some two dozen three or four times in an afternoon has been written by John Littlewit, proctor of the city who, like any anxious author, mingles with the audience to observe their reaction at the first perform-ance. It is 'The Ancient and Modern History of Hero and Leander' and, as if that was not enough, Proctor Littlewit has added to it, in the best tradition of the Elizabethan drama and its double-plots, 'The True Trial of Friendship between Damon and Pythias'. This is not the pair renowned in classical legend, but merely two friends of London's Bankside, a dyer's son and 'a wench of the Bankside'. For, as Leatherhead helpfully explains to Bartholomew Cokes, this performance is somewhat different to the 'printed book', the famous poem of Hero and Leander begun by Marlowe and completed by George Chapman. 'That,' says Leatherhead, 'is too learned and poetical for our audience. What do they know what Hellespont is?' So, in the modest author's words, he has 'made it a little easy and modern for the times, sir, that's all'. Jonson was of course in part making fun of what he considered the absurdities of contemporary drama, especially when judged by strict 'classical' notions of regularity and decorum. But there is no doubt that the

Ben Jonson, the Elizabethan playwright, whose work covered many contemporary issues of London life including alchemy, cut-purses, swindlers and gypsies as well as prostitution

THE FUN OF THE FAIR

Elizabethan audience had a happily undiscriminating dramatic appetite which was able to swallow ancient and modern, tragical and comical, historical and pastoral or any combination of these with great gusto and without any observable ill effects.

As Filcher and Sharkwell, Leatherhead's assistants, plant a flag and unfurl a sign to announce the performance, he himself muses on the audience's possible reaction and on other 'motions' which he has been privileged to present. For this is an audience which is at least as uninhibited as its grander counterpart in the 'legitimate' playhouse. 'All the foul in the Fair, I mean all the dirt in Smithfield', Leatherhead reflects, 'will be thrown at our banner today, if the matter does not please the people'. He fervently hopes that Proctor Littlewit's brainchild will be able to repeat the success of such outstanding productions as *Jerusalem, Nineveh, The City of Norwich* and *Sodom and Gomorrah*, the last embellished with the topical matter of the apprentices' riots which traditionally took place on Shrove Tuesday, usually in the Bankside and during which bawdy houses were often pulled down. But the greatest get-penny of them all, not surprisingly, was a show based on the Gun-powder Plot. 'I have presented that to an eighteen- or twenty-pence audience nine times in an afternoon.' And he has the experienced showman's explanation for his success with it: 'your home-born projects prove ever the best; they are so easy and familiar.' He fears that the latest production suffers from a common fault: 'They put too much learning i'their things nowadays; and that, I fear, will be the spoil o'this.' Jonson was perhaps getting in a sly dig here at those who complained of an excess of classical erudition in his own plays.

However, 'The Ancient and Modern History of Hero and Leander' goes down well, at least to begin with. The audience includes, besides the author himself, Bartholomew Cokes and the ragged group of urchins who have been following him around the fairground, Justice Overdo and various others. The price of admission is twopence but Cokes with lordly prodigality hands the keeper twelvepence. The show begins, with dialogue and commentary compounded in more or less equal parts of obscenity and fustian. Leander falls in love with the Bankside wench and asks her to put a candle's end in her window so that he may know her house by night. 'Fear not my gander,' replies fair Hero:

> I protest I should handle
> My matters very ill, if I had not a whole candle!

A single couplet from the concluding phase of the tragedy gives us a taste of Littlewit's skill in the elevated style:

> This tragical encounter falling out thus to busy us,
> It raises up the ghost of their friend Dionysius.

69

No one is as engrossed in these tragical goings-on as Cokes, and Jonson's point, that this kind of entertainment is fit only for the Cokes's who have more money than sense, is not particularly difficult to grasp. Nevertheless the rest of the audience sit through the performance with an indulgence which varies from the contemptuous to the affectionate. After all, Littlewit's 'motion' is, in its own way, as filled with London pride as *Bartholomew Fair* itself.

But all this is lost on Rabbi Zeal-of-the-Land Busy, who storms in to the tents of wickedness, bursting with indignation and roast pork. He is now an elder and prophet of 'the Brethren', which would have been any one of numerous Puritanical sects in Jonson's time. But, as we are told, he was not always one of the elect: 'He was a baker sir, but he does dream now and see visions'. He gave up his trade when he began to suspect that his cakes were being used for 'bridals, maypoles, morrices' and other such traditional festivities which the Puritans regarded as the works of Antichrist in the world. Although he has managed to gorge himself with roast pig 'with a reformed mouth, with *sobriety*, and humbleness' there is nothing else in the fair which escapes Zeal-of-the-Land's ferocious denunciation. Filled with the boundless confidence of one who 'derides all antiquity, and defies any other learning than inspiration', he holds forth with equal ardour against long hair and gay clothes, tobacco and bottle ale; even Lanthorn Leatherhead's toys are heathen idols and the gingerbread woman's wares a clutch of images in a 'basket of Popery'. The whole fair is nothing but the devil's market-place: 'the place is *Smithfield*, of the field of smiths, the grove of hobby-horses and trinkets, the wares are the wares of devils. And the whole fair is the shop of Satan.' He arrives at the puppet show breathing hell-fire, nothing daunted by his sojourn in the fairground stocks where he 'rejoiceth in his affliction, and sitteth here to prophesy the destruction of Fairs and May-games, wakes and Whitsun-ales, and doth sigh and groan for the reformation of these abuses'.

It is typical of Jonson's attitude to the Rabbi Busys of his world that, for all his dragon-like eloquence, the Rabbi is worsted in argument not by a more golden-tongued orator but by one of Lanthorn Leatherhead's wooden puppets. Many Puritans condemned the Elizabethan theatre because, among other things, men there dressed up in women's clothes which, according to the Bible, was an abomination in the eyes of the Lord. When Rabbi Busy adduces this argument against the puppets, one of them triumphantly raises its skirt to reveal that it has no sex at all. The Rabbi is dumbfounded: 'I am confuted, the Cause hath failed me!'

But the real-life equivalents of Rabbi Zeal-of-the-Land Busy and his brethren were not to be so speedily or ingeniously silenced. On the contrary their voices were heard more and more throughout the land, rising from a rumble to a roar till, thirty years later, with the outbreak of the Civil War and the ensuing victory of the Puritans, Rabbi Busy's prophesy of destruction came true. Then, for a time, the noise of the Fair would be stilled and no longer would the hopeful cry of the ballad seller be heard:

> Now the fair's a-filling!
> O for a time to startle
> The birds o'the booths here billing
> Yearly with Old St Bartle!

Instead, in the words of Lord Buckhurst later in the century:

> But Busy rallying, filled with holy rage
> Possessed the pulpit and pulled down the stage.

CHAPTER FOUR

White Magic and Black Witches

The medieval Catholic Church laid claims to many powerful kinds of magic which touched the lives of its members at every point. There was the magic of confession and absolution which assured the sinner in a voice of unshakeable authority that his transgressions were forgiven. There was the magic of conjuration and consecration by which ordinary materials and objects—oil, water, salt, crosses, rings, pieces of paper—could be invested with the power of God so that they protected the wearer from evil and misfortune. There was the magic of exorcism and healing whereby tormenting demons were cast out by the priest using the divine power granted to the true Church and the sufferer made whole again. And the magic of the sacraments gave shape and sustenance to a man's life, particularly the crucial sacrament of the Mass in which the bread and wine were truly and magically transformed into the body and blood of the Redeemer.

This magic was not of course the invention of the Catholic Church. In most cases it had taken over and adapted for its own purposes folk beliefs whose beginnings are beyond the reach of history. The Church in its wisdom saw that these beliefs prevailed because they fulfilled a deep and abiding need in the lives and minds of those who held them. In a world where for most people life was hard and precarious, where natural disaster was often both savage and inexplicable, the teachings of the Church may have offered an explanation which reconciled men to their misery, but its ritual magic held out the promise of power to alter their condition. If on any given occasion the magic failed, the failure could always be blamed on some defect in the performance or in the spiritual condition of the supplicant, not on the magic itself. And unlike science, in which one failure blots out the impact of a thousand successes, one apparent magical triumph cancelled out innumerable failures. The magic remained all-powerful and inexhaustible. The Catholic Church simply insisted that its source was always and only God. It did not try to beat folk beliefs to the ground; it merely joined them to its own vast and intricate system.

With the coming of the Reformation this faith was formally replaced in England by another brand of Christianity which differed from it in many important ways.

White Magic and Black Witches

We may sum up these differences in a single phrase by saying that the Church of England almost literally took the magic out of Christianity. It did its best to deny its flock access to these magical resources and certainly claimed no magical powers for itself. It abolished auricular confession and was opposed to exorcism and conjuration. In general it took the view that consecration was not an operation by which the actual nature of objects—oil, water, wine, bread or whatever—was miraculously transformed, but only an act by which certain articles were dedicated to the worship of God. From this it followed that no particular object, whether it was a cross, Bible or anything else, nor any particular form of words had magical power in itself. The sacrament of the Mass had to be understood symbolically, like all other rituals; the bread and wine did not actually change into flesh and blood. Feeding a horse on holy bread and water could not prevent it from being stolen. Prayers were not infallible charms but humble supplications to God which He might heed or not, in His divine wisdom and mercy. If God looked with favour on a man, he would prosper. If he did not prosper, then he should look closely into his own life, discover where he had gone astray and strive to mend his ways and please God. Constant prayer and strenuous effort were what the Protestant Church advocated. That was the true religion, and it had nothing to do with magic.

This new, official view offered cold comfort to the labouring poor. If a man's son died or his cattle were stricken, it was no real solace to be admonished to examine himself more closely and pray harder. God might be testing him or punishing him, but under the new dispensation there was virtually nothing he could do about it in either case. He was strictly forbidden to try and change God's mind and thereby alter his own state by having recourse to magic. But the need that was supplied by magic did not disappear just because of a *fiat* of the new Church. The conditions that gave rise to magical beliefs—the threat of sudden disaster from a hostile environment and the hope of some sort of control over it— still persisted, and if the Church no longer provided the magic, ordinary folk would look elsewhere for it. There is good reason to think that even before the Reformation, the mass of people was not particularly reverent as far as their attitude to the official teaching of Christianity was concerned. Many only went to church for the rituals of baptism, marriage and burial, as many do today. As for the behaviour of the congregation, this seemed to have been little different from their behaviour in a playhouse—they drank, spat, heckled the preacher and swore with little regard to their surroundings. What was important about the Catholic Church seems to have been not so much its official doctrine, but its claims to powerful magic. When these claims were implicitly withdrawn by the Elizabethan Church, they were taken up by other men and women who held out the same promises and offered the same services that the Catholic Church had earlier provided. These people were variously called 'cunning men', 'wise women', 'blessers', 'charmers', 'conjurors', 'sorcerers' or 'witches' and were familiar in virtually every village community in Elizabethan England.

'At this date' wrote Reginald Scot in 1584, 'it is indifferent to say in the English tongue "she is a witch" or "she is a wise woman".' Scot was an educated and humane observer, anxious to expose the so-called miracles claimed by the Catholic Church as well as to save harmless old women from the monstrous accusations of witchcraft often brought against them. As such it was no part of his purpose to draw a clear distinction between 'black' and 'white' magic. But we shall see that in the popular mind the difference was quite clear, because the white or 'blessing' witch served a very different psychological and social function from the maleficent or black witch. The same person could sometimes change from one to the other, but this did not alter the basis of the distinction.

The white witch could be of either sex, a cunning man or a wise woman. Both the Protestant and the Catholic Church condemned them, the former because it did not believe in 'good' magic, the latter because the white witch threatened its own magical claims. In some ways the white witch was a greater threat to the Church's authority than the black witch because his or her services were called upon more often. But here again we find the usual contrast between official theory and grass-roots activity. In 1583, the churchwardens of Thatcham in Berkshire sent for a cunning woman to find out who had made off with the communion cloth from the church, and in the previous year an Essex cunning man, Miles Blomfield, had been chosen as churchwarden. There are also several instances of clergymen themselves practising white magic during this period.

The cunning man or wise woman was very often an ordinary member of the village community who occupied a definite place in it and whose magical activities were only a side-line. Unlike in some primitive societies today, the role was not hereditary. Indeed it is difficult to understand just how one established a claim as a white witch. Sometimes being the seventh son of a seventh son or having some special distinguishing mark or quality such as a prominent birthmark or pro-tuberant eyes could help. The initial requirements seem to have been simply a certain amount of self-confidence together with the ability to make one's claims plausible; the latter would naturally be vastly enchanced by a successful miracle or two. Given the kind of situation in which he was consulted and the conditions within which he worked, it is no surprise to find that the cunning man had an impressive degree of success.

One great appeal of the cunning man was the comprehensiveness of his range. His magic could be harnessed to the service of any situation which his clients were likely to come across. There were charms to encompass everything, from getting rid of impotence to getting rid of rats. There were charms to banish toothache or protect one in battle, to win at dice or at love, to safeguard cattle from lightning or disease or make children sleep, to make corn grow or develop a person's musical abilities. An ever-popular commodity was the love potion, used by clients in all walks of life; a sinister variant of this was the draught of poison such as that which Dr Suckling's wife wanted the wise woman Mary Woods to brew in Norwich in 1613 to be administered to the doctor himself. If a woman wanted to know why her child had come out in sores or whether she would live longer than her husband or why her butter wouldn't turn, the cunning man or wise woman could not only tell her, but nearly always what to do about it as well. Among the most frequent services they rendered was the healing of sickness in human beings and animals. As a good many of their remedies were based on country herbs and practical psychology, it is at least possible that the white witch brought about more cures than a doctor who based his science on the theory of humours and who would often bleed a patient as soon as look at him. In any case there was a shortage of physicians at this time, especially in rural England. The white witch's charms and concoctions at least had the great merit of being fairly painless prescriptions—and their fees were usually much lower than those of the physicians.

The finding of lost or stolen goods and livestock was another of the white witch's skills very much in demand. For a poor peasant owning no land, the loss of a few sheep or a cow could be a very serious blow, and it was just the sort of misfortune which occurred fairly frequently. A rarer and more positive aspect of the search for lost goods was the search for buried treasure. This was an activity in which the cunning man was often assisted by a 'familiar' or spirit in animal form which he sometimes carried about within a ring or mirror; the familiar was necessary to exorcize the evil demon who usually kept watch over buried treasure; it is not perhaps surprising that nearly all efforts to locate buried treasure with the aid of the white witch failed.

Even walking on the water was not beyond the scope of the Elizabethan image, if the word of Thomas Ross is to be believed. In his *Natural and Artificial Conclusions* (1567), a little handbook so popular that no copies of the first two editions have survived, he gives the following instructions on:

How to walk on the water, a proper secret: For to do this, take two little timbrels and bind them under the soles of thy feet, and at a stave's end fasten another, and with these you may safely walk on the water unto the wonder of all such as shall see the same: if so be you often exercise the same with a certain boldness and lightness of the body.

This admirably lucid and simple advice, however, carried less than total conviction to at least one contemporary reader, who has scrawled on the margin of a copy of the 1581 edition: 'and if you do not sink you shall be sure to go upon the water'.

An illustration to accompany Thomas Hill's instructions on *How to walke on the water*. The instructions have the merit of simplicity rather than effectiveness

Other usual activities of the cunning man were fortune telling and the making of weather forecasts with particular reference to the requirements of farming. Before the countryman entered on any important transaction, the marriage of his daughter or a distant journey for example, he would consult the white witch who would use his skill to advise him with an appropriate degree of ritual. And finally, the cunning man would be consulted by anyone who had reason to believe that he had come under the influence—through curse, evil eye, bodily contact or other means—of a black witch and wanted to have the evil removed.

The scope of the blessing witch's activities therefore extended as far as the magic of the old Church. He also often provided something of the larger-than-life theatricality which the earlier Church ritual contained. Clients were often shown into special rooms, suitably darkened and furnished with objects such as magic beads, images, crystal balls and mirrors which were intended to produce an atmosphere of credulous awe. Occasionally the witch would wear a special item of dress or ornament such as a shawl or chain with a cross in imitation of a priest; and he tried to build around himself the same atmosphere of austere purity which, in theory at any rate, celibacy had given to the Catholic clergy. William Barckseale of Southampton, for example, prepared himself for the detection (sometimes success-fully) of stolen goods by fasting and praying for three days.

In 1569, Edwin Sandys, Bishop of Worcester produced a list of magical practices prohibited by the Church which offers a glimpse of the bewildering variety of diagnostic techniques employed in the service of magic: 'charms to cure men or beast, invocations of wicked spirits; telling where things lost or stolen are become by key, book, tables, shears, sieves; looking into crystals or other casting of figures'. This is the baldest summary and it leaves out more methods of healing and divination than it includes. It would take several pages merely to catalogue all the recorded methods in any detail, but it is worth pausing to look at some of the most important methods as well as some of the most improbable ones.

In the absence of any highly developed notion of *natural* cause and effect, we need not be surprised that the diagnosis of disease was often based on the view that an evil spirit was lurking within the sick person's body and needed to be exorcised by charms, conjurations and similar rituals. After all, it was quite usual for physicians to attribute their failure with a particular patient to the presence of an evil demon inside that patient. If such demons did exist, they could only be overcome by a more powerful magic. For the white witch this came from the Christian God who was mightier than the devil and his minions. On this the witch and the Christian minister were in agreement. The dispute arose as to the methods by which God's power could be invoked and manifested. For the white witch believed that this could be done through the use of specially 'consecrated' objects and appropriate rituals. The first essential was to establish the presence of the malignant spirit within the affected person. A common method of doing this was to measure the patient's belt, girdle or similar item of clothing. The assumption was that the article would vary in size according to the condition of the patient by a kind of sympathetic transference. Thus Elizabeth Mortlock, a wise woman of Cambridgeshire, began operations with prayers, then measured the girdle of the suspected patient from elbow to thumb while invoking God to tell her whether the person concerned 'be haunted with a fairy, yea or no'. If the answer was positive, the girdle would be shorter when she next measured it.

Other methods used were mainly methods of detection rather than of medical diagnosis. Bishop Sandys' list gives us some of the most usual ones. Many of the techniques were simple and required no special apparatus. Indeed, they were often practised by 'amateurs', though no doubt the cunning man dressed up the operation appropriately. One form of divination was done with a Bible and a key into the hollow of which each suspect's name was in turn inserted. The key was then put between the pages of the Bible. When the guilty person's name was inside the key, the Bible would begin to shake as soon as the key was inserted in it. Another equally simple and common method was divination by shears. For this, a sieve was pierced with a pair of shears which were then held by the point, with the sieve stuck in it. The name of each suspect was then mentioned, with the question whether he was guilty or no; when the culprit's name was mentioned, the sieve would begin to spin round. In another method clay balls containing suspects' names written on pieces of paper would be put in a bucket. The paper with the guilty person's name would unroll first. Other techniques were peculiar to a particular individual. Robert Harris of Maidstone practised divination simply by staring into people's faces, and Joan Moores, if we are to believe her, could prophesy by listening to frogs croaking. Thus in 1594, Cuthbert Williamson's eyes ran tears when he stood before a 'forspoken' or bewitched person. An eye drawn on a wall was alleged to make the guilty person's eye water when he stared at it. Perhaps the most gruesome forms of diagnosis and detection were those involving corpses, skulls and earth from freshly dug graves, all of which were used in the dangerous (because forbidden on pain of death) practice of raising the spirits of the dead.

When we move from diagnosis to prescription, the modes of operation become even more bizarre. The most straightforward remedies consisted of the utterance of certain magic spells, usually Christian prayers. We may see here the persistence of the notion that the language of religion had a special virtue which could be used for practical purposes. In 1528 Margaret Hurst described how she healed sick people by kneeling and praying for them to the Holy Trinity. She then prescribed five Paternosters, five Aves and a Creed for nine consecutive nights, followed by three more Paternosters, three Aves and a Creed and so on. For the ague she prescribed herbs, to be taken with holy water and accompanied by specified prayers. Mad dogs and their victims could be cured by feeding them with charms written on paper, and sick horses with charms hung from their manes. A man possessed by the devil could be cured by releasing a live bat in the room, whereupon the bat would carry the evil spirit away with him. One remedy for pains in the head was to boil a lock of the sufferer's hair in his urine and throw it on the fire. Not all recommended cures were as drastic as those for Anthony Wood, who was told to jump in the river to drown the evil spirits that caused his ague, and few were as macabre as the cure for goitre—the victim had to be touched by the dead hand of a freshly hanged corpse. Compared to this, the cure practised by Katherine Thompson and Anne Nevelson in 1604—to put a white duck's bill into the patient's mouth and intone charms—seems quite innocuous. Sometimes the white witch 'took on' the patient's affliction and cured her in that way. What lay behind all the diagnosis and the remedies prescribed was a need for external reassurance and a habit of mind as far removed as it is possible to imagine from that which we think of as 'scientific'.

From the middle of the sixteenth century to about the middle of the seventeenth recourse to white witches (and the hunting down of black ones) seems to have been fairly persistent in England. In 1549 one William Wycherley, arrested as a sorcerer, estimated that there were five hundred like him in the country, while thirty-five years later Reginald Scot reckoned that there were less than a score of parishes without a wise woman or cunning man. We are told that in Elizabethan Essex a cunning man was never more than ten miles away from any countryman. Part of their success was due, as we have seen, to the fact that they fulfilled a genuine need; the cures they recommended—the 'natural magic' of herbs and minerals—genuinely did alleviate suffering. There would also have been a proportion of people whose ailments cured themselves, but for which the cunning man could take the credit. As for the identification of those who had wished evil upon clients or the recovery of stolen goods, a certain amount of lucky guessing has to be allowed for. But the chief reason for the white witch's success in this respect is undoubtedly that his client came to him not for information he himself did not possess but for some sort of external confirmation of his own suspicions. The first question the cunning man asked his client was invariably: 'Whom do you suspect?' In a closed village community the number involved was bound to be small and it would require no exceptional skill to discover who was the most likely suspect. In the nature of the case it would be difficult to prove that the identification was wrong—how did a person prove that he had *not* cursed someone? Finally, as I have suggested, success would count for a great deal but failure could always be attributed to factors which would leave the white witch's reputation undamaged.

The question 'whom do you suspect?' took on a much more sinister overtone when what was at issue was not who had stolen corn or butter but who had cast a spell on another. And yet, in England at least, the identification of 'black' witches often rested on matters as trivial as these. For the most striking thing about witchcraft in England compared to developments on the Continent was the smallness of scale and the triviality of the charges involved. The witches in *Macbeth* could cause tempests and help to murder a king, but the real life 'witches' of Elizabethan England rarely claimed to perform or were accused of performing such spectacular deeds. One witch did claim at her execution to have been responsible for all the frosts and bad weather for some years past, but generally most of the claims and accusations were petty and personal. Twelve-year-old Agnes Browne was convinced that Joan Waterhouse had bewitched her by causing a black dog with an ape's face to haunt her; Agnes protected herself by uttering the name of our Lord. Margaret Harkett who was executed at Tyburn in 1585 picked peas from her neighbour's field and when asked to return them flung them down with a curse, after which no peas grew in his field. The wrath of a guardian demon apparently descended on one Peters of Devonshire and reduced him and his companions to ashes while they were digging for buried treasure. Philip Benny of Hereford knew that Mary Hodges was a witch because every night he saw her in her room making water in a dish and throwing it in the fire over crossed andirons. We are in an altogether different world from that described by the sixteenth-century Frenchman Jean Bodin who described a witches' sabbath where each witch, carrying a candle, kissed a huge black goat under the tail, while the devil commanded them to 'revenge or die'.

Indeed, disappointing as it may seem, it must be noted that as far as England is concerned, there is no evidence to suggest the existence of anything like an organized witch cult with covens, black sabbaths, midnight orgies and aerial transportation (a broomstick is mentioned only once in English witchcraft trials). What we do find are lonely old women living on the edge of poverty, often reduced to begging from their neighbours who looked on them with suspicion and resentment and whose guilty conscience probably troubled them a good deal. The fact that they were women is only to be expected because old women and childless widows were economically and socially the most vulnerable members of a small rural community. Often their only companions were a pet cat, a toad or a weasel. Sometimes they kept them in a pot of wool and called them affectionate names, Grizzell or Pyewacket or Sack-and-Sugar. These were transformed in the imagination of their accusers into their 'familiars' or puckrels, lent them by the devil to do his evil business. If in addition the lonely old woman had any distinguishing marks, a hump back or hair on her chin or a 'devil's teat' under her armpit, suspicion became near certainty; but once the accusation had been made a distinguishing mark was not difficult to find, nor was a familiar. For Matthew Hopkins, the notorious 'Witch Finder Generall' of the mid-seventeenth century, a mere fly settling on a suspect's shoulder was indubitably the suspect's familiar, and was strong evidence of her guilt.

If the activities of witches were local in scope, the proceedings against them were proportionately smaller in scale, compared to what happened on the Continent. Between 1558, when Elizabeth I came to the throne, and 1736, when witchcraft ceased to be a statutory offence in England, some 513 charges of witchcraft were examined in the Courts of the Home Circuit, which comprised Essex, Hertfordshire, Kent, Surrey and Sussex. There were 200 convictions and 109 persons were hanged. This is very different in scale from the 900 reported to have been burnt at the stake in Lorrain between 1580 and 1595 and the 1,000 at Como in the single year 1524. It has been suggested that one reason for the difference was that in England witches were generally tried for specific acts of evil against individuals, not, as on the Continent, for entering into a compact with the devil and thereby losing their immortal soul and becoming one of Satan's agents on earth. By a statute of 1542, witchcraft for the purpose of discovering treasure, injuring others or provoking unlawful love was made a capital offence without benefit of clergy. In 1563, the first law against witchcraft of Elizabeth's reign made the use of witchcraft resulting in anyone's death an offence punishable by death. For practising witchcraft resulting in a person's bodily harm, the first offence carried a penalty of one year's imprisonment and the pillory; a second offence was punishable with

Matthew Hopkins, 'Witch Finder Generall' of the mid-seventeenth century. Hopkins is recorded as using radical methods to secure a confession from those charged with witchcraft. These included depriving the accused of food and water, and confining them for long periods in uncomfortable positions

death. The penalty for practising witchcraft to provoke unlawful love was one year's imprisonment and the pillory for the first offence and life imprisonment and forfeiture of goods for a subsequent one. In the first year of James I's reign the penalty for a second offence became death, James being a far more fierce opponent of witchcraft than Elizabeth. Conjuring of spirits was a felony in all three Acts and the Jacobean Act added for good measure the capital offence of taking up a dead body for conjuring. In this last Act we can perhaps see the influence of continental ideas about a compact with the devil, for covenanting with spirits is also specified as a felony. But the cases which came before the court were usually particular offences against named individuals, not vague accusations of liaison with the devil.

On a national scale, then, the impact of witchcraft on English life was probably not very great. A.L. Rowse is probably right to say that far more people were hanged in Elizabethan England for cutting a purse or stealing a sheep than for witchcraft. But we need to note that there was a continuous prosecution of witches in Elizabethan and Jacobean England, rather than any intensive witch-hunt (though there were years such as 1612 when multiple executions of witches took place in Lancashire and Northamptonshire). Furthermore it appears that certain areas, notably Essex, were more given to witch-hunting than others, though this may have been due partly to the fact that fuller records survive for that area than for some others, and partly to the zeal of a particular witch-hunter such as the Essex Justice of the Peace, Brian Darcy. But we should also remember that the information we have relates almost entirely to those cases of witchcraft that came before the courts; in the nature of things we cannot know how many allegations of witchcraft were settled outside the judicial system; it is reasonable to assume that they were at least as many as were brought before it.

We have glanced briefly at what black magic in England was not and also at the laws concerning it. It is time to take a closer look at what it usually was and what kind of impact it had on those who were involved in it. As we have seen, the accused persons tended to be old, single women who often went the round of the village begging from door to door. This was a very different practice to that of the vagrant beggars, because the 'witch' was already known to those she begged from. She might be refused on certain occasions for a number of reasons. Perhaps the man who refused her charity believed her to be a malingerer, perhaps he himself was going through hard times (or thought he was), perhaps he simply couldn't be bothered. Whatever the reason, it is easy to imagine a situation arising where the old woman went off muttering to herself or lay in wait for an opportunity to pilfer or both. If shortly afterwards the person concerned suffered some misfortune, especially if it was something sudden or mysterious, his thoughts would go to the old woman whom he had denied. Before he even went to the cunning man to find out how to mitigate his distress he would have a pretty good idea who had cast the evil eye or tongue upon him. In the words of George Gifford, an Essex parson who was, like Reginald Scot, an enlightened and humane enquirer into the phenomenon of witchcraft: 'A man is taken lame; he suspecteth that he is bewitched; he sendeth to the cunning man; he demandeth whom they suspect, and then showeth the image of the party in a glass.' In *A Dialogue Concerning Witches and Witchcrafts* (1593) also by Gifford, one of the speakers admits that he cannot tell whether a witch has harmed him or not. His hog had died and so had five hens belonging to his wife. He may have displeased a certain old woman but he could not be certain. Not everyone in Elizabethan England was as forthrightly sceptical as the other speaker in Gifford's *Dialogue* who says roundly: 'The devil hath bewitched your mind.'

It is easy to understand why in a backward society some people would accuse others of witchcraft. As an explanation of sudden loss or suffering witchcraft had the great virtue of being an unfalsifiable theory, and a guilty conscience soon pointed the accusing finger at a known person. What is perhaps less easy to understand is why some people should claim powers of witchcraft for themselves. The risks were high—though perhaps lower in England than elsewhere because prosecutions were for specified acts of ill-will. But whatever the risks they were evidently felt to be worthwhile for there were many instances of people claiming to be witches, not all of them under duress. An extreme case perhaps was that of John Palmer who in 1649 confessed at St Albans to having transformed himself into a toad in order to torment one of his victims. Gifford cites the case of a butcher's boy who came out in sores; the cunning man learnt the suspect's name from the boy's father and advised the father to burn some of the boy's hair outside her house. When she returned, the suspected woman asked the boy to scratch her face till it bled (drawing a witch's blood was a popular method of overcoming her evil power). When he did this his sores healed. In 1670 Joan Townsend even offered to turn girls into witches if they laid down before the church font and forswore their Christian name seven times.

Among the many motives which we may attribute to those who accused themselves of being witches, the materialistic desire to relieve poverty may have been the most important, just as it may have been for those who took to the road as vagrants. For an old woman living by herself in an Elizabethan village the difference between bare survival and barely tolerable misery may only have been a handful of peas, a bag of corn, or a few eggs. A reputation for witchcraft might, within limits, be a useful way of ensuring that her neighbours did not let her go without too often. Another reason which might persuade a woman without much company that she was a witch was a conviction of excessive sinfulness. It is not a long step for a recluse from a sense of unforgivable sin to the feeling that if the devil was going to have her soul anyway she might as well be of the devil's party and

¶ Th e Apprehenſion and confeſsion
of three notorious Witches.

A rreigned and by Iuſtice condemned and
executed at *Chelmeſ-forde,* in the Countye of
Eſſex, the *5. day of Iulye, laſt paſt.*
1 5 8 9.
¶ With the manner of their diueliſh practices and keeping of their
ſpirits, whoſe fourmes are heerein truelye
proportioned.

In reality witches rarely claimed to perform spectacular deeds and were usually lonely old women on the brink of poverty. Their only companions were pets which were transformed by their accusers into 'familiars' sent by the devil

know it. But there could sometimes be a certain amount of confusion over this; a woman from Huntingdonshire who ended her days at the stake as a witch in New England confessed to having sold her soul to the devil in return for being able to pray more eloquently.

Related to the economic motive but distinct from it was the sense of power conferred on the witch by those who feared her. Again, the border-line between power feared and maleficence persecuted was a hazy one and the 'witch' herself could not always control the event or events which turned the community's violence against her. Perhaps a more powerful motive was the desire for revenge against a community which she felt had ill-treated her, on the part of someone to whom the usual means of revenge—the law, wealth, physical power, social standing and the like—were closed.

Once the suspect had been identified, it was not difficult to find evidence of her guilt. Apart from physical peculiarities already mentioned, which were invariably found, the alleged victim nearly always remembered at least one occasion when he had given offence to the 'witch' or might have done so. Others in the community would not be slow to come forward with corroborative evidence, for Elizabethan village life was harsh and those whose way of living differed from the set pattern of the majority were immediately regarded with suspicion. The 'witch' would be kept away from communal festivties—harvest ales, weddings and so forth—and then accused of harbouring a grudge for not being invited. And there would always be someone to say that he or she had seen the witch cursing—many lonely old women mumble under their breath—or perhaps a natural talent for swearing and cursing could in itself be a foundation for an accusation or conviction of magical powers; Sarah Brice of Hereford made a practice of kneeling in the churchyard when she felt the need to curse her neighbours.

When the complaint had been made and the suspect identified, the next stage was to obtain a confession from the accused person. Not every accused was as obstinate as Margaret Landish who in 1645 refused to confess that she was a witch and made 'a strange howling in the court to the great disturbance of the whole bench'. Though physical torture was hardly ever used in England to extract confessions of witchcraft (perhaps the accusers remained apprehensive to the end of the evil powers of the accused), the line between physical and psychological torture is notoriously difficult to draw. Witches were not hung by their feet or pressed with weights, though the custom of 'swimming' suspected witches was certainly practised in Elizabethan England. In this case the old woman was thrown into the water and pronounced guilty if she floated because this was a sign that the water, being the medium of baptism, refused to accept the evil one; if she drowned of course she was considered innocent—for all the good it did her.

Although an individual fanatic like Matthew Hopkins, the 'Witchfinder General' in the 1650s, was to anticipate modern methods of 'intensive interrogation' such as keeping suspects confined for long periods in uncomfortable positions and without food and drink, it is probable that most Elizabethan confessions of witchcraft were obtained by the psychological pressure put on the suspect. Consecrated bread which would choke a guilty witch, or boiling water or a hot iron which she could safely touch if she were innocent—these were still fairly straightforward ways of demonstrating the witch's guilt so that she confessed. Even more direct was the recommendation of one Zacharias, a cunning man of Hastings, who in 1593 advised sticking a knife in the buttock of an old woman suspected of bewitching a child. But the more usual process of extracting a confession is probably best illustrated by one of the more celebrated Elizabethan witch trials, that of Mother Samwell, her husband and her daughter, all three of whom were hanged for witchcraft in 1593. At first it was only the old woman who was accused of bewitching the children of Robert Throckmorton of Warboys in Huntingdonshire, in whose house she worked. The children broke out in fits at prayer time and screamed that Mother Samwell had bewitched them. The old woman very sensibly put down the accusation to 'pure wantonness' on the children's part, but soon the pressure began to build up; divines from Cambridge University came over to see her and the doctor whose treatment for the children was unsuccessful began to look on her with suspicion. One of the divines told the old woman in so many words that if she did not confess he himself would bring the wood and fire to see her burnt at the stake. When Lady Cromwell visited the children and scolded Mother Samwell, the latter answered back. Lady Cromwell grew ill, had bad dreams and died a year later. The old woman was arrested together with her husband and daughter. The woman who had earlier asked Lady Cromwell why she ill-treated her since she had done no harm now confessed that she had caused the lady's death—and she probably believed it. Earlier she had confessed to bewitching the children—'O sir I have been the cause of all this trouble to your children'—and her daughter was made to confess that she had been a party to the bewitching of Lady Cromwell—'as I am a witch and consenting to the death of Lady Cromwell, I charge thee come out of her'. As soon as the accused were hanged, all the children recovered. The worldly goods of the Samwells, worth some forty pounds in all, went to the lord of the manor, Sir Henry Cromwell.

It is probable that the courts in England were more lenient towards those accused of witchcraft than were the rural communities where they lived. Generally speaking, witch-hunts sprang from the grass roots, not as a result of pressure from those in authority. One of the speakers in Gifford's *Dialogue Concerning Witches and Witchcrafts*, a woman, says: 'If I had but one faggot in the world, I would carry it a mile upon my shoulders to burn a witch.' We can get some idea of what it was like merely to be accused of witchcraft from the fate of Agnes Fenn, a ninety-four-year-old woman who in 1604 was punched, beaten, pricked and then stabbed in the face with a knife by a group which included Sir Thomas Grosse, gentleman. A 'witch' could be dragged bodily from her own house and kicked, beaten and scratched in the open street; the necessity of drawing blood usually meant that the physical assault was severe.

In discussing both black and white magic we are dealing with an area of Elizabethan life where the line between those who were genuinely believed to have, or believed themselves to have, magical powers and the legions of counterfeiters is almost impossible to draw, since an imposter could have just as much 'success' as a 'genuine' witch. But we can glance briefly at a few examples of fairly obvious fraud. Reginald Scot exposed the fraudulent practices of Mildred Norrington of Westwell in Kent who claimed, in fits of apparently demoniacal possession, that her mother, Alice, kept two devils in a bottle and had already bewitched two men and a child to death through them. Adam Squier, Master of Balliol College, Oxford (1571–80) was accused by a group of irate Somerset men of having sold them a 'fly' or familiar spirit guaranteed to win for them in any dice game at the third try. After this, they had lost all their money and land. Squier managed to hang on to his Mastership because he had friends in high places. Not so fortunate were Alice and John West whose 'several notorious and lewd cozenages' were exposed in a pamphlet of 1613. One of their claims was that they were the King and Queen of the Fairies and could bestow wealth and happiness at their pleasure. Some idea of their mode of operation can be gained from evidence given at their trial on charges of pretending to introduce Thomas Moores and his wife to elfin royalty:

> They brought him into a vault, where they showed him two attired like the King and Queen of Fairies, and by them little elves and goblins, and in the same place an infinite company of bags, and upon them written 'This is for Thomas Moores', 'This is for his wife', but would not let him touch anything.

Their powers, however, were insufficient to save themselves from the pillory; Ben Jonson based a scene in his great comedy *The Alchemist* in part on their exploits. In another comedy *The Devil is an Ass*, Jonson drew some of his inspiration from the activities of John Darrel, a Puritan preacher, and one of the more spectacular charlatans in a period not notably lacking in them. Darrel had two doubtless laudable aims, to put the fear of God into atheists who disbelieved in devils and to show the world, now that the Church of England had renounced any claims to magic, that not only the popish priests could work miracles. His speciality was exorcism. He began by casting the devil out of a girl and followed this by casting out eight more devils. In Lancashire he exorcized demons out of seven people simultaneously. But his greatest success was at Nottingham with a young lad named Somers whom he had met at an alehouse at Ashby where Somers was playing and singing. Darrel displayed Somers in his fits, speaking with strange voices, foaming at the mouth and so forth. People came from miles away to see the possessed youth; some saw him speak with his mouth shut, others saw something running up his leg and into his mouth. The lad's belly under the coverlet swelled enormously and his movements and voice seemed totally out of his control. Popular excitement and enthusiasm were immense. To add to it, Darrel discovered in Somers a talent for identifying witches. In Nottingham alone Somers pointed to thirteen, most of them the usual old widows. But it was all too much for Somers who finally confessed that Darrel had taught him the whole bag of tricks, including using black lead to cause foaming at the mouth. All Somers had wanted was to get out of serving his period of apprenticeship as a musician. Darrel tried valiantly to make out that the devil had possessed the lad and tempted him into dissembling, appearing in the guise of a large black dog

Judith Philips, fortune teller and swindler, astride her victim, an unnamed 'rich churl in Hampshire'

(which a fellow Puritan preacher actually saw, if we are to believe him), but things were never quite the same again.

Even more intriguing is the case of Judith Philips, whipped through the City of London for defrauding a rich Hampshire man in Upper Samborne, near Winchester. Not satisfied with her first husband's meagre income, Judith Philips left him and set up as a cunning woman in Upper Samborne. Hearing that a rich and credulous farmer lived nearby, she made it her business to find out all she could about the man and his wife, including the fact that he was engaged in a lawsuit with a neighbouring landowner. She then went by night to the farmer's back garden and buried an angel and a silver sixpence under a hollow holly tree.

The next day the man's wife was sitting at her open front door when the cunning woman passed by and stopped to stare intently at her. When questioned, she said that the goodwife had a remarkably fortunate face. 'Have you not' asked Judith Philips 'a hollow tree standing near unto your house, with certain weeds growing about the root?' 'We have', was the answer, 'and what of that?' The cunning woman then asked to speak to the man of the house and was invited in. Again she gazed fixedly at the man's face and told him that she knew by certain signs on his forehead that he was involved in a lawsuit with some great man of the shire, and that he would win the case. This greatly heartened the farmer whose spirits were further raised when the cunning woman informed him that she could help him find much buried treasure that lay in his grounds if he undertook to defray her modest expenses. The farmer was naturally hesitant and wished to see some demonstration of Judith Philip's alleged powers. This was easily arranged. She took him by the hand and led him to the root of the hollow tree where, after some digging, he found the angel and the silver sixpence.

The man needed no more convincing. He promised to provide her whatever she needed for her operations, which included the substantial sum of fourteen pounds. The cunning woman then said: 'Now must I have the largest chamber in your house behung with the finest linen you can get, so that nothing about your chamber but white linen cloth be seen; then must you set five candlesticks in five several places in your chamber, and under every candlestick you must put an angel of gold.' All this was done. One further item was also supplied at Judith Philip's request, namely a brand new saddle with two girths.

All was now ready. The cunning woman ordered the couple to go into the yard and the man to get down on all fours. She then put the saddle on him, fastened it with the girths and rode him three times between the house and the holly tree. Her next commands were: 'You must lie three hours one by another grovelling on your bellies under this tree, and stir not, I charge you, until I come back again; for I must go into the chamber to meet the Queen of Fairies and welcome her to that holy and unspotted place.' The cunning woman then went inside the chamber, made a neat pile of the linen, candlesticks and money, and vanished into the night, pausing only to drape herself in some of the linen and make a brief appearance as the Fairy Queen, chanting appropriate incantations to the hapless couple quaking in the cold outside.

When the farmer awoke to the reality of the situation, he was too abashed to let the truth be discovered by his neighbour. Judith Philips might have escaped scot-free had her victim not ridden post-haste to Winchester seven miles away where he revealed the matter to an influential kinsman who organized a hue and cry immediately as a result of which the Queen of the Fairies was caught in mid-career, as it were.

The witchcraft craze in England did not long survive the scientific scepticism of the later seventeenth century. At least as far as the courts were concerned, more stringent standards of proof began to be called for (one judge remarked that it was not a legal offence to fly through the air) and it was not long before it became impossible to recognize with certainty an act of witchcraft. But though sceptism, which had existed almost from the beginning, spread to the courts as the century progressed, it does not seem to have affected popular belief in witches and witchcraft, which survived well into the nineteenth century and is hardly dead today. The biblical injunction 'Thou shalt not suffer a witch to live' continued to haunt the folk mind. Enlightened Christians like Reginald Scot tried to explain that this referred to those who secretly harmed their neighbours and those who deliberately pretended to have magical powers. They did deserve death. But others were either innocently accused or deceived themselves. Like Scot, Samuel Harsnet tried to expose both Popish and witchcraft 'miracles' for the frauds they usually were, while Gifford, as we have seen, thought the only witchcraft that really existed was that of the devil who bewitched the minds of the credulous. But though their humanity and scepticism finally triumphed in the courts and witchcraft trials dwindled in number and finally ceased, popular superstition lingered on: 'If you read the executions done upon witches, you shall see such impossibilities confessed as none, having his right wits, will believe'. Scot's despairing words were to remain true for a long time to come.

CHAPTER FIVE

Astrologers and Alchemists

Black and white magic were closely associated in the popular mind with the practice of alchemy. As we have seen, it is sometimes difficult to distinguish, where 'magic' is concerned, between genuine folk wisdom and psychological understanding on the one hand and self-delusion or sheer charlantry on the other. Similarly, among those who professed the arts or sciences of astrology and alchemy, it is virtually impossible to draw a clear line between real scientific experiment and inquiry and the most extravagant superstition.

Until late in the seventeenth century mathematical signs and symbols were looked on with suspicion as magical formulae—not always by the illiterate and ignorant— while terms such as 'mathematician', 'conjuror', 'astronomer' and 'astrologer' were more or less interchangeable. In his great satire *The Praise of Folly* (1511), Erasmus wrote of the arrogance of these self-proclaimed scholars: 'But those of them who feels most conscious of their own superior erudition, and regard with peculiar contempt the ignorance of others, are the mathematicians'. Pouring scorn on what appeared to be their unnecessarily elaborate apparatus of mysterious squares, circles, triangles and so on, 'with letters of the alphabet dotted here and there like soldiers in sentry boxes, first placed in one order and then in another', Erasmus went on to link mathematicians with another sort of 'figure caster':

> To this philosophical brotherhood belong all those who give out that they can foretell future events by observing the positions of the stars. And they predict occurrences of the most prodigious proportions. Talk of marvels of magic! Why, they dwindle to insignificance when compared with the astounding wonders which astrologers declare to us are about to be. Yet—fortunate men—they find gullible people enough in the world to swallow their wildest announcements!

Nearly one hundred and fifty years after Erasmus, we find John Gaule, a pamphleteer, remarking that almanacs were consulted by the common people more often than their Bibles.

Part of the Church's opposition to astrology was indeed due to its realization that it was to some degree in competition with the stargazers. Not only were priest and astrologer putting forward different explanations for the same observable facts of life and nature, but the effect of accepting astrological explanations tended to make the priest's role as pastor less important—when a decision was really vital one consulted the astrologer not the parson. It is clear that for about a hundred years, from the middle of the sixteenth century to the middle of the seventeenth, most people in England believed in astrology in one form or another.

In Elizabethan and Jacobean England, astrology was part of the general structure of belief of all classes of society, although it was the subject of much controversy as regards some of its details and uses. The Earl of Leicester asked Dr John Dee to consult the stars in order to fix an auspicious hour for the coronation of Queen Elizabeth. Anyone who could afford it had their children's horoscopes cast at birth and every village cunning man usually combined reading the stars with other kinds of divination; his clients neither understood nor cared about the difference.

Astrology was an ancient art when Greek civilization was young. It came to medieval Europe, like so much else, via the Arabs. Its immense prestige during the Renaissance period was partly due to the fact that its methods and assumptions fitted neatly into the general mental outlook of the time. From our present point of view the most important element in this was the notion, deriving from Aristotle, that the heavens were the eternal and perfect part of the universe while the earth was subject to change, disorder and decay. It was then reasonable to suppose that the perfect bodies influenced the imperfect ones, especially since in certain cases, as in the moon's action on the tides, the influence was readily observable. The planets seemed to move in perfect harmony and regularity, their circular motion being the very pattern of perfection. Earthly life on the other hand was so evidently lacking in these qualities. By plotting the positions of the planets, one would be able to predict their influence on happenings on earth. Of course this could only be done if there was an established body of knowledge as to which planets in which situations were favourable or unfavourable to terrestrial activities, and this is precisely what the ancient tradition of astrological lore provided. It constituted a system whose claim to authority was as weighty as that of the Church, whose idiom and ritual were no less arcane and whose savants were no less learned. The whole elaborate structure of the twelve zodiacal signs and the different 'houses' of the planets and the infinite conjunctions, oppositions, aspects and so on offered an image of order and solace to Renaissance man. It was part of the sense which he had inherited from the Middle Ages of belonging to a universal system of links and correspondences. 'If celestial spheres should forget their wonted motions', asked the Elizabethan divine Richard Hooker 'What would become of man himself, whom these things now all serve?'

A fortune teller. Together with 'blessers', 'charmers', 'sorcerers' or 'witches', fortune tellers would cast horoscopes, make weather forecasts and pander to the other requirements of country people

Not only was astrology absorbed into general belief, but its influence extended into practically every branch of human activity. 'These late eclipses in the sun and moon portend no good to us' declares old Gloucester in *King Lear*, 'Love cools, friendship falls off, brothers divide: in cities, mutinies; in countries, discord; in palaces, treason; and the bond crack'd 'twixt son and father'. His mind, like Hooker's, effortlessly makes the connection between domestic discord and civil strife and between these and the motions of the planets. In a different situation he might have pointed to the link between the stars and the more homely human activities, such as sowing and reaping. Thomas Tusser in his *Five Hundred Points*

93

of Good Husbandry (1573), one of the most popular agricultural handbooks of the time, advises the husbandman:

> Cut all thing or gather, the moon in the wane,
> But sow in increasing, or give it his bane.

The connection between astrology and agriculture was as plain to most people as that between navigation and the position of the stars—the influence of the planets on the weather was an observable fact. Less obvious but equally widely held was the belief that the planets influenced the growth and structure of plants and the nature of metals. Indeed, the planets were held to be the source of all physical change on earth as they sent down different quantities of heat, cold, dryness and moisture, the primary qualities associated with the 'elements' of earth, air, fire and water. Since these same elements and their associated qualities formed the basis of the human body, it is not surprising to find that astrology played a vital part in medical diagnosis and prescription. Every part of the body was supposed to be ruled by one of the twelve signs of the zodiac and diagrams of the Anatomical Man illustrated the popular almanac books of the time. 'Were we not born under Taurus?' asks the merry knight Sir Toby Belch of his dimwitted companion Sir Andrew Aguecheek in Shakespeare's *Twelfth Night*. An almanac would have told him the connection between revelling and the sign of the bull. 'Taurus? That's sides and heart', replies Sir Andrew with misplaced confidence, for if he ever did see an almanac the chances were that he could not follow it, except at a considerable distance. 'No sir, it's legs and thighs' says Sir Toby. As can be imagined, the supposed links between a man's health and the position of the stars offered an almost limitless field for the enterprise and ingenuity of the astrological quack. Some of them did not even need to see the patient; they could determine what was wrong with him merely by examining a specimen of his urine taken at a specified time. Shakespeare's Falstaff evidently consulted one of these 'piss prophets' as they were disrespectfully called, for in answer to his question 'Sirrah you giant, what says the doctor to my water?' his page replies: 'He said sir, the water itself was a good healthy water; but for the party that ow[n]ed it, he might have more diseases than he knew for.'

Until the middle of the sixteenth century, there was no important English work on astrology but there was a steady stream of translations from continental works which, thanks to the printing press, percolated rapidly down the social scale. The Cambridge pedant Gabriel Harvey mentions some of the most popular treatises in a contemptuous note: 'These be their great masters and in this manner their whole library, with some old parchment rolls, tables and instruments, *Erra Pater* their hornbook; the *Shepherd's Kalendar* their primer; the *Compost of Ptolomeus* their

Bible; *Arcandam* their New Testament.' The first of these dated from the Middle Ages and was allegedly based on the 'perpetual prognostications' of the Jewish seer Esdras. The second had been translated from the French, the third was a digest of the astrological sections of the second, and the fourth aimed at 'teaching the fatal destiny of every man' by a system of divination based on the letters of his name. Some astrologers were of course genuine scholars who could read treatises in Latin, Greek, Hebrew, and even Arabic; but most of them managed very well with versions of these four works and some on even less; almost at the very end of the seventeenth century a roving fortune teller caused alarm and despondency in Lincolnshire by telling people they were bewitched and assuring them that the end was nigh. Apart from some out-of-date almanacs, he appears to have based his predictions on a text-book on arithmetic.

Astrology and astronomy were interchangeable terms at this time; the full title of what we today call astrology was judicial astrology. It was divided into four principal sections of which general prediction was the most widespread. This consisted of relating planetary movements to future events not in any individual's life but in the whole movement of society. Thus crop failures, epidemics and civil strife were objects of general prediction. Two of the three main sections of early almanacs dealt with these matters (the third was simply a calendar with the fixed Church feasts marked). While such predictions were attended to with interest, they did not have anything like the impact of the other three branches of judicial astrology, all of which were generally tailored to the requirements of a particular individual. General predictions attracted widespread attention only when they were associated with some extraordinary celestial phenomena, such as the new star seen in the constellation of Cassiopeia in 1572, the comet of 1577 or the solar eclipse in 1652. Nativities were based on planetary positions at the time of a person's birth, and were kept up to date with 'annual revolutions' for every year. Then there were elections, which had to do with fixing on the appropriate moment for important actions. The characteristics of the client and his general situation as revealed in his horoscope were to be set against the position of the planets at a specified time in order to determine whether that time was auspicious for the action in question. The last and perhaps the most controversial branch of astrology consisted of the so-called horary questions. This was a method of determining the correct answers to questions based on the position of the stars at the time the questions were put.

If part of the great appeal of astrology was due to its comprehensive scope, a good deal was also due to its flexibility, or rather its unique combination of rigidity and complexity of scheme with flexibility of interpretation. To put it another way, the astrologer's calculations were elaborate and intricate, but if the prediction he made as a result turned out to be false, he could always demonstrate that this was not due to any fault in the system itself. An astrological figure was based on a map of the sky divided into the twelve zodiacal houses. Many factors could affect the accuracy of such a figure, the time and place when it was cast, the direction which the client or the astrologer faced, and so on. And once the figure was cast, it did not exist in isolation. In almost any important matter, other horoscopes than the client's would come into play, including the 'nativity' for the country as a whole at a given time. The opportunities for error—and fraud—were limitless. The ex-schoolmaster of Knaresborough, John Steward, confessed in 1510 that, although he pretended to consult an almanac to impress his clients, he could not make head nor tail of it. Steward specialized in the application of astrology to cases of theft. Five years before his confession, a carrier at St Ives consulted an astrologer on discovering that he had lost some money at an inn. On the basis of the astrologer's description, the carrier caused the inn-keeper's son to be arrested, but neglected to check the man for the discoloured teeth which the culprit should have had and ended up with a suit for wrongful arrest on his hands.

In his *Treatise against Judicial Astrology* (1601) John Chamber tells a story which has all the hallmarks of a traditional tale, and throws some light on the kind of description which an astrologer might give as guidance towards identifying the culprit in a case of theft. A man consulted an astrologer to find out who had stolen a silver spoon from his house. After due deliberation and divination, the stargazer pronounced that the guilty party was one who was born in a high place in the west, had long legs and a beak nose, wore a black coat and red stockings and spoke in a strange tongue. It was eventually discovered that the spoon had been taken by a bird, a Cornish chough, so that the astrologer's description of the thief turned out to be correct in all particulars. Behind the joke we cannot help feeling the element of solid common sense having its own back on the tortuous evasions of much astrological prediction. Nor was protest always merely verbal. When John Dee, whom we shall meet later in his role as alchemist, left his house in Mortlake on his second European journey, it was ransacked by the mob, who considered him a disciple of the devil but were too afraid to do anything while he was in England, while an even direr fate overtook 'Dr' John Lambe, the confidant of the Duke of Buckingham, whose astrological knowledge, in spite of his pretensions, was shown to be virtually non-existent when the Royal Society of Physicians examined him on it in 1627; Lambe was stoned to death by the mob in a London street.

Nevertheless the profession was not without its compensations. The production of astrological almanacs was a fairly profitable business for anyone with access to a printing press until two printers, Watkins and Roberts, were given the monopoly in 1571; in 1603 it passed to the Stationers' Company. But the most lucrative part of the profession consisted of personal consultation. Astrologers spanned almost the whole social scale of Elizabethan society, from village cunning men to the

Woodcut of title-page of *Astrologaster or the figure caster* by John Melton. Almanacs were often consulted more than the Bible by common people, for astrology constituted a system whose claim to authority was as weighty as that of the Church

associates of Court favourites. At the lower end of the scale they were often part-timers like the Nottingham cordwainer Edward Ashmore. But there were choice pickings to be had higher up. It was all very well for John Melton in his *Astrologaster or the Figure-caster* (1620) to ask scornfully why astrologers always lived in the back alleys of the city and to lump together the cunning man of Bankside, the shag-haired wizard in Pepper Alley and Mother Broughton in Chick Lane with the celebrated Dr Forman at Lambeth. But at his death (which he correctly predicted) Forman left £1,200 and at the peak of his astrological practice had about a thousand clients a year. Even more spectacular was the scale of

97

operations of Nathaniel Culpepper who is reported to have worked his way through an *average* of forty clients each morning. Fees for these sessions varied according to the importance of the issues involved. An ordinary consultation could cost two shillings and sixpence in London, though in the provinces payment was often made in kind. For finding a stolen mare the owner would have to pay one shilling, but if he was careless or unlucky enough to lose both horse and mare it could cost him four times the amount in consultation fees. William Lilly, the most celebrated astrologer of the seventeenth century, had nearly 2,000 clients in a good year, with individual consultations rarely lasting longer than fifteen minutes. Lilly claimed to have learnt astrology in a matter of eight weeks and his active career belongs to the second half of the century. For the Elizabethan and early Jacobean period, we are fortunate in having copious records of the life and adventures, astrological and amatory, of one of the most intriguing figures in a fascinating age, Simon Forman.

In his intellectual curiosity, his abundant physical and mental energy, his zest for life and in the diversity of his activities and interests, Forman typified many aspects of his age. Born in Quidhampton in Wiltshire in 1552, he was thrown on his own resources by the death of his father when he was a lad of ten, and by the apparent indifference of his mother. While working in Salisbury he persuaded a schoolboy who shared his lodgings to teach him in the evening whatever he had learnt at school during the daytime. This rudimentary education was apparently sufficient to enable Forman to work as a schoolmaster, for which he was paid £2 for six months' work. He was at Magdalen School, Oxford, for a brief while, during which he kept himself alive by acting as a servant to two Wiltshire gentlemen of libertine tendencies, later to become clerics. It was in the year 1579 that Forman, according to his own account, discovered that he possessed miraculous prophetic powers. These were, however, inadequate to prevent him being robbed of his books and other property in June of that year or being jailed for practising magic. He was released in July 1580, before he had completed his full term of sixty weeks and managed to make his way to London, probably offering his services as itinerant physician-cum-prophet. In London, he so impressed a patient, Henry Jonson, with his healing powers that Jonson invited him on a fortnight's visit to Holland. Here Forman learnt what he could about astronomy and medicine and on his return set up in practice in his native Wiltshire. But he was promptly ordered by the assize justices to abstain from quackery. It was probably to this prohibition that Forman owed his subsequent fame or notoriety, for it induced him to return to London in 1583 where he remained until his death in 1611.

Forman's London career brought him in close contact with all walks of Elizabethan society, from serving men and kitchen maids to eminent divines and peers—and particularly peeresses—of the realm. He was constantly in and out of prison—where he spent almost the whole of the year after he first came to

ASTROLOGERS AND ALCHEMISTS

Dr Simon Forman, an astrologer with an extensive, albeit dubious, repertoire and reputation

London—mainly because the College of Physicians kept hounding him for practising without a licence, but also because they claimed that his knowledge of astrology was non-existent. Be that as it may, it is clear from his papers that Forman himself believed implicitly in his own astrological powers, for he never took an important decision without 'casting a figure' for it. On several occasions Forman drew astrological diagrams to determine whether some woman or other would make him a suitable wife. But in a career of indefatigable philandering which lasted until his death he often consulted the stars as to the likely outcome of less permanent sexual relationships. Thus in April 1592 he abandoned a promising affair because the horoscope showed that the girl in question 'will prove a whore and bear outward in her behaviour a fair show, but she will play the whore privily'. His diaries record his copious copulations which he signified by his own code-word 'halek', and on more than one occasion Forman cast a figure to determine whether a given female would or would not 'halek' with him. Nearly always the stars were as kind to him as the women. When women consulted him, as they often did, as to whether or not they were pregnant, he took active steps to ensure they were.

During his London years, Forman combined the careers of physician, astrologer, alchemist, necromancer, philanderer and man-about-town in spite of constant harassment by the College of Physicians and others. In 1593 he was summoned before the College and declared that he needed no other help for the Ephemerides (almanacs) to cure diseases. In particular he did not much care for the fashionable treatment of blood-letting, nor for diagnosis by urine examination or 'paltry piss' as he called it. He was banned from medical practice and fined £5, which does not seem to have deterred him very much. He was proud of the fact that the year before he was summoned by the College of Physicians, when London was stricken by one of its periodic outbreaks of the plague, he had stayed behind to cure the sick and the poor while all the doctors had fled into the comparative safety of the country. It even moved him to verse:

> And in the time of pestilent plague
> When doctors all did fly,
> And got them into places far
> From out the city,
> The Lord appointed me to stay
> To cure the sick and sore,
> But not the rich and mighty ones
> But the distressed poor.

Forman's boast was justified, for he did stay behind and even caught the infection himself, though he was successful (or lucky) in his self-prescription and treatment. Throughout his career, even when he was consulted by the highest in the land, Forman remained accessible to his poorer clients, often giving them his services free.

A few examples of these services will illustrate how much astrology was a part of everyone's ordinary life in Elizabethan England. The place of astral prediction in marital and extra-marital life has already been indicated. Whether a woman was a virgin, whether she would remain faithful, whether a man was or was not the father of his wife's child—these and similar questions crop up constantly in Forman's casebooks, sometimes, as we have seen, involving him personally. Other questions related to the choice of trade, for which Forman drew up an elaborate set of rules. He even devised one set of rules for ascertaining whether or not a given house had been searched during the owner's absence, by no means an infrequent occurrence at a time of stringent religious and political censorship.

In an age whose favourite indoor pastime seems to have been litigation, it comes as no surprise to find that many clients sought astrological advice as to the outcome of lawsuits. Forman himself was involved in a series of legal actions against one Peter Sefton, a neighbour when Forman lived at Billingsgate. Among other things

Sefton claimed that Forman 'occupied a wench upon a stool, with many other false villains for the which I could have killed him with a good will' and also that he, Forman, had several whores and had killed two children. Matters came to a head when each was arrested at the other's suit. The legal rights and wrongs of the case are less interesting than the fact that Forman cast figures at several stages of the lawsuits to find out the result, and when the case was over he again consulted the stars to determine whether Sefton and he would continue friends. Clearly, as far as his astrological activities were concerned, Forman was no charlatan in the ordinary sense of the word.

In the middle ranks of Elizabethan society, we find Forman being consulted by divines, merchants and seamen on matters of public life and commerce. The eminent Elizabethan theologian, Hugh Broughton, made repeated inquiries as to whether or not he would be translated to a bishopric, as did Dean Blague of Rochester, whose wife was one of Forman's many conquests; it is sad to record that neither man became a bishop. Forman's meticulous records of his consultations illuminate for us an age where nearly all forms of success in public life, religious and secular, depended on the grace and favour of those in high places. Since the latter were themselves often engaged in power struggles with rival contenders, the path of the aspirant was doubly hazardous; no wonder he sought to impose on this chaos of uncertainty the reassurance of the orderly progress of the stars in their courses.

As navigation and the stars had always been closely associated, it is perhaps not very surprising that Forman had many clients who were connected with the sea. There was the woman whose husband went to sea with Essex, in 1597, who asked Forman whether she was destined to be a 'Lady' as a result of the expedition. (Essex had been granted permission by the Queen to confer a number of knighthoods on members of the expedition.) There were merchants such as Nicholas Leate whose overseas trading interests led them to consult the astrologer over the fate of a ship which was long overdue, or about the auspicious hour for sailing. Even marine insurance men habitually consulted astrologers. So did seamen, such as the famous Elizabethan sailor, Sir William Monson. Forman claimed that he had predicted to the very day and hour when Monson would meet a Spanish treasure ship. Evidently the prediction came true; although Monson did not succeed in capturing the ship he invariably consulted Forman whenever he put out to sea again. And Lady Hawkins, wife of Sir John Hawkins, sought the astrologer's advice in March 1595, just before the voyage to the West Indies from which neither Hawkins nor Drake returned.

Inquiries about missing ships and the fate of those who sailed in them remind us that this was a period when communications were bad and news slow and uncertain by both land and sea. Part of Forman's function was to act as a one-man missing persons bureau, casting figures to find out what had happened to lost husbands or wives, runaway servants and apprentices and the like. But one of the most frequent motives for consulting an astrologer, and one we have already met in the case of the cunning man, was to attempt to recover stolen goods or the search for hidden treasure. Forman could on occasion be more specific in his identification of a thief than the anonymous astrologer in the tale of the Cornish chough. When Martha Webb was robbed in 1601, he pronounced: 'He that stole it his name was Arnold, a gentlemanlike fellow; he was taken abed with two wenches. She heard of the gown and cloak. He is in Bridewell: he hath been burned in the hand before.' Yet such accuracy had its dangers; fifteen years earlier Forman had narrowly escaped being beaten up by one of the suspects as a result of his erroneous prediction in a case involving stolen goods.

By the mid-1590s, Forman was a figure of some note and influence, though he was still at loggerheads with the College of Physicians. In 1595, when he was again examined by the College, fined £10 and sent to prison, he was released six weeks later on the orders of no less a personage than Lord Keeper Egerton, who demanded an explanation from the College. In spite of this, he was charged by the physicians the next year with administering a potion which had killed his patient and was again imprisoned for two months. The year after that the Lord Mayor charged him with assaulting a woman and he spent a fortnight in one of the Counter prisons. When he was released he took the prudent step of moving from the city into Lambeth (he had often found it necessary to absent himself from his lodgings for short periods before) where he would be within the jurisdiction of the Archbishop of Canterbury and beyond the grasp of the meddling physicians. When Cambridge University granted him a licence to practise in 1603 (one of his sponsors being the Royal physician himself), his troubles with the College were nearly over, though four years later they heard complaints from his patients about his high fees and about some of his methods. It is possible that these complaints were deliberately engineered by the jealous doctors, for Forman's fees were by no means excessive by the standards of the time, and he often treated poorer patients free. He invariably received gifts at New Year and at other times from grateful patients, noble and humble; in 1604 they included a tin ladle, some apples, 'a chamber cushion' and a pair of gloves. Around this time Forman was prosperous enough to lend out money on goods received, but there is no evidence that he charged excessive interest. And we should note that the College of Physicians did not object to Forman because he practised astrology (so did a good many members of the College) but because he had (until 1603) no licence to practice medicine and because his astrological knowledge (according to the College) was bogus.

Forman died in 1611, but his greatest notoriety came posthumously four years later during the trial of Lady Frances Howard for the poisoning of Sir Thomas

Overbury. It was widely believed at the time that Forman had supplied her with poison through an intermediary, Anne Turner, who was later hanged. A contemporary ballad on the subject tells us that:

> Forman was that fiend in human shape,
> That by his art did act the devil's ape.

Intimate letters from Lady Frances to Forman (in which she addressed him as 'sweet Father') were produced in court, as well as leaden figures of a man and a woman in the act of copulation. But it seems clear that Forman's part in the whole squalid affair was confined to making love potions and magical figures whereby Frances Howard could compel the love of Robert Carr, the King's favourite. Nothing that we know of Forman's life and character suggests that deliberate poisoning was ever one of his activities, multifarious though these were. At the Overbury murder trial, it is said that Lord Chief Justice Coke was handed a manuscript book belonging to Forman containing the names of all Court ladies involved in amorous intrigues; he was about to read from it when he stopped abruptly; the first name in the list was that of his own wife, Lady Hatton.

Forman carried on his astrological and alchemical activities to the end of his life, combining them with a strenuous career as a man of 'halek' both with his wives (he was married twice, and his code-name for his wife was 'tronco') and others. (The entry for 9 July 1605, when Forman was fifty-three, is especially memorable: 'halek 8 a.m. Hester Sharp, et halek at 3 p.m. Anne Wiseman, and 9 p.m. halek tronco.' Forman seems to have been a virgin till the age of thirty and evidently determined to make up for lost time.) To the end he justified the phrase 'Oracle Forman' which a character uses of him in Jonson's *The Alchemist*. A week before his death, according to the astrologer William Lilly, Forman and his wife were having a meal in their garden house when she asked him which of them would die first (a question Forman was often asked by clients). 'Oh, Tronco, thou wilt bury me, but thou wilt much repent it' he replied, and when his wife asked him when this would be, his answer was 'I shall die ere Thursday night'. The following week he was in perfect health 'with which his impertinent wife did much twit him in the teeth'. After dinner on Thursday, he went down to the river and took a rowing boat to Puddledock. In the middle of the Thames, he collapsed, only saying 'An impost, an impost'. Sceptics have suggested that he may have commited suicide in order to prove himself right. He left £1,200 and a large number of children, mostly illegitimate.

Forman was both astrologer and alchemist, among other things, but I have ignored his alchemical activities as they can be observed in the life and adventures of another well-known Elizabethan, Dr John Dee. Astrology and alchemy touched at many points, not only because the same people often practised both but because their pursuit answered to many of the same needs, and the theoretical assumptions behind the activities overlapped a good deal. Thus we find, for example, the insistence in alchemical treatises on the desirability of performing the various operations during the most auspicious planetary conjunctions, an association between the seven recognized metals and the seven planets and so on. There were even sustained efforts to embody the planetary influence in some tangible physical form. Everywhere we come up against the realization that both astronomy and alchemy were widely regarded as essential parts of a wider system of ideas, though each had its sceptical critics.

The general objectives and methods of alchemy have already been briefly mentioned, but it would be useful here to take a closer look at its principles and practices, not only because they are fascinating in the insights they give into Elizabethan modes of thought, but also because, as with astronomy, some idea of what the alchemists were trying to do and the way they set about their business helps us to see more clearly the tremendous opportunities that beckoned the fraudulent practitioner.

When Chaucer, at the end of the fourteenth century, attacks fake alchemists in 'The Canon's Yeoman's Tale', the practice of alchemy in England was already well established. Early in the fifteenth century a statute laid down the death penalty for those who 'use to multiply gold or silver [n]or use the craft of multiplication'. But throughout the century licences to practise alchemy were being regularly granted by the sovereign. Occasionally someone would be caught practising the art without a licence but the punishment does not seem to have been very severe by the standards of the age.

The original alchemists did not think of themselves as magicians, but almost as scientists, attempting to achieve certain results by exploiting what they believed to be the laws of nature. All *matter*, they believed was one, and it was *form* which gave it variety; not only were metals, animals, and vegetables forms of the primitive elements of earth, air, fire and water, but these latter were themselves the basic forms of inchoate primal matter. Since we see all about us the forms of matter changing (seed into plant, egg into bird, wood into ash and so on) there was nothing inherently impossible or absurd in the notion that any form of matter could be changed into any other. These changes were thought of as part of the general pattern of life and growth, as the whole universe was a living process. Thus when a substance changed its form and took another (as when a heated metal changed its appearance and texture and lost its solidity) the process was conceived of in terms of death and resurrection, and the union of different substances as a marriage. These were not mere metaphors, or colourful descriptions of processes that could be more accurately defined in other terms. They correspond exactly to the categories of medieval and Elizabethan thought. Thus the process of transmutation and multiplication was a life-creating process, the 'generation' of new forms through the 'corruption' of the old. To create life, the first necessity was the soil, or raw material to sustain growth. The second was warmth, which the alchemist provided with various kinds of warm baths and dungbeds. Then there was the need for the active life-giving principle, which came from heaven, and which was thought of almost literally as a kind of breath which in metals manifested itself as two vapours rising up through the earth, one moist and one dry. Finally, a seed was needed from which growth could take place. This could be provided either by refining gold from base metals in which small quantities were present or by increasing the quantity ('multiplying') by various processes.

The four elements earth, air, water and fire, of which all substances were supposed to be constituted, were, so it was believed, to be found in their perfect proportions in gold, which was, therefore, eternal and indestructible ('whatever dies was not mixt equally' wrote John Donne). Thus the true alchemical inquirer was not led on by a sordid desire for wealth but by an urge to bring metals to their highest state, part of the greater urge to clothe all creation in the habit of perfection—as the search for the elixir of life, the other great alchemical quest, was prompted by the desire to banish the body's imperfections and bring it to a condition of perfect harmony.

Both the objectives of alchemy and the conditions in which it was practised made it a fertile field for charlatanry. As even the brief outline I have given will show, alchemy was compounded of more or less equal parts of what we would today call science and religion. To the science of chemistry, alchemy bequeathed little more than the idea of laboratory experiment and a few items of equipment whose modern descendants are still employed by the experimental chemist. Its aims and its basic assumptions about the world were so radically different from those of modern science that there was no more it could offer. The other part of alchemy influenced the creation and enlargement of various branches of mystical lore which are still alive and well today in many parts of the world. There were also those who considered the entire alchemical process as a symbolic system whose primary reference was not to metals and their transmutation but to the working of the human spirit within the gross body.

Of the twelve stages in the alchemical process, the first six were devoted to the making of the 'white stone'. These six were more or less identifiable chemical processes, most of them various forms of distillation. They had such names as calcination, dissolution, conjunction and putrefaction. In a treatise by George Ripley, one of the founding fathers of English alchemy, the second stage, dissolution, is described like this:

[It] maketh intenuate things that were thick also,
By virtue of our first menstrue clear and bright,
In which our bodies eclipsed been of light,
And of their hard and dry compaction subtilate,
Into their own first matter kindly retrogradate.

As even this small extract shows, clarity of exposition was not the chief virtue of the alchemical writers, nor did they intend it to be. They wrote in a deliberately obscure manner in order to restrict the secrets of their art to the chosen few, though this was hardly compatible with its dissemination through printing. Ripley's treatise, already a hundred years old, was presented to Queen Elizabeth in 1591. Not only did he and other alchemical authors develop a highly mystifying 'technical' vocabulary, but they also had an elaborate system of symbolism which sometimes had a vivid poetic life of its own. Thus apart from the symbolism of marriage and the life-process, we have the dragon that is to be slain—that is, imperfect matter whose form is to be changed, the green lion—a symbol for the devouring acid, the black cow—putrefying volatile matter, and so on. Both the technical jargon and the symbolism provided an excellent cover for the charlatan, a fact that Ben Jonson exploited to the full in his play *The Alchemist* (1610) which deals with the activities of Subtle, a fake alchemist and his assistant Face, during the absence of Face's master from his London house on account of the plague. The distinction between paraphrase and parody is impossible to draw when, for instance, Face comes in to tell Subtle how he has been superintending the experiment:

I have blown, sir,
Hard for your worship; thrown by many a coal
When 'twas not beech; weighed those I put in, just,
To keep your heart still even. These bleared eyes
Have waked to read your several colours, sir,
Of the pale citron, the green lion, the crow,
The peacock's tail, the pluméd swan.

The six later stages of the process were designed to change the white stone into the 'red stone' which is the true philosophers' stone, for it would transform heated mercury into gold. These processes were described in such obscure language that they almost defy intelligible interpretation. The two final stages were the critical ones: 'multiplication' or 'augmentation' of the elixir and 'projection' or transmutation of the base metal by casting the powder of the philosophers' stone. 'When do you make projection?' asked the impatient dupe Sir Epicure Mammon, to whom grave Doctor Subtle replies:

Dr John Dee, an eminent astronomer and mathematician as well as an alchemist, who may have been one of the models for Ben Jonson's impostor in his play *The Alchemist*

Son, be not hasty. I exalt our med'cine
By hanging him in balneo vaporoso,
And giving him solution; then congeal him;
And then dissolve him; then again congeal
    him.
For look, how oft I iterate the work,
So many times I add unto his virtue.

Needless to say the final stage of projection is never reached, and the penultimate stages are well-adapted for repetition as many times as the market will stand.

One of the models for Jonson's imposter may have been Dr John Dee, an eminent astronomer and mathematician as well as an alchemist. 'He used to distill egg-shells' writes the delightful seventeenth-century gossip John Aubrey, 'and 'twas from hence that Ben Jonson had his history of The Alchemist, whom he meant'. Dee himself appears to have been a sincere and dedicated alchemical experimenter, which is more than can be said for his associate Edward Kelly, an ex-apothecary who had been put in the pillory for digging up graves and practising necromancy and had his ears cropped for coining before he came to Dee. The spirit Ariel, whom Kelly invoked, instructed Dee to employ Kelly. This at least was Kelly's interpretation of the mystical language in which the spirits habitually addressed him. A sample follows:

Biab. Azien. Com. Selt. Gir. P. Ad.

Kelly obligingly translates, if that is the word, these gnomic utterances into terms such as these:

Understand the voice of winds, O you the second of the first, whom the burning flames have flamed within the depth of my jaws, whom I have prepared as cups for a wedding, or as flowers, in their beauty, for the chamber of righteousness, stronger are your feet than the barren stone, and mightier are your voices than the manifold winds.

As an undergraduate, Dee had been responsible for a production of a play by Aristophanes in which some of the effects were so ingenious that supernatural influence was suspected. In 1564 he instructed Queen Elizabeth in mystical matters and twenty-five years later, when he returned from a European sojourn of six years, she gave him money for his alchemical experiments. Dee's association with Edward Kelly lasted from 1582 to 1589, a period in which they achieved recognition throughout Europe, becoming known to four emperors. Between 1583 and 1588 they stayed at the court of the Emperor Rudolf in Prague, during which time the spirits were in continual converse with Kelly, who acted as Dee's 'scryer' or crystal-gazer. Among other things, they led him to discover certain books which Dee had burned three weeks earlier and also presented him with a 'stone of vision' (which was taken away by a spirit but later placed under his pillow by another). At one time the advice from the spirit world included the injunction that Dee and Kelly were to share their wives (Kelly had taken a wife reluctantly and only because the spirits had told him to). At least two astronomers of the later seventeenth century were convinced that Dee and Kelly had discovered the secret of the philosophers' stone. William Lilly affirmed that Kelly's sister had had some gold made according to her brother's prescription 'not thirty years since' while Elias Ashmole actually knew people who had seen Kelly heat a piece of a warming pan and turn it into pure silver which the ambassadors in Prague sent to Queen Elizabeth. And on the marriage of one of Kelly's serving maids, we are told that £400 of gold wire rings were given away to the guests. Even more impressive testimony comes from an eye-witness, Sir Edward Dyer, who saw Kelly put base metal into a crucible and heat it together with a small amount of the 'powder of the stone, whereupon it came forth in great proportion perfect gold to the touch, to the hammer, to the test'. One way to achieve this effect was to use a piece of gold-copper alloy with some of the surface copper removed by cementation. And it was not only Kelly who had mastered this technique; young Arthur Dee solemnly declared that his father had converted pewter objects into silver in Prague.

The demand for the services of such invaluable men was widespread. In 1588, a year for which many wonderful events had been predicted, Burleigh was trying to get Dee and Kelly to come back to England and also to obtain some alchemically produced funds to build up the English navy. Dee left for England but Kelly (who was now Sir Edward) was kept back by the Emperor Rudolf and died five years later, breaking his legs in an escape bid.

Whether Dee had the philosophers' stone or not, it is certain that towards the end of his life he had to sell his books to keep himself alive. He died in poverty in Mortlake in 1608. One of his alchemical recipes is reproduced in full below for the reader's edification:

Take a red dragon, courageous, warlike, to whom no natural strength is wanting, and afterwards seven or nine noble eagles, whose eyes will not wax dull by the rays of the sun, cast the birds with the beast into a clean prison, and strongly shut up, and under which let a bath be placed, that they may be incensed to fight by the warm vapour. In a short time they will enter into a long and harsh contention, until at length about the day fortyfive or fifty, the eagles begin to prey upon and tear the beast to pieces; and his dying, it will infect the whole prison with its direful poison, whereby the eagles being wounded, they will also be constrained to give up the ghost. From the putrefaction of the dead carcases, a crow will be generated, which by little and little putting forth his head, the bath being somewhat increased, it will forthwith stretch out its wings and begin to fly; but seeking chinks from the wings and clouds, it will long hover about; take heed that it find not any. At length being made by a gentle and long rain, and with the dew of heaven, it will be changed into a white swan; but the newborn crow is a sign of the departed dragon.

In making the crow white, extract the elements and distil them according to the order prescribed, until they be so fixed in their earth, and end in snow-like and most subtile dust, which being finished, thou shalt enjoy thy first desire to the white work.

Perhaps the aptest comment on all this is that of the sceptical Surly in Jonson's play:

> Sir, I'll believe
> That alchemy is a pretty kind of game,
> Somewhat like tricks o' the cards, to cheat a man
> With charming . . . . What else are all your terms,
> Whereon no one o' your writers 'grees with other?

But let us give the last word to Dr Dee noting, however, that his advice, worthy though it is, is far easier given than followed: 'Farewell, diligent reader; in reading these things, invoke the spirit of Eternal Light, speak little, meditate much, and judge aright.'

CHAPTER SIX

Low-Life on the Highway

If Tudor vagrancy had any one starting point, it may have been the disruption caused by the long drawn out travail of the Wars of the Roses. When, at their conclusion, Henry VII succeeded in his effort to abolish private armies, the immediate result was to drive out of employment many professional soldiers as well as servants of noble households who frequently had as much experience in the use of arms as the soldiers themselves. (Medieval drama provides many instances of complaints against the proud servants of noblemen who use their lords' livery as a cover for pillage and extortion.) A mid-fifteenth century ballad puts the point baldly but pithily:

> Temporal lords be almost gone,
> Households keep they few or none,
> Which causeth many a goodly man
> For to beg his bread:
> If he steal for necessity,
> There is none other remedy
> But the law will shortly
> Hang him all save the head.

Although the discharged soldier was a common enough figure on the medieval roads, his activities appear to have been more widespread and better organized in Tudor times. In 1589 for instance, soldiers returning from Drake's unsuccessful expedition against Portugal arrived in London just in time to create alarm and confusion during the festivities of Bartholomew Fair. Some of the city streets had to be closed off with iron railings and peace and order were not restored for six months. When we recall that soldiers on active service were badly paid (if they were paid at all) and discharged with only their weapons and their uniforms, we are unlikely to be surpised that so many of them turned to vagabondage or robbery with violence. They had the training, resources and opportunity to do little else.

The dissolution of the monasteries by Henry VIII probably added a few

111

One of a seventeenth-century series of engravings of beggars. Vagabondage became so acute during the Elizabethan period that it came to be accepted as a feature of social life

hundreds to this ever-growing army of vagrants. Not many of them are likely to have been monks, for most monks had pensions. Nor does the evidence suggest that monastic charity was responsible for keeping any large number of would-be vagrants off the roads; it was too sporadic and unsystematic for that. The really significant effect of the closing of the monasteries was that it threw out of work the large number of people who kept monasteries going from day to day—people such as gardeners, butchers, cooks, launderers and so forth. When the security of a roof over their heads was taken from them by the hammer blows of Henry's minister Thomas Cromwell, most of them had no alternative but to take to the roads with only their wits to keep them warm.

The Reformation also abolished the legal existence of itinerant friars and pardoners and turned them into vagrants in the eyes of the law. Proctors or collectors for charitable institutions, did, as we shall see, continue to travel the kingdom during Elizabeth's reign, but their activities offered a rich hunting ground for imposters.

Many vagrants would also have been recruited from the large number of peasants deprived of land and livelihood by changes in agriculture and forms of landholding which took place at the beginning of the Tudor era. With the shortage of labour resulting from the Black Death, wool-farming had received a strong impetus as it required fewer workers than husbandry. By the beginning of the sixteenth century, therefore, the English wool industry was strong and growing. Many landlords took to enclosing common lands for sheep pasture and forcing tenants out of their smallholdings. As one of the speakers in Sir Thomas More's *Utopia* (1516) exclaims:

> Your sheep that were wont to be so meek and tame, and so small eaters, now, as I hear say, be become so great devourers and so wild, that they eat up, and swallow down the very men themselves. They consume, destroy, and devour whole fields, houses and cities. For look in what part of the realm doth grow the finest and therefore the dearest wool, there noblemen and gentlemen, yea and certain abbots . . . leave no ground for tillage, they enclose all into pastures; they throw down houses; they pluck down towns, and leave nothing standing, but only the church to be made a sheephouse.

The process of evicting small landholders became easier because of a change from the medieval system of landholding, whereby even the humblest serf or villein had immemorial and virtually unchallengeable rights in the land in return for service, to a more individualistic system in which service was commuted for money and the peasant won the right to sell his labour in the open market. This worked very well for him when labour was scarce but was disastrous when, as in the later sixteenth century, the economy was growing more slowly than the supply of labour. 'What sea of mischiefs hath flowed out of this more than Turkish tyranny!' asks Robert Crowley eloquently in his tract entitled *Information and Petition Against the Oppressors of the Poor Commons of this Realm* (1549):

> What honest households have been made followers of other not so honest men's tables! What honest matrons have been brought to the needy rock and cards! What men children of good hope . . . have been compelled to fall, some to handicrafts and some to day labour, to sustain their parents' decrepit age and miserable poverty! What forward and stubborn children have hereby shaken off the yoke of godly chastisement, running headlong into all kinds of wickedness, and finally garnished gallow-trees!

Many of the men and women who had been ousted from their livings turned to a life of vagrancy and a large army of them were to be found thronging the Elizabethan highways, making travel an event not to be undertaken lightly.

It was certainly not an activity which any Elizabethan undertook for pleasure. Even in London, broad well-paved roads such as Cheapside and the Strand were the exception. Elsewhere in England, the four great Roman roads were the only thoroughfares that deserved the name. Virtually all the other roads were simply tracks which had been marked out by the feet of passing travellers or the hoofprints of their horses. Officially a Surveyor of Highways, appointed annually by each parish, was supposed to be responsible for the construction and maintenance of roads; every parishioner was compelled to work on the roads for eight hours a day during four consecutive days or, if he was one of the more substantial citizens, to provide horses and men for the work. Defaulters could be fined. No doubt this made the roads somewhat better than they had been before 1555, when they became the responsibility of the parish by statute. But this is not saying a great deal, for, as William Harrison complained 'The intent of the statute is very profitable, but in practice the rich evade their share, and the poor so loiter in their labour that scarcely two good days' work gets accomplished'.

Such as they were, these roadways connected the townships and hamlets of Elizabethan England. In winter they were almost impassable and in summer their dry rutted surfaces were a menace to horse and man alike. Often they ran alongside a narrow belt of cultivation, beyond which lay the thickly wooded countryside which still covered most of England, and which provided ideal refuge for the 'high lawyers' or footpads who preyed on the unfortunate traveller. Many of these were, as we have seen, discharged soldiers adept in the use of firearms, though they did not usually kill or wound their victims if the latter handed over their coin and goods without fuss. Very often they relied on ostlers and other inn-servants for intelligence about well-laden travellers and their itineraries. It was an easy matter for the ostler as he took the traveller's bag off his horse to judge how much it contained, and for the tapster to notice how much money the traveller had when he drew out his purse to pay for his drink. And an attentive ear at the dinner table could be very rewarding: 'It holds current that I told you yesternight', says the chamberlain to Falstaff's comrade-in-arms in *Henry IV* I, 'there's a franklin in the wild of Kent hath brought three hundred marks with him in gold: I heard him tell it to one of his company last night at supper . . . . They are up already and call for eggs and butter: they will away presently.'

The most celebrated highwayman of the day was Gamaliel Ratsey, whom we shall meet again. The son of a Lincolnshire gentleman, Ratsey had a good education and served with Essex in Ireland before he took to the highway. His

A hanging. Only the hardiest denizens of the underworld openly embraced a life of highway robbery as death on the gallows was the certain penalty if they were caught

career is so thickly barnacled with legend that it is almost impossible to tell fact from fiction, but Ratsey appears to have been something of a Robin Hood character who robbed the well-to-do and often helped the needy. In this he may have been influenced by a Cambridge parson whom he waylaid in a wood and compelled to preach a sermon before him; the reverend victim chose as his topic the Christian duty to show charity to the poor. Ratsey specialized in wearing several disguises on his expeditions, including one particularly horrible mask. After several years of highway robbery he was finally betrayed by his accomplices and hanged at Bedford on 26 March 1605.

Only the hardiest denizens of the underworld openly embraced a life of highway robbery; death on the gallows was the certain penalty if they were caught. Below the high lawyer, who was a full-time highwayman, came the 'ruffler', who went about begging, claiming to be a discharged soldier and seeking employment, but who would turn to robbing wayfaring men and women when it was safe to do so. 'Now these rufflers', says Thomas Harman, 'the outcasts of serving men, when begging or craving fails, then they pick and pilfer from other inferior beggars that they meet by the way, as rogues, palliards, morts and doxies.' Before we meet these interesting characters it is fitting that we should take a brief look at the uncrowned king of the vagrants, the upright man. Harman puts him 'the second in sect of this unseemly sort' below the ruffler but as, on his own admission, a ruffler had to serve a year's probation before he graduated to being an upright man, we may reasonably infer that his was the senior rank.

Everything we learn of the upright man confirms the impression of his supremacy. In the first place he did not so much beg as walk up to a cottager's door and demand money as his just due for long and loyal military service for his country: 'If he be offered any meat or drink, he utterly refuseth scornfully, and will nought but money.'

In the second place the unwritten law of the highway empowered the upright man to demand of any beggar he met whether he had been 'stalled to the rogue', that is, formally initiated as a beggar, and if so, by whom, when and where. If the answers he received were not satisfactory, the beggar would not only forfeit whatever money he had together with his best garment, but he would be taken to the nearest alehouse or 'boozing ken' where the upright man would call for a 'gage of booze' [a quart of ale] and pour it on the beggar's head with the words: 'I, G.P., do stall thee, W.Y.', to the rogue, and that 'from henceforth it shall be lawful for thee to cant [beg] for thy living in all places.' Finally, the upright man, not only had the right to help himself to a share or snap of any other vagrant's possession, but he also had what amounted to a *droit de seigneur* over anyone's woman. One of the earliest writers on the subject, John Awdeley, had this comment to make: 'And if he do them wrong, they have no remedy against him, no, though he beat them as he useth commonly to do. He may also command any of their women, which they call doxies, to serve his turn. He hath the chief place at any market walk and other assemblies, and is not of any to be controlled.' The stout truncheon or 'filchman' which the upright man always carried about him was as much the visible symbol of his authority as the metal-tipped staff of the sheriff's man—and probably more fearsome to the fraternity of vagabonds.

Harman is more expansive on the subject of 'doxies' than Awdeley who dismisses them curtly as 'their women'. 'These doxies' according to Harman 'be broken and spoiled of their maidenhead by the upright men, and then they have their name of doxies, and not afore. And afterward she is common and indifferent for any that will use her, as *homo* is a common name to all men.' Before a woman had been thus initiated by the upright man she is a 'dell', 'a young wench, able for generation and not yet known or broken by the upright man'. Harman has a brief but vivid sentence which reveals the origin of such women: 'These go abroad [out of doors] young, either by the death of their parents and nobody to look unto them, or else by some sharp mistress that they serve do run away out of service; either she is naturally born one, and then she is a wild dell.' When Autolycus, in Shakespeare's *The Winter's Tale*, sings 'heigh the doxy over the dale' he is perhaps expressing his taste for the mature woman rather than the inexperienced girl.

Other female vagrants included 'autem morts' who were women married in church, though Harman does not have any very high opinion of their marital fidelity, since they were often absent from their husbands for a month at a time: 'And they be as chaste as a cow I have, that goeth to bull every noon, with what bull she careth not.' 'Walking morts' on the other hand were not married, though they often pretended to be widows or to have husbands on active service. 'When these get aught, either with begging, bitchery, or bribery, as money or apparel, they are quickly shaken out of all by the upright men, that they are in a marvellous fear to carry anything about them that is of any value.' To thwart the upright man's activities they often left goods and money with various trusted alehouse keepers and others during their wanderings.

The last two classes of female vagrants commonly met with on the English roads were bawdy baskets, whom we have already met and at whom we shall take a closer look in the next chapter, and 'demanders for glimmer', who were women who travelled from place to place with false documents certifying that they had lost all their goods through fire. (We are reminded that fire was a constant hazard in an era when most houses were of timber and thatch.) If she did not always get money from tender-hearted folk, the demander for glimmer could nearly always count on malt, wool, bacon, bread and cheese, all of which were readily saleable commodities. And, like all female vagrants, they seem to have been, in Harman's words 'easily persuaded to liking lechery'. He goes on to say that an average demander 'would weekly be worth six or seven shilling with her begging and bitchery'.

Nor must we forget the younger generation, the children of vagrants, called 'kinchin coes' if they were boys and, if girls, 'kinchin morts'. They served a variety of purposes, including wriggling through small openings to pilfer, distracting attention while the parents went about their nefarious business, and looking suitably pathetic in order to soften the hearts of the villagers. Instances are not lacking of children being deliberately mutilated to increase their potential earning capacity as recipients of charity. When very young, these children were carried tied up in sheets and slung on their mothers' backs. 'The morts their mothers carries them at their backs in their slates, which is their sheets, and bring them up savagely, till they grow to be ripe: and soon ripe, soon rotten.' Clearly Harman had no sympathy to waste on those who were born into a life of vagrancy.

Among the most fearsome wanderers on the Elizabethan roads was the 'Abraham man' or 'Tom O'Bedlam', who claimed to be lately released from Bedlam asylum. He is dealt with in a later chapter on the treatment of the insane in Elizabethan times. Then there was the 'prigger of prancers', known to our more prosaic age as a horse thief, whose activities were largely concentrated on fairs and markets. But there were a number of other principal types of vagrant, with such colourful names as 'palliards' (or 'clapperdudgeons'), 'whipjacks', 'dummerers' and 'counterfeit cranks'.

A 'rogue' was originally a vagrant who went about with forged papers, apparently seeking a long-lost relative or bearing an important letter to a gentleman in a neighbouring shire; all he wanted was money to help him get there, as he had been waylaid and had lost all his. Sometimes the rogue would even carry papers certifying that he had been whipped for vagrancy and was now being sent back to his parish, some convenient distance away. (Under Elizabethan law a convicted vagrant was whipped and returned to his parish.) 'And all this feigned, because without fear they would wickedly wander, and will renew the same where or when it pleaseth them; for they have of their affinity that can write and read.'

The clapperdudgeon or palliard was a beggar born. He was easily recognized by his long patched cloak, high-heeled shoes or 'stampers' and the wooden dish he carried at his girdle. Often he had a wooden staff tipped with iron. His doxy followed him carrying a covered pack containing whatever she contrived to filch on her wanderings. She had a needle and thread stuck in her cap and as she walked she knitted or made string balls or shirt-strings. Sometimes she told fortunes or professed to diagnose and prescribe for women's and children's ailments. While the palliard was begging at the door his doxy would be on the lookout for any poultry feeding in the garden; she would feed them with bread stuck on a hooked pin tied to a thread.

Palliards came in two varieties, the genuine and the artificial. The latter showed considerable artistry in the way they adorned (if that is the word) their bodies with sores, called the great cleym. Dekker's description of their procedure in *O Per Se O* is vivid and precise enough to deserve quoting in full:

> They take crowfoot, spearwort and salt, and, bruising these together, they lay them upon the place of the body which they desire to make sore. The skin by this means being fretted, they first clap a linen cloth, till it stick fast, which plucked off, the raw flesh hath ratsbane thrown upon it, to make it look ugly; and then cast over that a cloth, which is always bloody and filthy; which they do so often, that in the end in this hurt they feel no pain, neither desire they to have it healed, but with their doxies will travel, for all their great cleyms, from fair to fair, and from market to market, being able by their maunding [begging] to get five bords, that is, five shillings, in a week, in money and corn. Which money they hide under blue and green patches; so that sometimes they have about them six pound or seven pound together.

The artificial palliards went about begging in twos or threes and appear to have uttered their eloquent lamentations in the form of rounds, one voice taking up the plea before the other had quite finished:

> Ah, the worship of God look out with your merciful eyne! One pitiful look upon sore, lame, grieved and impotent people, sore troubled with the grievous disease, and have no rest day nor night by the canker and worm, that continually eateth the flesh from the bone! For the worship of God, bestow one cross [coin] of your small silver, to buy him salve and ointment, to ease the poor wretched body, that never taketh rest; and God to reward you for it in heaven!

This touching appeal usually ended with the Lord's Prayer and as many Ave Marias as were necessary to touch the hearts and pockets of passers-by. According to Awdeley, the genuine clapperdudgeon would occasionally set upon the spurious one and rob him of his takings, though one would imagine that the beggar who was sound in wind and limb could well take care of himself against one who was actually wounded or crippled.

The whipjack was one of the many varieties of vagrant who carried a counterfeit licence, in this case testifying that the bearer had suffered severe losses at sea through shipwreck or piracy. These would always have been incurred well away from where they were begging. 'These fresh-water mariners, their ships were drowned in the plain of Salisbury' remarks Harman curtly. He confiscated the forged licences and earnings of several whipjacks in his capacity as a Kentish Justice of the Peace, and one group confessed that they had bought their licence for two shillings from a sailor in Portsmouth. These licences were often forged skilfully enough to pass the most careful scrutiny. Harman ruefully notes that confiscating licences is ineffectual because 'they will not be long without another. For at any good town they will renew the same'.

The dummerer was a real or pretended mute, usually, we are told, the latter. 'Therefore of these many' says Harman, 'and but one that I understand of hath lost his tongue indeed.' He relates how, on a visit to a priest in Dartford, he found a dummerer at the priest's door, with seals and certificates testifying to his plight. But one of the seals Harman recognized as one he had himself bought at Charing Cross. He therefore hurried home, knowing that the dummerer would have to pass that way. In due course the dummerer arrived, in the company of a palliard 'which palliard I saw not at Dartford'. They had been detained by a surgeon called Wostestowe, who was convinced that they were both counterfeiters. The surgeon made the dummerer open his mouth and tried to pull forward his tongue, which the dummerer held doubled. After some time he succeeded, but the man still would not utter a sound. Harman helpfully suggested that two of the man's fingers be tied tightly, with a stick inserted between them, which would be rubbed up and down till the dumb man spoke. 'Sir' said the surgeon, 'I pray you let me practise another way'. The surgeon's way consisted of tying the man's wrists with a halter and suspending him from a roof-beam till 'for very pain he required for God's sake to let him down'. Harman thereupon confiscated the man's money and distributed it to the needy poor of the area and sent the man with his servant to the next Justice, to be whipped and pilloried 'and none did bewail them'.

The last portrait in our rogues' gallery is in some way the most spectacular. This is the counterfeit crank. These were men and women who went about the country pretending to be epileptics, 'for the crank in their language is the falling evil'. They wore filthy rags about their heads and carried a piece of soap on their person which

¶A Caueat or Warening,
FOR COMMEN CVRSE-
TORS VVLGARELY CALLED
Uagabones, set forth by Thomas Harman.
Esquiere, for the vtilite and proffyt of his naturall
Cuntrey. Augmented and inlarged by the fyrst author here of.
Anno Domini. M. D. LXVII.

¶ *Vewed, examined and allowed, according vnto the*
Queenes Maiestyes Iniunctions.

¶ Imprinted at London in Fletestrete at the signe of the
Falcon, by Wylliam Gryffith, and are to be solo at his shoppe in
Saynt Dunstones Churche parde. in the West.
Anno Domini. 1 5 6 7.

Title-page from Harman's *Caveat for Common Cursitors*. In his capacity as a Kentish J.P. Harman
had plenty of experience of the various tricks used by the many different kinds of vagabond

they conveyed into their mouths at opportune moments to produce a most realistic effect of epileptic foaming. In 1566, when Harman was checking the proofs of his book on vagrants (he was in lodgings at Whitefriars at the time), a counterfeit crank came to his door. He was naked above the waist except for an old leather jerkin which had more holes than leather. His head was wrapped round in filthy cloths, and his beard too was tied up in rags. He carried an old felt hat as a begging bowl. His face was smeared with fresh blood from the eyes downward, as though he had just fallen in a fit and injured himself. His clothes, such as they were, were spattered with fresh mud. Harman asked the man what ailed him. 'Ah, good master' he replied, 'I have the grievous and painful disease called the falling sickness'. He explained that he had fallen in a ditch where he had lain all night. A kindly old woman had offered him a wash in her rain-water butt in the morning, but he had refused, because, he said 'if I should wash myself, I should fall to bleeding fresh again, and then I should not stop myself'.

This explanation stirred Harman's suspicion and he questioned the man more closely. He learnt that his name was Nicholas Jennings, a native of Leicestershire and a sufferer from epilepsy for the past eight years. His father too had the disease and (curiously) 'my friends before me'. He claimed to have spent a year and a half in Bedlam asylum. 'Why, wast thou out of thy wits?' inquired Harman, to which Jennings replied 'Yea, sir, that I was'. When Harman asked Jennings the name of the keeper at Bedlam he answered that it was John Smith, which, to say the least, showed a lack of imagination on Jennings' part.

The conscientious Kentish gentleman, having ascertained from Jennings that the keeper and several other members of the Bedlam staff were well aware of his epilepsy, sent his servant to the asylum to verify what he had heard. The servant returned with the information that no such person as Jennings had been in Bedlam, that there was not and never had been a keeper named John Smith and that no inmate was released until he was fetched away by his friends.

At this point in the story, Harman's activities as author become curiously involved with his personal experiences as investigator of vagrants. He sent for the printer of his book, told him about the counterfeit crank and asked him to set a servant to observe the crank's activities. The printer obligingly provided two lads who trailed Jennings to the Temple, where, having begged till noon, he retired to a field behind Clements' Inn. Here he redaubed his face with blood from a bladder which he carried about him, and put fresh mud on his clothes. He then returned to his begging. At nightfall Jennings crossed the water to St George's Fields and thence to Newington, where one lad followed him while the other went to report matters to his master the printer. The latter went with the boy to Newington where he charged the local constable to take Jennings into custody for the night. They compelled him to wash himself and asked him what money he had. Jennings

Nicholas Jennings as Gentleman and Beggar from *Groundworke of Conycatching*. He was apprehended in a number of disguises including a counterfeit crank and a whipjack claimed to have only twelvepence, but the lads who had seen him at his begging trade earlier in the day knew better. Under threat of whipping, the counterfeit crank reluctantly produced various sums from different parts of his person, totalling nearly fourteen shillings, no inconsiderable sum at a time when the daily wage of a master mason or carpenter would be about eightpence.

The constable and the printer then stripped Jennings naked and saw him to be a handsome fellow with flaxen hair and unblemished skin. 'Then the goodwife of the house fet her goodman's old cloak, and caused the same to be cast about him, because the sight should not abash her shamefast maidens, neither loath her squeamish sight.'

Later that night the constable set out with a search party to apprehend certain rogues and upright men who were reported to be spending the night in a nearby barn, and the printer accompanied him. This gave Jennings his chance. He had already drunk three quarts of beer and told the goodwife he wished to go out at the back 'to make water, and to exonerate his paunch'. She let him go, believing that he would hardly try to escape, clad as he was in nothing but an old cloak. But Jennings, casting modesty and the borrowed cloak to the winds, ran naked through the fields to his own house, which, it later turned out, was not far away.

That was on All Hallows Eve, 31 October. The next time the printer saw Jennings was at Whitefriars on New Year's Day. He hardly recognized the fellow, for he was now dressed in a smart black frieze coat, a new pair of white hose, a fine felt hat and a shirt of Flanders linen which cost as much as sixteen shillings. In the meantime, as it transpired, he had been putting in a spell as a whipjack in various parts of the country with certain associates. This time his story was that he was a hat-maker who had unfortunately lost all his money but, if he could only borrow the wherewithal to pay for his night's lodging, he would seek work among the hatters on the morrow.

When he said his name was Nicholas Jennings, the printer was sure of his man. He pretended to be about to lend him some money and talked him into walking along till he found a constable, whom he promptly asked to arrest Jennings. The constable was reluctant to do so, seeing how respectable Jennings looked. So they went along to the ward alderman's deputy who also tended to believe Jenning's story, but finally consented to commit him to the Counter on the understanding that the printer would be liable to any costs and damages if it turned out to be a case of false arrest.

In the morning one of the printer's boys identified Jennings as the counterfeit crank. Jennings tried to brazen it out to the end, giving a false address, but at last his real lodging, where he lived with his wife, was discovered and turned out to be a very well-furnished residence. After three days in the Counter he was removed to Bridewell where he was stripped and attired in his crank's disguise, to the

This is the fygure of the counterfet Cranke, that is spo-
ken of in this boke of Roges, called Nycholas Blunt
other wyse Nycholas Gennyngs. His tale is in the xvii.
lefe of this booke, which doth showe vnto all that reades
it, woundrous suttell and crafty desett donne of & by him.

Nicholas Jennings was finally caught and punished, spending time in the Counter and at Bridewell,
before being put in the pillory at Cheapside

astonishment of the governors. He was then put in the pillory at Cheapside where he had to stand alternately in his finery and in his beggar's rags. After this he was whipped at the cart's tail from Cheapside to his own door with a picture of him displayed in front of the cart. Finally, he was taken to Bridewell and released after some time on condition that he gave up his wicked ways. 'And his picture remaineth in Bridewell for a monument.'

Such were the rogues, beggars and vagrants who roamed the roads of Elizabethan England. To what extent they formed an organized anti-society is open to question. That they had some sort of hierarchy among them we have already seen. But how efficiently this operated, given the wide open countryside and scattered towns and villages the vagrants travelled through, and the seasonal character of their vagabondage (from summer to harvest-time was the peak period) is a question impossible to answer. Conscientious investigators such as Awdeley and Harman would have us believe that the society of the road was as tightly knit as that of Elizabethan England as a whole. But against this we must remember, first, that their information may have come from those who had their own reasons for making the 'anti-society' appear more efficient and formidable than it actually was, and secondly, that, like all Elizabethans, the authors had a passion for classification. But after making allowances for these and similar considerations, it may be safely concluded that some sort of organization and pecking order did indeed exist actively among these more or less permanent denizens of the road. Certainly it was efficient enough, on the testimony of the Somersetshire Justice of the Peace, Edward Hext, for eighty rogues to rob a man of a cartload of cheese he was taking to a fair and for three others to stay at an alehouse for three weeks, during which time they ate their way through twenty sheep.

The alehouse played an important part in the life of a thief and the vagrant. It is necessary to distinguish the alehouse very clearly from the inn, which was an altogether more respectable establishment, usually spacious and standing in the town's main thoroughfare, with a wine licence, stabling and guest rooms where men and women of standing would often meet. The alehouse on the other hand could often be the back kitchen of a mean dwelling, standing in some obscure back street and was frequently unlicensed. To the wanderers on the road it was a hotel, social club, information bureau, brothel, playhouse and, most important, receiving centre for stolen goods.

The Elizabethan alehouse should more properly be called a beerhouse, for it was the change from ale to beer which brought about the decline in domestic brewing for home consumption and the consequent rise in the number of alehouses. Beer kept longer and tasted better than ale, though it was more difficult to make. But the alehouse-keeper could buy on credit from the brewer and his only capital investment was for a few benches and tables for customers in his kitchen. For a

Woodcut from the title-page of *The Praise, Antiquity and Commodity of Beggary, Beggars and Begging* by John Taylor, showing three grades of vagrant. It is difficult to assess to what extent the many types of vagrant formed an organized anti-society, but it seems safe to assume that some sort of organization and pecking order existed among them

poor peasant or craftsman living on the edge of subsistence, an alehouse could be a very useful source of extra income. Many of them let out their barns to vagrants for a penny a night. For the growing number of vagabonds and for day-labourers receiving a money wage the alehouse was the only centre of refreshment and society. It is not therefore surprising that from the beginning of the sixteenth century there was a steady increase in the number of English alehouses. When the first parliamentary statute designed to regulate them came into force in the last year of Edward VI's reign, there were at least 20,000 alehouses in England; when Charles I came to the throne in 1625 there were over 33,000.

Alehouses were not only places where stolen goods could be safely stored, but in many of them they were openly sold. Sometimes the alehouse-keeper acted as pawnbroker or moneylender, even instigating robbery, as when Nicholas Sill was persuaded to steal sheep by the keeper of the White Hart at Canterbury. The overnight accommodation offered was none of the best, lodgers sometimes having to share a bed with the keeper and his wife. But the advantages of being away from the constable's or the Justice's scrutiny and the inexpensiveness of the amenities outweighed any such discomforts. And sometimes there were other and less usual compensations. At Mother Borden's alehouse at Chelmsford her daughter offered her services to customers at a price, while one of the attractions of a Canterbury alehouse was Black Bess, a Negro whore.

Many voices were raised against the abuses, real or imagined, which took place in alehouses. 'The true and principal use of inns, alehouses and victualling-houses is twofold' wrote Michael Dalton in *The Country Justice* 'viz., either for the relief and lodging of wayfaring people travelling from place to place about their necessary business, or for the necessary supply of the wants of such poor persons as are not able by greater quantities to make their provision of victuals; and it is not meant' he continued sternly, 'for entertainment and harbouring of lewd or idle people to spend or consume their money or time there'. That this last is indeed what usually happened at alehouses there is plenty of evidence to suggest. Any two Justices of the Peace could license an alehouse if the applicant could produce two sureties and recommendations from parishioners. At Milton in Essex, the applicant bound himself not to 'suffer any suspicious persons, vagabonds, barrators [cheats or promotors of quarrels], quarrelers or thieves' to stay on his premises nor to allow any unlawful games 'as bowls, tennis, dice, cards, tables [backgammon]' nor, revealingly, to permit 'any company eating, drinking, or playing in the time of any sermon or service of the parish church'. Alehouse-keepers were also made liable for a number of requirements such as not allowing bastard births on their premises, not serving meat in Lent and not allowing prostitution. We may be sure that these regulations were far more often breached than observed. Sometimes alehouse-keepers openly defied the law, and not always with such unhappy results as with Edward Bettes of the Saracen's Head at Gosfield who harboured Roger Banstead and Thomas Lawrence in spite of the local constables warnings; the pair robbed Bettes of money and goods to the tune of £8. The Buckinghamshire Justice of the Peace who wrote to Cecil complaining about alehouses was hardly exaggerating: 'I do think [them]' he wrote 'to be the very stake and stay of all false thieves and vagabonds.' Many a young man of promise could end up as a vagrant by over-frequenting an alehouse, like Thomas Carr of Billericay, who in 1600 was charged with 'living idly, following no trade to live by, being a lusty young man that goeth from alehouse to alehouse spending his time'. In general, though preachers inveighed against the vices of idleness and drunkenness, the more serious threat posed by alehouses as far as the authorities were concerned was that they gave refuge to undesirables. But I cannot resist quoting the case of one Essex parishioner who was so drunk at church on New Year's day that 'he was not able to go of his legs and so was led home'. His punishment was to sit on his knees in the church porch with three empty ale pots before him holding a white wand till the end of the second lesson, and then to enter the church and repeat aloud after the minister certain public words of penitence set down in writing!

Notwithstanding frequent denunciations, repeated regulations, raids and closures of individual premises, alehouses continued to flourish throughout this period because, as we have seen, they served a variety of needs among a section of the community not otherwise catered for. Without them, the outcasts of Elizabethan England would have been deprived of their chief source of physical, professional and social sustenance. Since one so often hears complaints and criticisms about Elizabethan vagrants, let us make some amends by listening, finally, to an impassioned sermon on behalf of thieves and vagabonds preached (under duress, it must be confessed) by a certain Parson Haberdyne, at the behest of certain thieves, who waylaid him at Hartley Row in Hampshire, robbed him and made him preach to them on the spot. Whatever he lacked in theological orthodoxy, the good parson certainly made up for in presence of mind and flair for paradox. Here, in full, is the text of his sermon, which it would be pleasant to believe actually was preached, though there is a suspiciously similar incident told about the highwayman Gamaliel Ratsey:

I greatly marvel that any man will presume to dispraise thievery, and think the doers thereof to be worthy of death, considering it is a thing that cometh near unto virtue, being used of many in all countries, and commended and allowed of God himself. The which things, because I cannot compendiously show unto you at so short a warning and in so sharp a weather, I shall desire you, gentle audience of thieves, to take in good part these things that at this time cometh to my mind, not misdoubting that you of your good knowledge are able to add much more unto it than this which I shall now utter unto you.

First, fortitude and stoutness of courage and also boldness of mind, is commended of some men to be a virtue; which being granted who is it then that will not judge thieves to be virtuous[ed]? For they be of all men most stout and hardy and most without fear. For thievery is a thing most usual among all men; for not only you that be here present, but many other in divers places, both men and women and children, rich and poor, are daily of this faculty (as the hangman of Tyburn can testify).

And that it is allowed of God himself, as it is evident in many stories of [the] Scriptures; for if you look in the whole course of the Bible, you shall find that thieves have been beloved of God. For Jacob, when he came out of

Mesopotamia, did steal his uncle Laban's kids. The same Jacob did also steal his brothe[r] Esau's blessing. And yet God said, 'I have chosen Jacob and refused Esau'. The children of Israel when they came out of Egypt, did steal the Egyptians' jewels of silver and gold, as God commanded them so to do. David, in the days of Abiazar the high priest, did come into the temple and did steal the hallowed bread. And yet God said, 'David is a man after mine own heart'.

Christ himself, when he was here on the earth, did take an ass and a colt that was none of his; and you know that God said of him, 'This is my beloved Son, in Whom I delight'.

Thus you may see that God delighteth in thieves. But most of all I marvel that men can despise you thieves, whereas in all points (almost) you be like unto Christ himself. For Christ had no dwelling-place; no more have you. Christ went from town to town; and so do you. Christ was laid wait upon in many places; and so are you. Christ at the length was caught, and so shall you be. He was brought before the judges; and so shall you be. He was condemned; and so shall you be. He was hanged; and so shall you be.

He went down into Hell; and so shall you do. Marry, in this one thing you differ from him, for he rose again and ascended into heaven; and so shall you never do, without God's great mercy, which God grant you! To whom, with the Father, and the Son and the Holy Ghost, be all honour and glory for ever and ever. Amen.

Thus the sermon being ended, they gave him his money again that they took from him, and two shillings to drink, for his sermon.

CHAPTER SEVEN

Autolycus and His Tribe

In addition to the professional criminal and vagrant, there were all over the country many hundreds of men, women and children who eked what living they could from trades which, though not themselves illegal, often offered opportunities for part-time robbery or fraud. These people were almost as diverse and inventive as the professional villains. They included pedlars, tinkers, jugglers, bearwards, strolling players, conjurors, minstrels, fortune tellers, exorcists and alchemists, to say nothing of collectors for various charities who had, or pretended to have, due authorization for their activities. They were the ragged and colourful tassels on the outer fringe of the Elizabethan underworld.

Neither pedlars nor tinkers stood very high in the estimation of the communities they served. But the pedlar was often the only regular link with the outside world in towns and villages which were cut off from each other by roads no better than rutted tracks in dry weather and marshy troughs when it rained. In places too small to have shops (and these would include most English villages of the time) he would be linen-draper, hosier, glover, perfumier and stationer rolled into one: In *A Winter's Tale*, Autolycus describes his wares as follows:

> Lawn as white as driven snow,
> Cypress black as e'er was crow,
> Gloves as sweet as damask roses,
> Masks for faces and for noses;
> Bugle-bracelet, necklace-amber,
> Perfume for a lady's chamber;
> Golden quoifs [head scarves] and stomachers
> For my lads to give their dears;
> Pins and poking-sticks [ironing rods] of steel;
> What maids lack from head to heel!
> Come buy of me, come, come buy, come buy,
> Buy lads, or else your lasses cry; come buy!

The 'swigman' or 'swadder', as the pedlar was called; a colourful figure who was often the only link with the outside world for those living in the more remote towns and villages

131

He is here clearly supplying the feminine luxury trade, with wares which he has, as likely as not, come by honestly. It was not unusual, if we are to believe Thomas Harman, one of the earliest investigators, for the upright man to unload his booty on to a pedlar, either for safe keeping or at prices unilaterally decided by the upright man, who, we may remember, was the uncrowned king of the highway.

There were gradations within the ranks of pedlars. To judge by the contents of his pack, Autolycus was fairly well placed. In addition to the items specified the typical pedlar would carry sheets of the latest ballads, gory, scurrilous or romantic, which told of singing fish or betrayed lovers or usurers' wives giving birth to money bags. Lower down the scale was the 'Irish toyle', who carried small items such as laces and pins in his wallet and who made a speciality of calling at houses when only children or servants were in, so that he could badger them into buying a pennyworth of lace in exchange for ten times its value in wool or grain.

But whatever his rank the 'swigman' or 'swadder', as the pedlar was called, had a supplementary source of income into which Autolycus again gives us a glimpse. 'My traffic is sheets' he announces blithely, 'when the kite builds, look to lesser linen'. For as the kite snatched scraps of household linen to line his nest, so the swigman helped himself to whole sheets which provident housewives conveniently laid out on hedges to dry. We also get some idea of how Autolycus spent his leisure hours when he explains his ragged clothes as the result of gaming and whoring. The simple country clown and his lass were legitimate prey in his own eyes, whether he practised his lawful trade or his less lawful ones, such as stealing from hedges or picking pockets. Beating and hanging were the ultimate punishments, but Autolycus's attitude to them is more casual than would have been that of his counterparts in real life.

The female counterpart of the pedlar was the bawdy basket who, as her name implied, offered more for sale than the laces, pins and ribbons she carried in her basket. 'And as they walk by the way, they often gain some money with their instrument by such as they suddenly meet withal.' Like the Irish toyle, the bawdy basket dealt as far as she could with servants and children and like him reckoned to get a shilling's worth of bacon or cheese for a pennyworth of pins.

Bawdy baskets did not work in partnership with swadders very often. Instead, they were great favourites of the upright men, who sometimes helped them to rob other denizens of the road. The experience of a lame beggar to whom Harman talked was doubtless not unique. As he was hobbling along a Kentish lane one day the beggar found his way blocked by an upright man and a bawdy basket. 'This knave oweth me two shillings for wares he had of me half a year ago' said the bawdy basket to her companion. The poor man's protestations that he had never set eyes on the woman in his life did not save him from being beaten up by the upright man and robbed of all he had, which was fourteen pence. As they left him lying by the roadside, the bawdy basket added insult to injury: 'Why' she said 'hast thou no more? Then thou owest me tenpence still; and, be well assured, that I will be paid the next time I meet with thee.'

Harman and Greene were voicing no more than popular belief when they asserted that the tinker made more holes than he mended. At a time when metal ware was expensive the tinker obviously performed a useful task, and because of this he found it easy to obtain access to a house, or at least the yard, for an hour or two, which made pilfering relatively risk-free. Sometimes the tinker left his bag of tools at an alehouse and turned to straightforward begging for a while. Tinkers' reputation for drunkenness followed them everywhere and they were not above selling their doxies' garments for the price of a drink. They evidently changed partners more often than other wanderers and frequently worked with a female companion who would hang about in the yard of a house where the tinker was at work in order to make off with a pewter pot or pan or whatever else lay conveniently to hand.

Sometimes their operations were on a larger scale and their methods more direct, for they were reputedly some of the roughest members of the roadside fraternity. There was a tippling tinker and his dog who took on four palliards and two rogues ('six persons together' as Harman helpfully elucidates for us) on the highway and robbed them of £4, hiding in a wood for a couple of days in order to avoid capture. 'Thus with picking and stealing, mingled with a little work for colour they pass their time.' Because he could visit houses regularly for long periods and because he could carry a large variety of tools and implements without arousing suspicion, the tinker was well equipped for picking locks—which was called 'the black art'. Greene's story about the tinker who visited the village of Bolton-in-the-moors has

A pedlar would travel the country not only selling to people, but also stealing from them to finance his leisure hours spent gambling and whoring

133

the ring of a folk tale about it, but it is the sort of folk tale which was far more likely to be the product of communal experience rather than communal fantasy; certainly many of its details have an air of homely authenticity.

For some time the village of Bolton-in-the-moors in Lancashire had suffered a series of mysterious robberies. No one could say for certain who the culprit was, but it was not long before the finger of suspicion was pointing at a visiting tinker who seemed to be getting accustomed to a style of living rather more lavish than his work alone could account for. The villagers took their complaint to the knight of the manor, who promised 'both redress and revenge'.

Not long after, the tinker called at the knight's house in search of work. The knight was extremely affable, and called out to the cook to bring out whatever pots and pans needed mending. While the tinker was at work (duly regaled with a blackjack of ale) the knight fell into genial conversation with him and asked him about the uses of the various tools in his bag, taking great care not to let the tinker realize that he had seen the bunch of skeleton keys which he carried. When the tinker had finished, the knight expressed himself very well pleased with the work, congratulated him on his skill and asked him how much he would have for his pains.

'But two shillings—of your worship' said the tinker, highly flattered, whereupon the knight answered that this was far too little for such a skilled craftsman. He gave him twice the sum and, hearing that the man was on his way to Lancaster, asked him to carry a letter to the gaoler there concerning a certain felon. The tinker willingly agreed and went on his way.

The end of the tale is fairly predictable. The tinker carried the letter straight to the gaoler as soon as he arrived in Lancaster, boasting of the courtesy and hospitality he had received at the knight's hands. The gaoler read the letter, solemnly assured the tinker that the knight had commanded him to offer the bearer of the letter 'the best entertainment I may' and promptly clapped him in irons. The letter of course was a *mittimus* committing the bearer to custody, and we can almost see Greene rubbing his hands with moralistic relish as he tells us that 'when he [the tinker] heard the *mittimus*, his heart was cold, and had not a word to say; his conscience accused him. And there he lay while the next sessions, and was hanged at Lancaster, and all his skill in the black art could not serve him'.

Another group of vagrants, though not perhaps essential to the life of rural communities, nevertheless played an important part in bringing to them the only entertainment they were likely to have outside of Maytime revels and the occasional ducking or pillorying. Minstrels, jugglers, acrobats and strolling players had travelled the roads for centuries, and before Henry VIII dissolved the monasteries, they had depended on the charity of the monks, if not their patronage. But the new Church of England was less hospitable in its attitude than the old faith and during the Elizabethan period the livelihood of these itinerant entertainers became more precarious than ever.

The most affluent among this group were probably the strolling players. The 'Act for the Punishment of Vagabonds' passed in 1572 made life easier for the better sort of players, who were protected by being officially recognized as servants of some nobleman, but almost certainly harder for the scores of others, for it took away from ordinary gentlemen the right to support troupes of players, restricting it to the nobility. Those who were not accredited members of such a troupe ran the risk of being arrested as rogues, vagabonds and sturdy beggars. The Act specifically mentions common players of interludes, and minstrels, as well as bearwards, jugglers, tinkers and pedlars.

Despite this Act, strolling players, both authorized and otherwise, continued to

Travelling players visiting a manor (*c.* 1610) from Moyses Waler's *Album Amicorum*. Gaining access to some gentleman's mansion led to opportunities for petty pilfering

135

roam the countryside till at least the end of the century. In 1605 Gamaliel Ratsey, the celebrated highwayman, was hanged. The event produced the customary spate of pamphlets purporting to recount Ratsey's life and opinions, in one of which we hear of the highwayman's encounter with a troupe of strolling players. The episode gives a shadowy glimpse of the conditions under which the players lived and worked.

One night Ratsey arrived at an inn where he learned that a company of players was staying. Ratsey called one of the leading players to his chamber and learned that the troupe was attached to a certain nobleman. He thereupon gave the players a lecture on acting (not unlike Hamlet's advice) and went on his way. A week later he came upon the troupe again but the players did not recognize him as he was in one of his many disguises. They were at a different inn and now pretending to be the servants of a different nobleman, who was better known in that particular locality: 'For being far off, (for their more countenance) they would pretend to be protected by such an honourable man, denying their lord and master; and coming within ten or twenty miles of him again, they would shroud themselves under their own lord's favour.'

Ratsey ordered them to put on a private performance for himself and rewarded them liberally. But the next day he caught up with them on the highway and retrieved his money, adding a sermon on their idle profession for good measure. He even went through a mock ceremony of knighting one of the players—'kneel down, rise up, Sir Simon Two-shares-and-a-half'—and told him that next time he should play under his (Ratsey's) warrant.

Strolling players frequently had better opportunities for petty pilfering than tinkers, pedlars and the like, especially if they were lucky enough to gain access to the mansion of a country gentleman or lord. Two of Middleton's plays, *Hengist, King of Kent* and *It's a Mad World, My Masters*, feature strolling players in their role as confidence tricksters. The latter play contains an elaborate trick in which the players (who are in fact, con-men disguised as players and are led by the nephew of the country knight who is to be their victim) nearly succeed in a large-scale robbery. Even when some of the gang are apprehended and brought into the very hall where the others are performing, they evade exposure by pretending that the arrest is all part of the play and that the constable who has brought them in is merely one of the players. They even succeed in trussing up the constable while they make their escape, and only the untimely ringing of a stolen alarm-watch gives them away. Though such virtuosity was doubtless exceptional, it is clear that in the lower reaches of their profession, it was not easy to distinguish between strolling players who were part-time con-men and con-men who were part-time strolling players.

It was possible for players attached to successful London companies such as

A minstrel would normally travel alone, and required a licence, frequently forged, in order to travel from place to place

Shakespeare's to make a handsome living and aspire to being gentlemen or even knights. One of the most famous of them, Edward Alleyn, founded Dulwich College, though he did not succeed in his attempt to get a knighthood. But the condition of the common players was much closer to that described by a gentlemanly 'character' writer of the time:

> The statute hath done wisely to acknowledge him a rogue, for his chief essence is *a daily counterfeit*. He hath been familiar so long with outsides, that he professes himself (being unknown) to be an apparent gentleman. But his thin felt and his silk stockings, or his foul linen and fair doublet, do [in him] bodily reveal the broker. So, being not suit-able, he proves a motley.

For all the hazards of their trade, the strolling players had the security, however minimal, which came from travelling together and belonging to a common profession. This could not be said of the bearwards, minstrels, jugglers and conjurors who usually travelled alone (though, as we shall see later, they sometimes had an accomplice in the audience). They too needed a licence to travel from place to place (only gentry and nobility could leave the parish without one), though these could be forged (at a price) and appear to have been serviceable for quite long periods of time. The bearward took his bear on a chain, making it dance, tying it to a stake for the assembled throng to cast stones at it, among other diversions. What these latter were we can gather from a handbill for an entertainment at the famous Bear Garden in London:

> Tomorrow being Thursday shall be seen at the Beargarden on the Bankside a great match played by the gamesters of Essex who hath challenged all comers whatsoever to play five dogs at the single bear for £5 and also to weary a bull dead at the stake; and for your better content shall have pleasant sport with the horse and ape and whipping of the blind bear.

The travelling bearward could not of course boast the extensive menagerie which the London ring afforded, but the pattern and purpose of the entertainment were alike, and there were stray dogs everywhere.

As for minstrels, the term covered a wide range of musical entertainers, from those such as Autolycus and Ben Jonson's Nightingale who sang the ballads they carried for sale, to impromptu singers, fiddlers and pipers. One of the best-known minstrels was called Anthony Now-now, from the chorus of one of his songs. The minstrels, like the strolling players, were reasonably safe if they could boast the livery of a nobleman; far from preventing them from taking to the road, it gave them a degree of security when they did so. Their less fortunate brethren had to depend on luck and cunning or on a forged passport. In either case their favourite haunts were taverns, alehouses and fairs. The ballads they sang varied from moralizing tracts or cautionary tales to the sort of things at which the honest Puritan, Philip Stubbes, waved his pious fists: 'bawdy songs, filthy ballads and scurvy rhymes, serving for every purpose and for every company.' One of the purposes for which they served was of course to engage the attention of the listeners while the cutpurse or pickpocket went about his business. Another was to whet the prospective client's appetite before he went to that part of the alehouse which customarily served as a brothel. There is a story of a character named Barnes of Bishops Stortford in Essex who used to stand outside the door drumming up custom for the performance of his two young sons who, 'one in a squeaking treble, the other in an ale-blown bass', gave a non-stop recital of bawdy ballads, obliging with an encore on the most obscene lines and stanzas. According to Henry Chettle who tells the story, father and sons earned up to twenty shillings a day, most of it derived from their share in the takings of the nip and foist. And in *Greene's News both from Heaven and Hell* Richard the bricklayer's wife complains bitterly that she might have married a minstrel who would have got

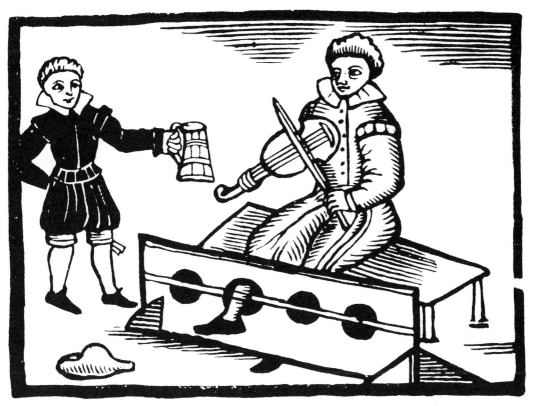

A fiddler in the stocks, perhaps because he entertained his listeners while his accomplice cut their purses

more money in a week with his fiddle than Richard could get in a month with laying bricks.

The underhand dealings of jugglers, conjurors, exorcists and their like were exhaustively documented by Reginald Scot in a substantial volume called *The Discovery of Witchcraft*, published in 1584 and one of the books which James promptly ordered to be burned when he became King of England in 1603. As the title indicates, Scot was primarily interested in witchcraft, not because he did not believe in witches but because he considered it a blasphemy to attribute to witches powers possessed only by God, and because he was outraged by the torments inflicted on simple old women who were accused of or confessed to being witches. For some ten years before his book was published he had served as a Justice of the Peace in his native county of Kent and many cases involving alleged witchcraft had come before him. In several instances he was able to demonstrate that the witchcraft was no more than elementary chemistry, ventriloquism or collusion, helped along by intense popular credulity. (Though occasionally the populace showed a sturdy scepticism: at Brenchley, the Vicar accused Margaret Simons of casting a spell on him so that his voice was affected, but the parish at large remained firmly convinced that his low voice was due to 'the French pox' and would not attend Communion until he had obtained medical clearance from two doctors.)

In investigating such allegations, Scot also uncovered many tricks used by jugglers, conjurors, exorcists and alchemists. He made a clear distinction between those who practised legerdemain only for the sake of 'mirth and recreation, and not to the hurt of our neighbour' and those who arrogated supernatural powers to themselves 'to the abusing and profaning of God's name'. The latter was generally more lucrative and Scot was unremittingly scornful about it, giving grounds for his scepticism with a range of examples and a precision of detail (including illustrations) which identify him as an investigator in the field rather than an armchair theorist.

The inter-connection between jugglery and witchcraft is well illustrated by the story of Brandon the juggler which introduces the section of Scot's book devoted to jugglery, though strictly speaking the tale does not involve jugglery at all. Brandon, in the King's presence, painted a dove on a wall and seeing a pigeon on a rooftop, repeatedly stabbed the picture uttering 'magical' incantations until the pigeon dropped down dead. Brandon was instantly forbidden to perform this feat any more 'lest he should employ it in any other kind of murder; as though he whose picture so ever he had pricked must needs have died, and so the life of all men in the hands of a juggler; as is now supposed to be in the hands and wills of witches.' The story was still fresh in people's minds at the time Scot was writing, and he goes on to explain how it was done. The pigeon had been observed always to perch on that particular rooftop and had been previously drugged by the juggler with *nux vomica* which killed it in half an hour or so. We catch a glimpse of the true researcher in the marginal note which tells us: 'This [i.e. the effects of the poison] I have proved upon crows and pies.'

The art of juggling proper is divided by Scot into three main branches: with balls, with cards, with money. In each of these were tricks which could be performed by the juggler alone and others which required an accomplice. For instance, the pigeon trick might be assisted 'by a confederate who, standing at some window in a church steeple or other fit place, and holding the pigeon by the leg in a string, after a sign given by his fellow, pulleth down the pigeon and so the wonder is wrought'. Many of the tricks which Scot analyses had been the stock-in-trade of jugglers for centuries and still survive today on shady pavements and in the back rooms of pubs. Some of them in their practical details bring vividly before us the conditions of everyday life in Elizabethan England. For example, the trick of throwing a coin into a pot and making it move towards the juggler (by tying a black hair to a hole in the coin's edge) reminds us how dark it must have been indoors most of the time. 'This feat' says Scot helpfully 'is the stranger if it be done by night, a candle placed between the lookers-on and the juggler; for by that means their eyesight is hindered from discerning the conceit.'

Other tricks have an oddly modern ring to them, as for example 'How to tell what card any man thinketh . . . how to make one draw the same, or any card you list', 'how to pull laces innumerable out of your mouth, of what colour or length you list', 'to throw a piece of money away and find it again where you list' and so on. It is worth noting that these activities were not always offered as mere entertainment but often as evidence of supernatural powers or used to the possessor's advantage in crooked games of cards and dice.

The juggler thus shades off imperceptibly into the conjuror, witch or magician whose services could be made use of in several ways by a credulous rural community. At a time when the detection of crime was sporadic, inefficient or non-existent, those who claimed to have the power to track down stolen property were much in demand. One such character named Pope produced a striking effect by telling a man as soon as he walked into the room that he had come to say his horse was stolen. He would then, for a fee, give exact details as to when and where the stolen animal could be recovered. Sure enough, his predictions were always fulfilled, mainly because the guesswork had been taken out of them by his business associate, Stephen Taylor, who had earlier stolen the horse and hidden it at a pre-arranged place. This simple procedure was particularly successful in isolated areas with bad roads because pursuit was difficult and concealment easy.

One of the most spectacular conjuring acts of the Elizabethan juggler was called 'the decollation of John the Baptist' and was performed with great success by a juggler named Kingsfield at Bartholomew Fair just two years before Scot wrote his book. It was adapted for theatrical use and may indeed have originated in stage practice. It consisted of displaying an apparently decapitated body with the head still alive at its feet. The original illustration makes the basis of the display clear even without the elaborate verbal description which contains suggestive hints such as 'put about his neck a little dough kneaded with bullock's blood, which being cold will appear like dead flesh, and being pricked with a sharp round hollow quill, will bleed and seem very strange'. Perhaps the most helpful advice Scot gives regarding this particular act is contained in his final sentence on it: 'Not to suffer the company to stay too long in one place.'

Sometimes, in his desire to dazzle the audience with his magical powers, the conjuror fatally overreached himself. At a tavern in Cheapside one conjuror gathered a large crowd about him by announcing, in a voice somewhat slurred with ale, that he was about to stab himself in the belly with a dagger and remain alive.

To cut off ones head, and to laie it in a platter,
which the iugglers call the decollation of Iohn Baptiſt.

The forme of ỹ planks, &c.

The order of the acti-on, as it is to be ſhew-ed.

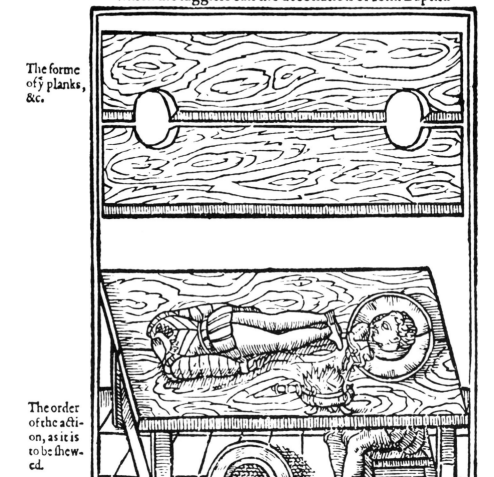

One of the most spectacular conjuring acts was 'the decollation of John the Baptist' and consisted of displaying an apparently decapitated body with the head still alive at its feet

Autolycus and His Tribe

To the astonishment of the onlookers he thrust his dagger deep into his stomach, causing a vivid stream of scarlet to spurt forth. Astonishment turned to consternation, however, when the performer, still bleeding, staggered into St Paul's churchyard and fell down dead. Essential preparations for the feat included wrapping linen around the belly and wearing a protective plate over that, then fixing a false chest and belly 'coloured cunningly', complete with 'paps, navel, hair etc.' over the plate, with a bladder of blood attached to the underside (calf's or sheep's blood is specified, as ox blood would be too thick). But the unfortunate conjuror of Cheapside was too drunk to remember to wear his protective plate. Not surprisingly, the marginal note warns: 'But herein, see you be circumspect.'

We have already noted that the practice of alchemy had a venerable ancestry by the time Chaucer's canon's yeoman spoke of 'that sliding science' and of his master who could turn all the ground between Southwark and Canterbury upside down and transform it into silver and gold. In Elizabethan times the upper ranks of alchemical experiment included several serious scientists and men of learning such as Thomas Hariot and John Dee. The lower reaches were occupied, as always, by the real-life counterparts of Jonson's Subtle and Face, the smooth operators in *The Alchemist* who contrived to hoodwink a representative cross-section of society with the promise of astronomical returns on investment. The fact that in Jonson's play London is the centre of operations is evidence enough that the lure of alchemy was not felt merely by gullible peasants in small villages. Queen Elizabeth herself engaged an alchemist named Lannoy to produce 50,000 gold marks per annum for her.

Basically, practical alchemy, with its twin objects of multiplication and transformation offered undreamed-of riches through the 'philosopher's stone' and the promise of perpetual youth through the elixir of life. Both endeavours were gateways to charlatanry on an impressive scale, especially in and around London. Multiplication was the power to increase the quantity of a given substance, or make barren metal breed, transformation the power to turn base metals into gold.

The travelling alchemist (who could also be a conjuror, exorcist or juggler as the occasion demanded) could not of course carry the elaborate equipment of London operators such as Face, Subtle and Dol Common, who were fortunate to possess a fixed if temporary 'laboratory'. But the itinerant alchemist, too, had at his command the full resources of an impressive-sounding technical vocabulary, with a grand title for each of the twelve stages of the art, from calcination to projection. 'Infuse vinegar' said Subtle to his assistant Face

> To draw his volatile substance and his tincture,
> And let the water in glass E be filtered
> And put into the gripe's egg. Lute him well;
> And leave him closed *in balneo*.

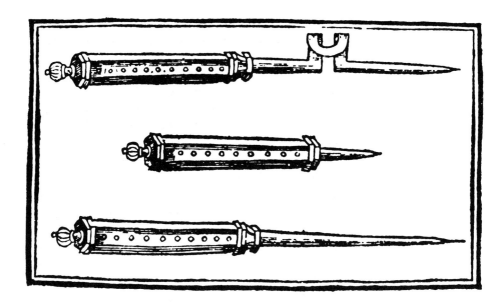

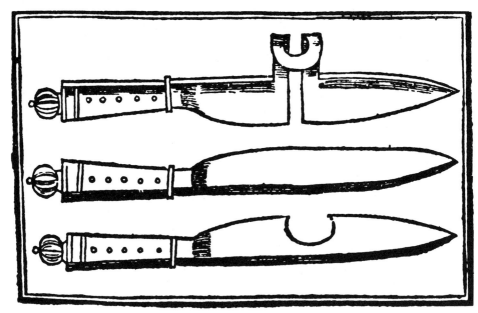

Tricks to cut off your nose and thrust a bodkin into your head and through your tongue (from Scot's *Discoverie of Witchcraft*)

The misfortunes of a Kentish yeoman at the hands of an itinerant alchemist illustrate the possibilities open to the latter. Having ascertained that the yeoman was a man of substance, the alchemist struck up an acquaintance with him, ostensibly to pay court to his daughter. To enchance his eligibility as a suitor he offered to increase his prospective father-in-law's fortunes by alchemy. For his first trick he needed only a ball of wax into which he inserted two angels in the yeoman's presence, delivering them to him for safe keeping. What he handed to the yeoman was not, however, the original ball of wax but another in which he had secreted several more angels. After some days the ball of wax was opened according to the alchemist's instructions and the contents thereof gladdened the heart of the honest yeoman, who was easily persuaded to repeat the experiment, this time with all the money he possessed as well as whatever he could borrow. Difficult though it sounds, the alchemist not only contrived to get it all into a wax ball, but palmed another on to the yeoman as before. To avoid any possibility of fraud, the alchemist insisted that the ball of wax be locked up in a box with two separate locks, the yeoman and himself each having the key to one lock only. With a solemn warning that the alchemy would fail if the box was forced open a second before the appointed time, the learned man went back to London, promising to return. It need hardly be added that he did not return. Several months later the yeoman forced the box open, only to discover that the alchemy had indeed failed. But at least the credit of the art was saved—till the next gull happened along.

Some of the most interesting characters on the vagabond 'fringe' were the Proctors or Fraters who were supposed to have authorization to collect alms on behalf of others, such as lepers, who were prohibited from begging or were unable to beg for themselves. They also collected on behalf of charitable institutions, church repairs and even certain public works. Before the Reformation they were familiar figures throughout the land and had papal authority to reward the donors of charity with pardons and indulgences. Although the sale of indulgences ended in England with the Reformation, it is probable that the number of proctors did not grow much smaller, as proctors' licences were only one of a number of authorizations given to several groups of vagrants recognized by the authorities as more or less legitimate—such as university students during vacation time and those who had incurred losses by fire and sea. Curiously enough, one of the commonest forms of licence was that which authorized the collection of ransom money for those who had fallen prisoner to the Turk; a regular collection was taken at St Paul's for this purpose.

The proctors of some of the larger institutions did not go out on the road themselves but employed factors to do the work for them, appropriating to themselves a portion of the money collected. This was all the easier as there was no regular or systematic keeping of accounts, and the collectors themselves in turn did

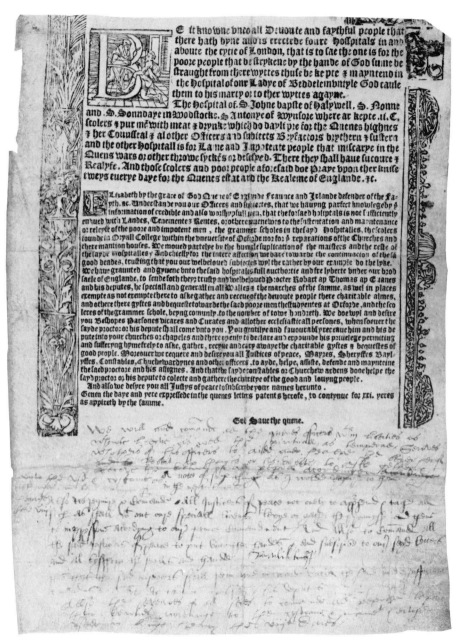

A proctor's licence. Forged licences were so common that the position of 'jarkman', or forger, was often a full-time one

not find it difficult to withhold some of the takings from the chief proctors. An even more lucrative way of turning a dishonest penny was to get hold of a forged licence. These were so plentiful that Awdeley speaks of a special class of crook called the 'jarkman' who was a full-time forger of passports or licences. Though many of these vagrant tricksters had some pretensions to literacy (since their livelihood often required it) it is possible that those with a special gift for impressive calligraphy turned to forgery as a full-time occupation. Forgers repeatedly came before the Justices during the Elizabethan period. In 1569 the Privy Council particularly required London alderman not only to give full details about the bearer of a licence, the route and the term of validity, but also that 'the passports would be so discreetly sealed, subscribed and written as they should not easily counterfeit the same, which, as it is reported, some of them can readily do, and do carry about with them certain counterfeit seals of corporate towns, and such like to serve their purposes in that behalf'. Harman underlines the necessity for this warning with his accounts of the frequent removal of counterfeit licences from vagrants. Considering that the ability to decipher elaborate handwriting was far from common, it is easy to understand Harman's advice to accept any licence unless it was printed or bore the Great Seal of the Privy Council. How casual the imitations could be we learn from Dekker's statement that seals were carved on the end of a stick, usually depicting the head of a dog, a horse or a unicorn, but without the circle around the figure which genuine seals had. Solomon's dictum about those who give to the poor lending to the Lord was the usual all-purpose inscription, and Dekker adds that wherever the bearer was found he 'is sure to have at least one hundred miles to go to his home'.

Collections were usually taken by the proctor or his agents outside church after service and at other public gatherings. If the proctor's contemporary reputation was even partly justified, some of the proceeds must have been spent in the way described by the Kentish Constable who recounted his experiences with half-a-dozen alleged collectors for charity. Hearing a commotion from the local 'spital house' after midnight, this constable went along with a neighbour to investigate. Prudently standing by the wall, they heard a good deal of drunken swearing and laying of bets and presently saw six hefty men lurching out to the back garden where they started playing a variation of pitching horseshoes, using an axle tree as the target and betting on the outcome. The moon shone bright and clear on this disreputable scene while indoors the goodwife prepared a delectable roast pig for the gamblers. It was not long before the contestants fell into an argument and then to blows.

At this point, according to the constable, he and his companion rushed in to part the combatants who promptly fell upon them. The woman then came running out of the house to assure the constable that his assailants were thoroughly respectable folk, all proctors and factors of spital houses 'and that they had tarried there but to break their fast and would ride away immediately after, for they had far to go and therefore meant to ride so early'. The constable was less than convinced by this explanation of their early rising. While the woman of the house was elaborating on it, however, the neighbours, roused by the commotion, came in and made off with the roast pig which, as far as the officer of the law was concerned, was nothing more than poetic justice. What is perhaps worth noting about the incident is the impunity with which the proctors, real or pretended, turned on the constable. Making due allowance for Dutch courage, this suggests as much a confidence in their licence as in their physical superiority, though understandably it was the latter that was most in the constable's mind as he saw them off the parish: 'By my troth I was glad I was well rid of them. . . . For they were so strong and sturdy that I was not able to stand in their hands.'

To complete this cavalcade of part-time rogues in Elizabethan England we shall now glance briefly at those who made a speciality, though by no means an exclusive one, of fortune telling, the wandering tribe, quite distinct from the home-grown English rogue in the eyes of most contemporary observers—'that wicked sect of rogues, the Egyptians'.

CHAPTER EIGHT

Minions of the Moon

In Ben Jonson's *Masque of the Gypsies Metamorphosed*, presented before King James I in August 1621, a stage direction reads: *Enter a Gypsy, leading a horse laden with five little children bound in a trace of scarves upon him. A second, leading another horse laden with stolen poultry: The first leading Gypsy speaks, being the Jackman.* In language as colourful as his appearance, the Jackman proceeds to introduce himself and his company: 'Room for the five princes of Egypt' he cries, 'mounted all upon one horse like thy four sons of Aymon . . . . Gaze upon them as on the offspring of Ptolemy, begotten upon several Cleopatras in their several countries.' He then tells of a gypsy child, offspring of a sheriff's daughter and a gypsy captain, who is an expert in many skills: ''Tis true he can thread needles o'horseback or draw a yard of inkle [tape] through his nose: but what's that to a grown gypsy, one of the blood and of his time, if he had thrived.' Jonson's account was probably based not so much on first-hand experience of gypsies as on a literary tradition that had been well established in England for nearly a century. But in its essential details it is confirmed by other historical records of the alleged origin, appearance and reputation of 'the offspring of Ptolemy'.

On the unfrequented country roads of sixteenth-century England, the sight of a band of 'wretched, wandering wily vagabonds calling and naming themselves Egyptians' would have been almost as spectacular and certainly more outlandish than their appearance on stage. With their swarthy faces often painted red or yellow, their fantastic costumes made up of embroidered turbans and brightly coloured scarves worn over shreds and patches and with little bells tinkling about their feet as they rode, the gypsies formed a special class of vagrants, at once exotic and familiar, in the England of Elizabeth. Although, as we shall see, they were subjected to official persecution of unremitting if erratic brutality, these early immigrants survived well beyond our period as a cohesive group with a life-style very little affected by the society around them.

It was long believed that the gypsies were descendants of the ancient Egyptians, a notion they themselves did nothing to dispel, no doubt because, in the words of a late seventeenth-century pamphlet, Egypt was 'a country which anciently outvied all the world for skill in magic, and the mysterious black arts of divination'. Xenophobia was endemic throughout Europe in the sixteenth and seventeenth centuries; a reputation for supernatural powers might help to offset the worst aspects of persecution. Many gypsies also optimistically sought refuge by claiming to be on pilgrimage in expiation for crimes committed in the past.

As far back as the eleventh century gypsies turned up in Greece as ventriloquists and fortune tellers. There are records of them in other parts of Europe, notably Bohemia, during the next two hundred years. But it was not until the beginning of the fifteenth century that the great migration of gypsies into Europe took place, possibly as a result of the hardships suffered by them when the Mongol Emperor, Tamerlane, overran India in 1398. On their long drift westward gypsy tribes passed through Armenia into the heart of the Byzantine Empire. Then we hear of them in the great European cities, Hamburg, Rome and Paris. In 1427 the civic authorities of Paris refused admission to the people of 'little Egypt' and shut them up at La Chapelle as *cajoux*—undesirables. This seems to be the first recorded instance of an 'official' European hostility towards the Romany people. It was one to be repeated with increasing savagery. By the time Henry VIII was on the throne, the gypsies had reached England. (Under the name of Saracens they had perhaps made their way to Scotland even earlier.) Before long the first laws designed to extirpate them appeared on the English statute book.

Deceiving simple folk by pretending to read palms as well as committing graver crimes like robbery with violence were accusations commonly made against them, especially in official pronouncements. 'An Act concerning Egyptians' passed in 1530 spells out very clearly the danger to the commonwealth that the authorities felt was represented by the dark strangers:

> For as much afore this time diverse and many outlandish people calling themselves Egyptians, using no craft nor fact of merchandise, have come into this realm, and gone from shire to shire and place to place in great company and used great subtle and crafty means to deceive the people, bearing them in hand, that they by palmistry could tell men and women's fortunes, and so many times by craft and subtlety have deceived the people of their money, and also hath committed many and heinous felonies and robberies to the great hurt and deceit of the people that they have come among.

The penalties proposed had the merit of a brutal simplicity, reflecting official belief that wholesale expulsion was the solution to the problem. No more gypsies were to be allowed into the country and those already in England were ordered to depart the realm within sixteen days, on pain of forfeiture of goods and imprisonment. If

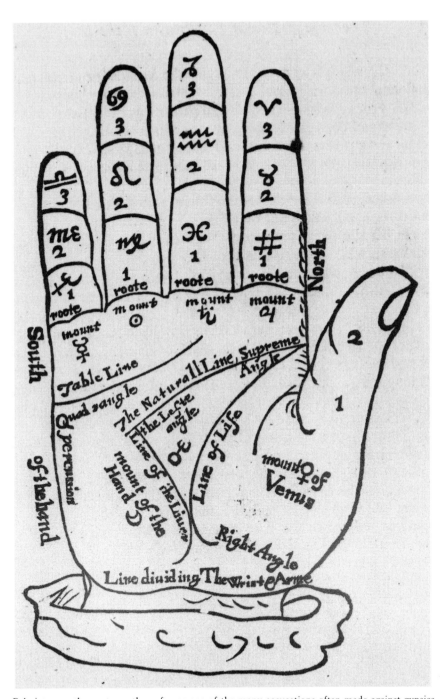

Palmistry, or the pretence thereof, was one of the many accusations often made against gypsies

the goods taken turned out to be stolen property, they were to be restored to the rightful owners; otherwise they were to be equally divided between the King and whoever apprehended the gypsies.

In the treatment of gypsies, as elsewhere in Elizabethan law enforcement, we find the familiar contrast between official severity and grass-roots inefficiency or unconcern. Six years after this Act was passed, Henry VIII's chief minister Thomas Cromwell warned local officials who 'little regarding their duties towards His Majesty, do permit them [gypsies] to linger and loiter in all parts, and to exercise all their felonies, falsehoods and treasons unpunished' that His Majesty was gravely displeased at their dereliction of duty. In spite of a royal pardon for a murder committed by a band of gypsies, given on the strict understanding that they and all their tribe left the kingdom forthwith or be hanged without trial wherever they were taken, they had not done so. Cromwell therefore charged the Lord President of the Marches of Wales (to whom the letter was addressed) and his officers to see to it that any gypsies who were caught were taken immediately to the nearest port and despatched 'upon the first wind that may convey them to any part of beyond the seas'. If they refused, they were to be summarily executed and the letter expressly instructed that no notice should be taken of 'any commission, licence or placard that they [the gypsies] may show or allege for themselves'. This suggests not only the existence of the trade in forged licences which has already been noted (we may remember that the speaker in Jonson's masque is the Jackman, a counterfeiter of seals) but also perhaps that some local officials at least were not averse to granting gypsies a licence, if only to see them safely off the parish. Unfortunately for the gypsies no other 'part of beyond the seas' was noticeably more hospitable to them than England.

The lot of the gypsy was even harder than that of the indigenous vagrant, for the law could literally hound him out of the country. Thus we hear of one group of gypsies shipped from Boston to Norway, closely followed by a second group who were arrested and searched by the Boston constables, whose spokesman noted with disgust that 'nothing could be found upon them, not so much as would pay for their meat and drink'. Even their horse, in the writer's opinion, was not worth four shillings. When the gypsies were examined, it appeared that they had been lately released from Marshalsea prison in London with strict orders to take ship at the nearest port. Their reception at ports nearer to London can perhaps be guessed at from the way they were treated at Boston. And according to the letter in which the story is told, the constables drove them out of town towards the next ports, Hull and Newcastle, 'here being no shipping for them'.

However, deportation, confiscation of goods and imprisonment did not seem to have the intended effect of ridding the land of gypsies. In 1554 another Act was passed, which complained that 'divers of the said company and such other like

Gypsies on the road. These 'Egyptians', also known as 'the offspring of Ptolemy' and 'Moon men', 'be light fingered and use picking, they have little manner and evil lodging and yet they be pleasant dancers'

persons, not fearing the penalty of the said Statute, have enterprised to come over again into this realm using their old accustomed devilish and naughty practices and devices, with such abominable living as is not in any Christian realm to be permitted, named or known'. This time the Christian realm sought to protect itself by imposing a fine of £40 (a very considerable sum) on any person knowingly bringing in a gypsy. Those who were already in England who did not leave within forty days were to be executed as felons without sanctuary or benefit of clergy. The only exception made was in the case of any gypsy who would abandon his 'naughty, idle and ungodly life and company, and be placed in the service of some honest and able inhabitant'. The threat of a felon's death may have been effective in the short term, for twelve years later (after an important extension of the statute which we shall note later) Thomas Harman gave thanks to God that through wholesome laws the memory of gypsies had been clean extinguished and devoutly wished for a like consummation in respect of the home-grown vagabond. But neither the memory nor the presence of the nomadic bands was to be extinguished quite as cleanly as Harman imagined. A pamphlet called *The Art of Juggling* published in 1614 points out that in spite of the number of gypsies executed, 'yet notwithstanding all would not prevail; but still they wandered as before, up and down, and meeting once a year at a place appointed; sometimes at the Devil's Arse in Peak Derbyshire, and at otherwhiles at Ketbrooke by Blackheath, or elsewhere as they agreed still at their meeting'.

During the years immediately following their arrival in England, the gypsy bands were easily classifiable as unwanted immigrants and treated as such. Official energy was directed entirely towards rounding them up and expelling them. But after they had roamed the land for a decade or two a new problem faced the authorities. How were they to treat gypsy offspring who were born in England and were therefore technically true-born Englishmen? An added complication was the fact that some English vagrants, attracted by the exotic appeal and reputation for supernatural powers enjoyed by the Romany folk, went around the country pretending to be gypsies. For instance, on 27 November 1618 a witness deposed before two Justices at Manchester that on his way to Heppenstall fair in Yorkshire he met a company of counterfeit Egyptians one of whom he believed was called William Waller. Waller, a shoemaker of Newcastle-upon-Tyne, was examined and duly confessed that he was born in Newcastle and that he 'travelled under the pretence of counterfeit Egyptians'. The change which the nomadic life provided from the humdrum routine of small-town existence was doubtless one reason why such respectable tradesmen joined the gypsies temporarily or permanently. But sheer poverty would have been the main spur to small craftsmen to take to the life of the road and risk the penalties that went with being caught as a counterfeit gypsy. About the same time as the Waller case the Manchester Constables' Accounts also record a payment of two shillings and eight pence 'for whipping of eight counterfeit gypsies that were taken with a private search'. Only a year after Elizabeth ascended the throne, lawyers at Dorchester Assizes were arguing learnedly that the 'Egyptians' on trial there could not be charged with felony because they had come into England from Scotland and had not therefore come from across the seas.

The first statute against gypsies passed in Elizabeth's reign took a very short way with these complications. It was passed in 1562 and was called 'an Act for the punishment of vagabonds calling themselves Egyptians'. The phrasing is significant, for it seems to take note both of the genuine gypsy and the fake. The Act began by noting an element of doubt in the earlier statute as to whether native-born Englishmen who counterfeited the apparel and speech of gypsies could be punished in the same way as the foreign vagrants. It then reaffirms the earlier statute but added that all persons taken in disguise in the company of gypsies would be regarded as felons and suffer death as well as forfeiture of lands and goods without benefit of clergy. Only children under fourteen and prisoners in custody were exempted.

Whatever the statutes proclaimed, most contemporary observers made a clear distinction between gypsies and English vagabonds. We have already noted how Harman looked forward to the fate of the former befalling the latter. Dekker has a touch of patriotic fervour as he writes:

Look what a difference there is between a civil citizen of Dublin and a wild Irish kern, so much difference there is between one of these counterfeit Egyptians and a true English beggar.

But Edward Hext, a Somersetshire Justice of the Peace writing to the Lord

Wandering gypsies, with their strange dress, language, culture and habits, were viewed with such suspicion by the Elizabethan world that statutes were even passed condemning them

Treasurer in 1596 draws a comparison between the two groups from which the native rogues come off worse: 'But upon peril of my life', he writes, 'I avow that they [gypsies] were never so dangerous as the wandering soldiers and other stout rogues of England, for they went visibly in one company, and were not above 30 or 40 of them in a shire.' We shall see later that Hext may have been mistaken both about the number of gypsies and their travelling habits; certainly there were few instances of large bands of gypsies being taken into custody, though this did not necessarily mean that they did not travel in large bands; one possible alternative explanation is that local constables simply preferred discretion to valour and let the larger groups pass through the parish without attempting to arrest them.

So far we have looked at the gypsy folk chiefly in relation to the law, both because it is the laws against them which make us most forcefully aware of their presence and because evidence given in various courts provides much of what is known about them. But it is time to take a closer look at the gypsies themselves, and we may begin with a glance at their strange speech. On their travels from the east, the original Romany tribes had acquired a distinctive dialect by borrowing words from virtually every language en route. It was not long before this dialect acquired its characteristic English form, often confused by ordinary people and literary commentators alike with the canting language of native vagabonds, though the two actually had little in common. One of the earliest accounts of English gypsy language is found in a book published in 1547 and reprinted fifteen years later. It is expansively titled *The First Book of the Introduction of Knowledge* and Chapter 38 'treateth of Egypt and of their money and of their speech'. The author, Dr Andrew Boorde, gave up holy orders for medicine, travelled abroad several times and was imprisoned at least twice, so that he may have had first-hand acquaintance with gypsies. Boorde had a contemporary reputation, at least among his opponents, for inebriety and loose living which, together with his somewhat jocular style, may have given us the epithet 'Merry Andrew'. His chapter on 'Egypt' runs to barely two pages of blackletter text, most of which consists of English phrases and their Romany translations, and suggests that his encounters with gypsies took place in taverns or alehouses, which fits very well with what we know about both the author and his subject. 'Will you drink some wine?', 'Sit you down and drink' and even more emphatically 'Drink, drink for God's sake' are three of the thirteen phrases offered and others include 'Give me flesh' and 'Maid, come hither, hark, a word'. About the gypsies' money all we are told is that 'Their money is brass and gold' but one sentence of Boorde's solitary paragraph on gypsies is worth quoting for its air of crisp and cheerful tolerance: 'The people of the country' Boorde writes 'go disguised in their apparel, contrary to other nations; they be light fingered and use picking [pockets], they have little manner and evil lodging and yet they be pleasant dancers.' The last phrase suggests one of the reasons why in spite of official hostility the gypsies continued to be accepted by the populace. Boorde's chapter is decorated with a charming woodcut of a gypsy which, if authentic, would undoubtedly have been the earliest such illustration in England. But the very same woodcut is used to illustrate a native of Gascony in another chapter of Boorde's book and twice more (in the second edition) to depict natives of Saxony and Spain; and our confidence in its authenticity is finally shattered when we learn that at least fifteen years before *The First Book of the Introduction of Knowledge* was published, the identical woodcut had been used to portray the allegorical figure of Imagination in a morality play. After this it comes as no surprise to find that the woodcut illustration to Chapter 7 of Boorde's book, which is offered as a portrait of the author, had been used earlier as a portrait of John Skelton, the poet Laureate—at least it accounts for the laurel wreath on his head.

It is worth noting that the confusion between the gypsy language and the canting tongue continued into the eighteenth century. *The English Rogue*, first published in 1665 gives, as Romany speech, a vocabulary which is almost wholly that of English vagrants, as does the life of Bamfylde Moore Carew published in the next century. About the gypsy language itself, two things give us a glimpse of their attitude to life. One is that the word *merripen* stands for both life and death and the other that there is, according to Barrow, no word for glory in the Romany tongue.

As suggested above, Boorde's references to the gypsies as pleasant dancers indicates one of the sources of their attraction for country folk, understandably not touched on in the statutes. It is possible that Morris dancing, that archetypal survival of English folk life, was originally 'Moorish' dancing, brought to the village greens of England by the wandering strangers. Thomas Dekker explicitly compares the appearance of the gypsies with that of Morris dancers: 'Their apparel is odd and fantastic, though it be never so full of rents: the men wear scarves of calico or any other base stuff, having their bodies like Morris dancers, with bells and other toys, to entice the country people to flock about them.' With their many coloured scarves flying in the wind and the music of their bells lilting upon the summer air, these dancing 'Egyptians' brought colour and theatricality to many an English village, creating a larger-than-life spectacle which, as we have seen, Ben Jonson thought fit to set before a king. Perhaps in the minds of many country people a stolen fowl or sheep was not too high a price to pay for all this glamour and gaiety.

If the desire for entertainment drew the common people to the gypsies, their association with witchcraft and sorcery was an even more powerful magnet. Official opposition to the gypsies was undoubtedly due in part to the Church's attitude to what it saw as heathenish superstition. Gypsy bands were often suspected of harbouring popish priests in disguise. But the very paganism which brought down the wrath of the Church on the gypsies was one of the reasons why ordinary people

Kemps nine daies vvonder.

Performed in a daunce from
London to Norwich.

Containing the pleasure, paines and kinde entertainment
of *William Kemp* betweene *London* and that Citty
in his late Morrice.

Wherein is somewhat set downe worth note; to reprooue
the slaunders spred of him: many things merry,
nothing hurtfull.

Written by himselfe to satisfie his friends.

LONDON
Printed by *E. A.* for *Nicholas Ling,* and are to be
folde at his fhop at the weft doore of Saint
Paules Church. 1600.

Thomas Dekker describes the appearance of gypsies with that of Morris dancers, '. . . the men wear
scarves of calico or any other base stuff . . .'

tolerated them and made use of the services they offered. For as we have already seen, beneath the pieties of official Christianity there lay in Elizabethan life a deep vein of belief in demons and spirits, witches and their familiars. The gypsy fortune teller tapped this vein with great skill and subtlety. Though nearly all the evidence we have comes, not surprisingly, from hostile witnesses, this in itself indicates the appeal of the gypsy as diviner, especially to women. We can turn once more to Harman for a representative view. He speaks of gypsies as 'deeply dissembling and long hiding and covering their deep deceitful practices, feeding the rude common people, wholly addicted and given to novelties, toys and new inventions; delighting them with the strangeness of the attire of their heads, and practising palmistry to such as would know their fortunes.' And Dekker, with the characteristic cynicism of the Londoner, tells how on fair days and feast days these 'moon men' (so called because they were both 'mad' and changeable) practised palmistry, often predicting imminent misfortune—a prophecy fulfilled when the listener discovered that his purse had been cut.

But for all that, in a community where a young girl's marriage prospects formed the most momentous consideration of her life it is not difficult to imagine why the services of those who professed certain knowledge on such matters were so eagerly sought after. Dekker is only one of many who linked the gypsies' claims to tell fortunes with their thieving, and there is no doubt that the two activities often went together. Late in the seventeenth century a pamphlet was published called *Strange and Certain News from Warwick* which purported to be 'a true relation how a company of gypsies in Warwickshire chose one Hern for their king, who, being accused for deceiving a maid of 10 shillings under pretence of telling her fortune, solemnly wished before a magistrate he might be burned if he had it'. Hern, the anonymous author tells us, was once master of a good trade in London till a disastrous fancy for the gypsy life overtook him. After some years he came to Warwickshire, a county by this time thoroughly 'Romanized'. The traditional annual election of the gypsy king was about to take place and Hern duly succeeded to the title, though not without a broken arm sustained in the traditional wrestling match against another contender for the crown. Then, resplendent in his royal robes, he selected for himself a buxom queen and set up his headquarters in the village of Badford where he gathered a large clientele among whom were many 'young wenches (that neither hope nor wish nor dream of anything but husbands)'. According to the writer, King Hern soon found a chance to trick one young wench of ten shillings under the pretext of telling her fortune. When she discovered her loss she 'began lamentable exclamations as loud as an Irish hubbub' till her father had the gypsy king and queen arrested by a constable and brought before a magistrate. It was here that Hern took his rash oath 'that he might be burned that night if directly or indirectly he had meddled with any of the girl's money or knew what was become of it'. In spite of this eloquent protestation, Hern and his queen were remanded in custody where they refused a bed and lay on straw (apparently because of the gypsy fear of contamination by the *gorjo* or outsider). But we are told that he covered the straw with rich blankets of his own. The story ends with the expected tragedy illustrating the foreseeable moral. During the night the straw caught fire burning the gypsy king to death and nearly roasting his queen alive; 'a sad example', concludes the pamphleteer with soulful relish, 'that should warn all people from wishing such curses upon themselves, nor neglect or forsake their honest employment to engage in such wicked courses and society, which ever terminates in bitterness and misery'. The story may perhaps be too good to be true, for no reference to it has so far been discovered in local registers and records, which is curious since the pamphlet assures us that the fire nearly destroyed Warwick gaol and was eventually put out by fire-fighters breaking through the house of an alderman who lived next door.

While most contemporary observers of low life mention the gypsies, and court records are full of references to their misdeeds, we owe to Thomas Dekker the first extended account of their life and habits. In *Lanthorn and Candelight* (1608) he,

Gypsy children on horseback from the Roxburghe ballads. They often rode more than one to a horse. Riding was learned early in their lives and was a useful skill for people who often needed to make a quick getaway

too, begins with the customary note of disapproval of the moon-men, who are, he says crisply, 'beggarly in apparel, barbarous in condition and bloody if they meet advantage'. But very soon the enthusiastic chronicler of the life about him takes over from the earnest moralizer and finger-wagging gives way to vivid description. For instance, the beggarly apparel, on Dekker's own admission, includes gay scarves and bells to say nothing of the exotic headgear and rich cloaks which covered them. Dekker also adds the intriguing comment that the gypsy women 'like one that plays the rogue on the stage' commonly wear 'rags and patched filthy mantles uppermost, when the undergarments are handsome and in fashion'—a comment that suggests a certain degree of first-hand acquaintance with the subject. As the entrance in Jonson's masque shows, gypsies often rode more than one to a horse with the elder children carried in panniers or tied together. Gypsy children acquired the art of riding very early in life, a useful skill for a way of life that brought them into many situations where a quick getaway was desirable.

Although in Edward Hext's opinion gypsies never travelled in groups of more than thirty or forty to a shire, it is difficult to be certain how accurate or representative his information was. Dekker tells us that they were 'commonly an army of about four score strong' and more plausibly that on entering a county they divided into groups of four, five or six, the leading group leaving a trail of twigs for the others, thereby diminishing the threat they presented to the local community. The author of a pamphlet called *Martin Markall, Beadle of Bridewell* (1610) asserts that 'they go always never under an hundred men and women' in the Peak district of Derbyshire. He also tells us that the first gypsy king and queen of England were called Giles Hather and Kit Callot, both of which had long been traditional English names before gypsies arrived in England. Though there is mention of a gypsy group of 180 in Staffordshire in 1539 and though nearly 200 were arrested in the North Riding in 1596, most gypsies were taken in small groups, so that Dekker's account is probably true.

As for the charge that gypsies were 'bloody if they meet advantage', Dekker reinforced this with the remark that 'nothing can satisfy them but the very heartblood of those they kill'. But the strength of the accusation is somewhat softened when we discover that the victims of the bloodthirstiness Dekker has in mind are 'innocent lambs, sheeps, calves, pigs'. Together with fortune telling, stealing of livestock was the activity most often associated with gypsies and there is no reason to doubt that the one reputation was less well deserved than the other. Having stolen a sheep or fowl the gypsies would make off to a deserted place where one of them, using a long knife called a skene which was carried under the mantle by the women, slaughtered the creature while the rest gathered round in a circle till the 'massacre' was completed. If a stranger happened along, the group pretended that there was a woman in labour. If this failed to disarm suspicion (as well it might) the group would lay the blame on the actual thief and even hand him over to an officer of the law. But Dekker adds that they usually managed to rescue the prisoner while he was on his way to the gaol and, given the calibre of the local constable commonly found in Elizabethan England, this is not difficult to believe.

A darker tint appears in Dekker's account of how gypsies, when they entered a district, commonly stayed in the barns and outhouses of remote villages where the owners dared not deny them lodging for fear of having their buildings and hayricks burned to the ground. But the same allegation was usually made against English vagrants, particularly discharged soldiers, and there is no reason to suppose that it was peculiar to the moon-men. For good measure Dekker takes care to tell his readers that 'these barns are beds of incest, whoredom and adulteries, and of all other black and deadly-damned impieties', which is strangely similar to what Thomas Harman had to say about the domestic arrangements of native vagabonds. The gypsy ceremony of divorce, where the couple casually shook hands over the carcase of a dead animal, would have shocked the righteous and heightened the general reputation for loose living always associated with vagrant communities by more settled ones. It is curiously transformed in Awdeley's account of a 'patriarco' or hedge priest. (The word 'patriarco' may be a version of 'pattering cove' from the pre-Reformation priest's custom of muttering the words of the paternoster up to 'lead us not into temptation'.) According to Awdeley, the patriarco solemnized a marriage between native vagrants 'which is after this sort: when they come to a dead horse or any dead cattle, then they shake hands and so depart every one of them a several way'. This sounds much more like a gypsy divorce than a marriage. At any rate Harman will have none of it. Having noted that a 'patriarco' was supposed to make marriages, he denies the existence of such a person among English vagabonds on the grounds that marriages hardly ever took place among them: 'For I put you out of doubt that not one amongst a hundred of them are married; for they take lechery for no sin, but natural fellowship and good liking love.'

Life for the gypsy in Elizabethan England was as hard as it was for the English vagrant though the former was somehow more exotic and evidently held great appeal. Although Justices of the Peace rarely relaxed their severity towards them, the gypsies survived because they brought into the lives of the people a sense of mystery and excitement which could not often be found elsewhere. When the gypsies entered a village with their jackman or captain at their head, decked in all their finery, bells jingling and tabors playing, it is easy to imagine the villagers rushing out to see them, leaving their houses open to robbery by some of the gypsy band—though at the next fair day they could probably retrieve their lost goods, albeit at a price. In the villages the curious could see the gypsy conjuror spit fire, eat flax and draw coloured ribbons from his nose, while another gypsy was picking

With their colourful attire and distinctive music, gypsies would often draw the villagers from their homes, diverting their attention with tricks and dancing while accomplices picked their pockets

a villager's pocket of a gilded nutmeg or a row of pins even as he read his palm. Churchwardens and constables might bribe them to avoid the parish, but the motley bands were never far away for long. Their ranks were augmented by *gorjos* who joined them seeking work or excitement or both and by the 'by-blows of young wenches' [illegitimate children] which popular tradition and the occasional historical record speaks of. Let Ben Jonson who introduced us to the 'offspring of Ptolemy' utter our farewell to them, with the Jackman's song from his masque:

> From the famous peak of Derby,
> And the Devil's Arse there hard by,
> Where we yearly keep our musters,
> Thus the Egyptians throng in clusters.
>
> Be not frighted with our fashion,
> Though we seem a tattered nation;
> We account our rags our riches,
> So our tricks exceed our stitches.
>
> Give us bacon, rinds of walnuts,
> Shells of cockles, and of small nuts,
> Ribbons, bells and saffroned linen,
> All the world is ours to win in.

163

Knacks we have that will delight you,
Sleights of hand that will invite you
To endure our tawny faces
And not cause you cut your laces.

All your fortunes we can tell ye,
Be they for the back or belly:
In the moods too, and the tenses,
That may fit your fine five senses.

CHAPTER NINE

Counter and Clink

One autumn evening in the year 1616, William Fennor, poet, performer and pamphleteer was taking the air in a London street when a merchant accidentally ran full tilt into him and nearly knocked him into the gutter. As Fennor himself relates:

> I, for his unexpected courtesy, not forgetting to give him the good time of the night, up with my sword, scabbard and all, and took him a sound knock o'erthwart the pate, and if the most headstrong ox that ever was sacrificed in St Nicholas Shambles had received but half such a blow, it would have staggered him. But he, like a valiant and provident tradesman, bare it off with his sinciput and shoulders and ran away.

Mindful of the possible consequences of his action, Fennor prudently made his way back to his lodgings as fast as he could, but not fast enough to escape the arresting officers who clapped him on the shoulder with the ominous greeting: 'Sir, we arrest you in the King's Majesty's name, and we charge you to obey us.' These two 'pewter-buttoned, shoulder-clapping catchpoles' disarmed Fennor and took him forthwith to the Compter or Counter in Wood Street, one of the three London prisons so named. While waiting for his release Fennor improved the time by setting down his prison experiences which were published under the title of *The Counter's Commonwealth or a voyage made to an infernal island discovered by many captains, seafaring men, gentlemen, merchants and other tradesmen.* In this pamphlet Fennor works his hyperbole and his infernal and diabolical analogies to the point where they become counter-productive, so to speak, but his account is one of the chief sources of our information about Elizabethan and Jacobean prison life, an experience undergone by a surprisingly wide range of inhabitants. As the mocking epigraph addressed to the reader has it:

> It is enough to know, too much to see,
> That in the Counter there is room for thee.

THE ELIZABETHAN UNDERWORLD

Nearly every well-known playwright of the day—among them Marlowe, Dekker and Massinger—spent some time inside prison. Dekker too has left a record of his experiences but Fennor earns the self-advertisement with which he embellished the title-page of *The Counter's Commonwealth*: 'the conditions, natures and qualities of the people there inhabiting, and those that traffic with them, were never so truly expressed or lively set forth.' Elizabethan prisons, of which there were fourteen in London, in many respects constituted the underworld of the underworld, where those whom chance, greed, malice or misfortune had pushed to the bottom of the social heap struggled as best they could against a system of extortion and corruption of frightening proportions. Before we go inside the Counter with Fennor and other unfortunates, let us pause to take a brief look at the reasons why and the manner in which so many people ended up in prison.

In Elizabethen times, a man or woman could be put in prison for virtually any offence. Vagrancy, petty theft, being out of a parish without lawful cause and with no visible means of support, slander, debt, assault, disorderly conduct, suspicion of witchcraft—the list was virtually endless. Two of the commonest causes of imprisonment were debt and assault. In a city where the lure of quick profits seemed to infect all classes of society and get-rich-quick schemes of fantastic elaborateness abounded, it is hardly surprising that so many found themselves entangled in debt, while assault was the rule rather than the exception until the forces of law enforcement became efficent and adequate. As for the way people landed in gaol, nothing could be simpler. Anyone, provided he had the means, could swear out a warrant against anyone else and have him arrested—as Fennor was arrested, at the suit, presumably, of the London merchant whom he had so rashly knocked o'erthwart the pate. The number of those arrested would almost certainly have been greater if the guardians of law and order had been anything other than bumbling, sporadic and haphazard in their activities.

The incredible inefficiency of Elizabethan law officers, especially at grass roots level, is attested not only in the drama of the time but in innumerable well-authenticated incidents and documents. Dogberry, Elbow and Dull are probably the most realistic characters that Shakespeare ever drew, and we encounter their like again and again in Elizabethan life and literature. No less a person than Elizabeth's chief minister Burleigh had first-hand experience of law officers in action. On his way into London one day in 1586 he observed at almost every town end a group of men gathered under the eaves of an alehouse. At first he thought they were either waiting for a drink or sheltering from the rain, but by the time he reached Enfield the rain had stopped and it occurred to him that the group gathered there might be the watch, waiting to apprehend some dangerous villain (this was the year of Babington's conspiracy against the Queen). Stopping his coach he asked one of the men why they were there. 'To take three young men'

Two pretended fortune tellers in the pillory; this seemingly trivial crime, like petty theft, vagrancy and even debt, was harshly punished in Elizabethan England

came the prompt answer. When further questioned as to how the wanted men (who were indeed suspected of being involved in the conspiracy) could be identified, 'Marry' said they, 'one of the party hath a hooked nose'. 'And have you,' asked the chief minister, 'no other mark?' and the cheerful answer was 'No'. Small wonder that Burleigh wrote somewhat tartly to Mr Secretary Walsingham, who had overall responsibility for law enforcement and peace keeping:

Surely, sir, whosoever hath the charge from you hath used the matter negligently; for these watchmen stand so openly in plumps as no suspected person will come near them, and if they be no better instructed but to find three persons by one of them having a hooked nose they may miss thereof.

And thus I thought good to advertise you, that the justice that had the charge, as I think, may use the matter more circumspectly.

It is not surprising that law enforcement was inefficient when we consider that those responsible for it, especially at the lower levels, were expected to work long hours for little pay, with scant esteem from their fellow citizens. The village constable was commonly regarded as a figure of fun, a compound of self-importance, ineptitude and wilful idleness. 'A constable' noted John Earle in his book of characters *Microcosmographie*:

is a viceroy in the street, and no man stands more upon't that he is the king's officer. His jurisdiction extends to the next stocks, where he has commission for the heels only, and sets the rest of the body at liberty. He is a scarecrow to that alehouse, where he drinks not his morning draught, and apprehends a drunkard for not standing in the king's name.

We are irresistibly reminded of Dogberry's immortal words as he gives his assistants their charge: 'You shall comprehend all vagrom men; you are to bid any man stand in the prince's name.' 'How if a' will not stand?' inquires one of his seconds-in-command pertinently. 'Why, then,' comes the magisterial answer, 'take no note of him, but let him go, and presently call the rest of the watch together, and thank God you are rid of a knave.' There can be little doubt that a good many of Dogberry's colleagues adhered to this advice and the philosophy that lay behind it: 'If you meet a thief, you may suspect him, by virtue of your office, to be no true man; and, for such kind of men, the less you meddle or make with them, why, the more is for your honesty.' We can well believe John Aubrey when he assures us that Dogberry was drawn directly from life. In 1616 the Court of Quarter Sessions at Wiltshire received a petition from a constable requesting release from his duties on the grounds that he was unable to read and had to go two miles to the nearest scrivener for help in understanding the warrants he received. James Gyffon, Constable of Albury in 1626 gives, understandably, a more flattering picture of his office in his *Song of a Constable*:

> A constable must be honest and just,
> Have knowledge and good report,
> And able to strain with body and brain,
> Else he is not fitting for't.

But the rueful advice to his fellow-parishioners with which he concludes implicitly acknowledges the true state of affairs:

My counsel now use, you that are to choose;
Put able men ever in place;
For knaves and fools in authority do
But themselves and their country disgrace.

Minor London law officers probably had to be smarter than their provincial brothers, if only because they generally had to deal with a superior class of villainy. Fennor's arrest was reasonably straightforward but not infrequently the arresting officers had to resort to various forms of subterfuge in order to capture their prey. Occasionally they would try the 'soft' approach, inviting the intended victim into a tavern or ordinary and then explaining that they were only carrying out their jobs and so forth. If these methods failed or were considered inappropriate, the sergeants might go disguised as merchants, courtiers or councillors in order to effect an arrest. Often this was done in complicity with the person at whose suit the arrest was to be made. One particular group of creditors, having finally managed to fix a meeting with a particularly elusive debtor, agreed to bring with them a councillor and a scrivener to draw up some sort of agreement. Instead, however, they brought along two sergeants suitably disguised; in addition half-a-dozen more sergeants lay in hiding outside the debtor's door. When the creditors arrived the debtor was in the company of a group of his own men. The sergeant disguised as the councillor asked for a private meeting and no sooner had the debtor got rid of his men than the 'councillor' entered into conversation with the debtor and the 'scrivener' went to the window and fired a loaded pistol which the debtor provided for his own protection. At this signal the rest of the sergeants rushed in with drawn swords and surrounded the debtor, who had to choose between paying his debts or accompanying the sergeants to prison forthwith. On this occasion he paid his debts.

The story is one Fennor claims to have heard in prison. He tells also of a Norwich man who was heavily in debt to certain Londoners and who, though he often came up to London, did so in such a secretive fashion that they could never get close to him while he was in the city. He would only speak to them from the security of his window and he particularly instructed his servants not to let in anyone in satin doublets, taffeta-lined cloaks and ruffs such as merchants wore. Presumably the Norwich man was avoiding not only the merchants who were his creditors but wily sergeants disguised as merchants. In despair the creditors went to the Counter in Wood Street and promised the arresting sergeants a handsome reward if they could bring their debtor to book. One of them undertook to do so and succeeded by ascertaining that the man received weekly letters from Norfolk brought by a porter who had free access to the house to deliver them. Wearing a porter's long coat and red cap with a rope about his shoulders the sergeant went to the house just before the regular porter was due to arrive, carrying what he claimed were letters from Norfolk for the gentleman who lodged there. He was directed to the man's chamber and knocked on the door, whereupon the Norfolk man peeped through the keyhole to make sure that it was in fact the porter. Satisfied he let him in and tore open the letter inscribed to him; while he was doing so the sergeant pulled his mace out of his pocket and arrested him. The arrested man went quietly to the Counter where, according to Fennor's informant, he eventually died.

Then there was the merchant who arranged to transport himself and his worldly goods secretly to the Low Countries in order to escape his creditors. He planned to take his baggage in wooden vats and asked his maid to go out and fetch a couple of coopers to mend them. But the faithless wench who was in the pay of the man's vigilant creditors told them everything and when the 'coopers' arrived they turned out to be sergeants who not only made the merchant pay everything he owed but a fee for themselves as an insurance against further actions.

Stories such as this, and there are scores of them, illustrate not only how frequent were indebtedness and attempts to evade payment, but how much initiative and capital expenditure were required in order to recover one's debts, lawful or otherwise. Some idea of the hazards facing a gentleman up from the country and arrested for debt for the first time can be gained from the sergeants' typical manner of dealing with such a case. They would take him to a tavern near the Counter where they wined and dined at his expense, assuring him all the while how reluctant they were to be arresting him and how they would try to put in a good word for him with his 'adversary'. Presently one of them would leave on the pretext of fetching this adversary in order to settle the matter, but instead would go along to Cheapside and similar well-frequented places in the city inquiring whether the gentleman concerned was indebted to anyone there. If he found someone, the sergeant would tell him that he happened to know where he was and would undertake to arrest him, for a fee. He then went to the Counter and entered a fresh action against the unfortunate gentleman after which he returned to the tavern with the news that the adversary was too busy to come for at least three or four hours yet. If the gentleman wished, the sergeants would stay with him till the adversary arrived, for a consideration; otherwise they would be obliged to take him to the Counter. By supper time they would still be there and eventually the gentleman would have to pay twenty shillings a night to lodge with one of the sergeants and avoid being imprisoned; but unless he was very lucky he would end up in the Counter anyway when all his money was gone, which, at the rate it was being leeched out of him, would not be very long.

Prison sergeants seem to have had a widespread and unenviable reputation for cruelty as well as for corruption and extortion. 'I have seen them come dragging in a poor man by the heels' Fennor's anonymous informant tells him, 'that his head hath knocked against the stones for a quarter of a mile together, and so battered and martyred that a man could scarce know whether he were a man or no.' The sergeants also appear to have been adept at the art of playing both ends against the middle. When they discovered that a man was in debt they would go to him even without a warrant and threaten to inform his creditors of his whereabouts unless paid to keep quiet. On the other hand, after they had already been paid to arrest a man, they would, if they had reason to believe that the intended victim would be suitably grateful, send word to him in advance to stay out of the way when they came to arrest him. Sometimes, they would actually meet the man for whom they had a warrant, take a pair of 'angels' as a bribe and let him go, telling the man who had paid them for the warrant that they could not find the suspect. Most sergeants were not prepared to issue a warrant unless they were paid much more than the official fee of one shilling. No wonder Fennor calls them the 'most ravening and cruel monsters of our land'.

But whatever the sufferings of the poor prisoner on his way to gaol, they were mere flea-bites compared to what he had to undergo once he was actually inside prison. Each of the city's fourteen prisons had its different grades of accommodation and which one a prisoner ended up in depended not on the nature of the offence he was charged with or the severity of the sentence but entirely on how much money ('garnish' was the technical term) he was prepared to lay out in bribes to gaolers, keepers, tipstaffs and others. At the Counter the three grades of lodging, in descending order, were the Master's Side, the Knight's Ward and the appropriately named Hole. When a prisoner first arrived he was allowed his choice of quarters and, provided he could pay for it, he usually chose to be put in the Master's Side. First, however, his name was entered in the prison register or 'Black Book' and at each doorway till he reached the Master's Side he had to pay a turnkey anything from a shilling to half-a-crown for the privilege of having the door opened. Finally, he came to the hall of the Master's Side, fittingly decorated with a tapestry depicting the story of the Prodigal Son. Here the prisoner had to part with two shillings more under threat of having his hat and cloak and other items of apparel forcibly taken from him. This done he was at last shown to the luxury of his own cell on the Master's Side, a narrow cobweb-festooned room with some straw and a pair of dirty sheets and a candle-end for illumination. And this was the best grade of accommodation which the Counter boasted.

The food and drink in this part of the prison were not inadequate by contemporary standards. Fennor had meat at every meal and claret to wash it down with, as well as plenty of tobacco. The only snag was that each of these items called for a further instalment of garnish and at his very first meal Fennor was compelled to accept the honour of paying for the food and drink of all the other prisoners on the Master's Side, to say nothing of the keepers and the vintner's boy who poured out the claret. After dinner there was more garnish to be paid if the prisoner was to avoid being locked up in his cell. There was even a resident who guaranteed to get a case speedily heard at the Court of the King's Bench with an acquittal to follow, all for a beggarly forty shillings; but as the attorney himself had not yet succeeded in getting out of the Counter it is unlikely that he inspired much confidence in his prospective clients.

As long as the money lasted, life on the Master's Side was quite tolerable. But since everything had to be paid for over and over again it was clear that no one could afford to stay there very long, especially as the sergeants were diligent in adding new warrants to the original charge wherever they could do so. For three or four weeks the prisoner was permitted and even encouraged to eat, drink and be merry on credit, but after that he had only the choice of paying up or being transferred to the Knight's Ward, the next stage down in the Counter. Needless to say the change of attitude on the part of the keepers when the prisoner's funds were on the point of running out was marked by every observer. 'Art thou poor and in prison?' enquires Dekker eloquently. 'Then art thou buried before thou art dead. Thou carriest thy winding-sheet on thy back and down the house. Thou liest upon thy bier and treadest upon thy grave at every step. If there be any hell on earth, here thou especially shalt be sure to find it. If there be degrees of torments in hell, here shalt thou taste them.' In his powerful play *The Roaring Girl*, Thomas Middleton is equally eloquent but more explicit on the poor prisoner's lot when garnish has reduced him to pennilessness:

> Bedlam cures not more madmen in a year
> Than one of these Counters does; men pay more dear
> There for their wit than anywhere. A Counter!
> Why, 'tis an University! . . .
>   With fine honey'd speech
> At's first coming he doth persuade, beseech
> He may be lodg'd with one that is not itchy,
> To lie in a clean chamber, in sheets not lousy;
> But when he has no money, then does he try,
> By subtle logic and quaint sophistry,
> To make the keepers trust him.

Conditions in the Knight's Ward, though less comfortable than in the Master's Side, were still tolerable, though here, too, everything from a cup of wine to a breath of fresh air was obtainable only after payment of the inevitable garnish. Shortage of funds compelled Fennor to take a cell immediately adjoining the unwholesome privy (jakes, to use the down-to-earth Elizabethan term). The consequences of refusing to pay garnish are illustrated by the case of Richard Vennor, nicknamed 'England's Joy' because he issued playbills advertising a spectacular theatrical entertainment under this title and then absconded with the takings. Vennor thoroughly deserved John Manningham's description of him as 'the grand cony-catcher with golden spurs and a brazen face' and had been in and out of prison throughout most of his colourful career. On one occasion he flatly refused to pay any extra to be let into the Master's Side at the Wood Street Counter, claiming that he was too old a hand to be caught by such keepers' tricks: 'For howsoever you may fetch over young gulls for their money, *I* will not be so caught. What I call for, I will make a shift to see discharged. Otherwise, I determine to pay nothing. And so resolve yourselves.' The chamberlain or chief keeper on the Master's Side was not over-impressed by this forthrightness and removed Vennor's cloak from his room while he lay sleeping. In the morning Vennor, learning from his fellow-prisoners what had happened, demanded the return of his cloak from the chamberlain who replied that he would be happy to do so as soon as he received his garnish. Vennor thereupon managed to smuggle a letter out to a friend asking him to go to the nearest Justice and swear out a warrant for felony against the chamberlain. When the warrant was duly served, the chamberlain offered Vennor his cloak back but the latter refused to accept it unless it was accompanied by an undertaking that he would be exempted from any further payment while in gaol. Although this was reluctantly given it did not do Vennor as much good as he evidently hoped, for shortly afterwards he died in the Hole, the keepers having thrust him in there without blankets during winter time.

It was just as easy to die of starvation as of cold in the Hole, and the Twopenny Ward was only fractionally better. 'Where shall the wretched prisoners have their baskets filled every night and morning with your broken meat?' asks Dekker in *A Rod for Runaways*, referring particularly to the plight of poor prisoners during times of plague, 'These must pine and perish. The distressed in Ludgate, the miserable souls in the Holes of the two Counters . . . how shall these be sustained?' There were no regular public funds set aside for the provision of food and drink and poor prisoners were entirely dependent on citizens' legacies and Christmas treats. It goes without saying that many such legacies benefited the keepers as much as or more than the prisoners. Near the end of Queen Elizabeth's reign the prisoners in the Hole at Wood Street Counter produced a petition which paints a brutal picture of abject misery:

In all lamentable manner most humbly beseech your good Worship, we, the miserable multitude of very poor distressed prisoners, in the Hole of Wood Street Counter, in number fifty poor men or thereabouts, lying upon bare boards, still languishing in great need, cold and misery, who, by reason of this dangerous and troublesome time, be almost famished and hunger-starved to death; others very sore sick, and diseased for want of relief and sustenance, by reason of the great number which daily increaseth, doth in all humbleness most humbly beseech your good Worship, even for God's sake, to pity our poor, lamentable and distressed cases; and now help to relieve and comfort us with your Christian and godly charity against this holy and blessed time of Easter.

An equally pathetic complaint was made to the Lords of the Council by the poorer inmates of Fleet prison in 1586. Among other things they alleged that the warden, Joachim Newton, who was later accused of murder, had sold the gaolership to the highest bidder. The victualling and lodging was let by Newton to 'two very poor men' who 'being also greedy of gain, lived by bribery and extortion'. It was as a corrective against such abuses that the great Elizabethan Poor Law Act of 1601 ordered the levying of a weekly rate in London for the relief of poor prisoners.

Virtually all the abuses with which the Elizabethan penal system was riddled arose from the fact that those entrusted with its day-to-day management received pitifully inadequate remuneration for their labours. No doubt there was corruption even among well-paid officials, but the sheer pervasiveness of bribery and extortion suggests that totally inadequate financial provision had been made for the running of prisons. In 1593, for instance, out of a total of 1,651 prisoners discharged, no fewer than 285 arranged their release by bribing keepers. One enterprising deputy warden named Bambridge actually made a door in the prison wall through which prisoners could pay their way to go through to freedom. One of them made use of this exit several times for the mutual benefit of the keepers and himself. The prisoner, Thomas Dumay, made several trips to France to obtain wine at wholesale rates for the warders. The credit was obtained against bills drawn on Richard Bishop, one of the tipstaffs at Fleet prison. At first the bills were honoured but after Dumay had obtained an exceptionally large quantity of goods on credit, Bishop refused to redeem the bills. When the merchants went in search of Dumay he was already in prison, so there was little point in having him arrested.

Wood Street Counter was one of the most notorious of London's prisons, though the Fleet, Newgate and the Clink did not lag far behind. It was founded in 1555 and its first inmates came from Bread Street prison where the keeper, who had already been punished for cruelty to prisoners, nevertheless continued to cheat them of victuals and to lodge known thieves and whores at fourpence a night. We can get a fair idea of the kind of pickings that were to be got out of prison contracts from the action of one Mr Greary who, at the end of the seventeenth century, offered to pay the warden £1,500 per annum for the victualling concession; there were at the time some 2,000 prisoners out of whom he reckoned he could make well

The. Metropolitan Prison of London Called NEW GATE

Newgate was the only London prison intended for those charged with criminal offences and for most of them it was a melancholy last stop on the way to the gallows

over twice the amount he offered. In the light of such evidence, Fennor's outraged expostulation against warders, jailers, keepers, tipstaffs and all their quality is not unjustified: 'They imitate ravens, kites and crows, that feed upon the corruption, stinking garbage, and guts of any carrion lyinig in the fields . . . . But for one man like a cannibal to feed upon the other, what more monstrous and worse than cruelty is this, which every day is seen in this place!' It would have been little consolation to the hapless prisoners to have known that a statute dating from the reign of Henry VI, and still in force in the time of Elizabeth I and James I, stipulated that one groat (about four old pence) was all that any prisoner could be charged, under pain of a fine of £40 plus thrice the sum unlawfully charged; it is difficult to imagine that this law was ever enforced in any of London's prisons. Indeed in the Counter, as we have seen, when shortage of funds compelled a prisoner to transfer from the Master's Side to the Knight's Ward he had to pay garnish all over again for the several doors that had to be opened.

Conditions in the Hole (the equivalent quarter of the Fleet prison was grimly nicknamed Bartholomew Fair) were as brutal and squalid as can be imagined. 'In this place' writes Fennor

a man shall not look about him but some poor soul or other lies groaning and labouring under the burthen of some dangerous disease; the child weeping over his dying father, the mother over her sick child; one friend over another, who can no sooner rise from him, but he is ready to stumble over another in as miserable a plight as him he but newly took his leave of. So that if a man come thither he at first will think himself in some churchyard that hath been fattened with some great plague, for they lie together like so many graves.

The rapacity of the keepers pursued the prisoners even in death, for 'some, say they, will not stick to take fees of dead men, and scarce let the coffin go out of their gates before his friends hath paid his fees'. The charity of citizens such as Robert Dowe who in 1612 left a trust to provide £20 annually for paying poor prisoners' debts and the more immediate charity of citizens who provided free meals or dropped food and coin through the prison gratings was all that the wretched inhabitants of the Hole and its counterpart in other prisons could look forward to. Even giving alms to prisoners was not without its hazards, for one Thomas Hoggs was detained in prison for nine months by the keepers simply for dropping money into the prison grating. Sir Thomas Overbury's grim epitome of contemporary prison existence was all too accurate: 'it is an university of poor scholars, in which three arts are chiefly studied—to pray, to curse, and to write letters.'

It is almost inconceivable that anyone would let himself fall into the clutches of Elizabethan prison officials if they could possibly avoid doing so. But the indisputable truth is that nearly all prisons contained a quota of 'voluntary' prisoners, those who, for one reason or another, had contrived to get themselves jailed. Fennor describes them succinctly:

> Others there are that are voluntary and such are they that come in of purpose, who, if it please themselves may keep themselves out; of which I find four kind of people, that are good subjects to this commonwealth of the Counter, and they are these: the first, your subtle citizen; the second, your riotous unthrift; the third, your politic highwayman; and the fourth and last, your crafty mechanic.

The first group, 'the firmest leg the body of this commonwealth doth stand upon', consisted of merchants who over a period of years had carefully built up a reputation for reliability and creditworthiness. They would then obtain several hundred pounds' worth of goods from several different purveyors at once, sell the lot and retire to the country. When the creditors had taken writs out against them they returned to the city and let it be known that they had become bankrupt as a result of trusting plausible young gallants and allowing them credit. They asked their own creditors (through a bankrupt intermediary) to allow them a period of grace in order to build up their ruined fortunes and repay their debts. The creditors promised the intermediary that they would not use the poor merchants too harshly and he then told them the debtor's whereabouts. As soon as they learned this the creditors promptly had the defaulting merchant arrested and clapped in gaol, which was of course exactly what he had wanted all along; having the wherewithal to lead a comfortable life in prison, he would not budge until his creditors had agreed to a settlement of debts on his own terms.

> What cares he for actions, executions, judgements, statutes or any other writs! He hath enough to keep himself in prison, and will make them come to composition with him as he list himself, or they get none at all. So his creditors at last, seeing his resolution so fixed and settled, will, though, very loath, take one quarter of their debts rather than lose all— and, it may be, not half of that in money, but young gentlemen's bonds, and desperate debts that God knows whether they will ever recover one penny.

Then there was the 'riotous unthrift' who, relying on the kindness and generosity of friends, had himself arrested on a bogus charge by arrangement with an accomplice, and let his friends learn that he was languishing in gaol for a debt of a few pounds. If the friends acted according to his expectations they would lend him the sum required to free him, which the young gallant speedily shared with his accomplice, not forgetting an angel for the arresting sergeant who was of course in the plot all along. But on at least one occasion the plan misfired. After the third or fourth time of paying to free a young man from prison his friends ran out of either patience or funds, with the result that the gallant found himself in the Hole for two or three years—'and if at last he had not got off clear by his own industry he might have been a prisoner there while this time, for all of them'.

Fennor seems to have got his third and fourth categories mixed up, for the type of cheat he describes as 'the politic highwayman' was probably the 'crafty mechanic', and vice versa. The first of these committed a highway robbery in Newmarket Heath or some such place outside London and rode post haste into the city to discover that the hue and cry had been raised. He instantly got himself arrested on some minor misdemeanour, rightly reasoning that a prison was the last place anyone would search for a man wanted for a crime committed only a few hours earlier.

The *modus operandi* of the crafty mechanic was simply a variation on that of the riotous unthrift. They were prisoners who had been released from the Hole by means of charitable legacies and who felt their freedom too sweet to be savoured only once. So once a year (usually around Christmas or Easter when the legacies came in) they arranged to be arrested for a matter of thirty or forty shillings, which was duly paid to them out of the legacies and which they shared with their accomplices. 'These base tricks are usual' writes Fennor, and he continues with predictable piety 'though they be not looked into or corrected, for it is an extreme wrong, first to the party that gives it, in cheating of him, and, secondly, in defrauding other poor prisoners that lie in for due debts.'

In prison then, as almost everywhere else in Elizabethan society, there was one law for the rich and one for the poor. Life in the Master's Side could be, as we have seen, as comfortable as life outside for those who had money. The inmate could eat and drink as he pleased, smoke whenever he had a mind, have his friends in for an evening's gambling or a wench from the stews to warm his bed. He could even practise a trade in prison. The most privileged class of prisoners were the three hundred or so who dwelt in the vicinity of Fleet prison in an area called The Rules, presumably because there were hardly any. These were dwellings on both sides of Ludgate Hill up to the Old Bailey as far as Fleet Lane and back along Farringdon Street, to the prison entrance. Although the inmates of these houses were officially on the prison register they were, to all intents and purposes, free citizens, with the inestimable advantage that they could not be arrested (because technically they were already in prison). Most of them were arrested, or arranged to be arrested for debt and naturally they paid handsomely for their fortunate position.

Although the Elizabethan penal system was a blatant instrument of exploitation and oppression, it is worth remembering that the links between criminals and their

A gaoler from an engraving from Mynshul's *Essays and Characters of a Prison*, Links between
criminals and their custodians were often close for many gaolers were often pardoned criminals.
'They imitate ravens, kites and crows, that feed upon the corruption. . . .'

custodians were closer then than they are in our society. The gaolers themselves were often pardoned criminals and a condemned prisoner who was willing to act as hangman could thereby escape with his life. 'Thou shalt have the hanging of thieves and so become a rare hangman' Prince Hal promises Falstaff. And the experience of imprisonment for debt or brawling was so common that it does not seem to have had any social stigma attached to it. When Ben Jonson was imprisoned in 1605 for giving offence to King James' Scottish courtiers in the satirical play *Eastward Ho!*, he wrote to Lord Salisbury for help, but was much more shamefaced about being imprisoned for writing a play than for being in prison itself: 'The cause (would I could name some worthier) . . . is, a (the word irks me, that our fortune hath necessitated us to so despised a course) a play, my Lord. . . .' No such apologetic coughings and splutterings troubled Thomas Nashe whose view of the Counter was that 'a gentleman is never thoroughly entered into credit till he hath been there; that poet or novice, be he what he will, ought to suspect his wit, and remain half in doubt that it is not authentical, till it hath been seen and allowed in Unthrift's Consistory . . . . I protest I should never have writ passion well, or been a piece of a poet, if I had not arrived in those quarters.' Later in the same energetic pamphlet, entitled *Strange News*, Nashe was even more emphatic about the value of a sojourn in prison as part of a young man's education:

> Trace the gallantest youths and bravest revellers about town in all the by-paths of their expense, and you shall infallibly find, that once in their lifetime they have visited that melancholy habitation . . . there is no place of the earth like it, to make a man wise . . . . I vow if I had a son, I would sooner send him to one of the Counters to learn law, than to the Inns of Court or Chancery.

No doubt there was in his attitude a desire to make a virtue out of a necessity by accepting the fact that a professional writer's life was hazardous in Elizabethan times and that he was more likely than not to land in gaol for libel or debt sometime or other; nevertheless beneath Nashe's hyperbole there seems no trace of a feeling that a prison sentence was anything to be ashamed of.

Indeed the very phrase 'prison sentence' can be misleading when applied to this period. Life in prison could, as we have seen, be bad enough, but it was not usually considered as a form of punishment so much as of detention or custody. Of all the London prisons only Newgate was intended for those charged with criminal offences, and for most of these Newgate was a melancholy last stop on the way to the hanging tree. Because the machinery of law enforcement was not equipped to keep a constant watch on accused or suspected persons, prisons were used to detain them until they were either brought to trial or released. Whether a person was imprisoned for a criminal offence, for political reasons or for debt or assault, it was never for a specified period. Those who were accused of political crimes were detained until they could be proved guilty; if this was not possible but the suspected persons were considered dangerous they could be detained in prison indefinitely. As for felons, they were held until trial and execution or, rarely, release. Sometimes an accused man refused to plead either guilty or not guilty of the charge of felony, for by doing so he could safeguard his property which was automatically forfeit to the Crown on conviction of felony. The law's answer to this evasion was *la peine forte et dure*—pressing to death by stretching a man's body and heaping weights upon it. In Elizabethan and Jacobean England this was a form of execution rather than of torture; it was not until the eighteenth century that it came to be used as a means of extracting a plea from the victim. In the first two decades of James I's reign forty-four people in Middlesex alone, including three women, were pressed to death, in addition to over 700 who were hanged.

With Fennor as our guide we have made a tour of the Counter in Wood Street. Conditions in other London prisons did not vary a great deal. Garnish was levied in them all in spite of repeated regulations forbidding it, and the general rule prevailed that a person got what he paid for. The only fees which keepers were authorized to charge were for committal and discharge of prisoners and for not putting a prisoner in fetters. At Fleet prison the fees varied according to the social status of the prisoner; a poor man would be committed free of charge, but a duke, duchess or archbishop would have to pay £10. In fact offending archbishops and lesser clerics were more likely, in Elizabethan times, to end up in the Clink rather than the Fleet. The Clink was within the Borough of Southwark and, from being a prison for offences committed locally, it had become specifically associated with those on charges connected with religion; it was conveniently situated near the residence of the Bishop of Winchester. The Clink is supposed to have got its name from the sound made by prisoners' fetters but it is difficult to see why one prison out of so many should be singled out for this distinction; one would have expected it to be Newgate, where criminals were often put in chains.

Food and accommodation varied little from prison to prison but a great deal in different parts of the same prison. The keepers at the two Counters were commanded in 1606 to keep two tables, at one of which a meal would cost a prisoner ninepence, at the other fivepence; these were for the Master's Side and the Knight's Ward respectively. From a list authenticated by the Privy Council in 1592 we learn that a prisoner who was 'an esquire, a gentleman or wealthy yeoman' could, for a weekly charge of ten shillings ('and so rateably according to the receipt of a nobleman or knight') treat himself to the following menu:

Bone of meat with broth
Bone beef, a piece
Veal roasted a loin or breast or else one capon
Bread, as much as they will eat
Small beer and wine claret, a quart

On 'Fish Days', 'this is the proportion for eight or nine at a table of gentlemen or yeomen':

Butter, 2 dishes
Ling, a jowl and
of seafish or fresh fishes, 3 good dishes or 4 or
as the market will serve.

Gentlemen could dine alone or with their friends and be waited on. At the other end of the scale poor prisoners tried to stretch their funds by cooking for themselves and Dekker paints the scene at meal time for us:

But the time of munching being come, all the sport was to see, how the prisoners . . . ran up and down, to arm themselves against that battle of hunger . . . some ambling downstairs for bread and beer, meeting another coming upstairs carrying a platter . . . proudly aloft full of powder beef and brewis [bread soaked in boiling salt-beef potage] . . . . Every chamber showing like a cook's shop, where provant was stirring.

Buying food in the prison, like everything else, was an expensive business and prisoners tried to buy direct from the street through the grated windows. In 1620 the inmates of the King's Bench prison rioted partly because the Marshal, Sir George Reinell, walled up such a window. They complained to the Privy Council 'of a window shut up by Sir George Reinell whereby they were debarred from taking in their victual out of the street and consequently compelled to take their victual from Sir George Reinell's servants to their great charge and inconvenience as being far dearer, than that which they could buy abroad [i.e. from the street]'. Sir George's reply that the window had been shut up for the security of the prisoners carried less than total conviction.

As for the prisoners in the Hole they had to rely on legacies, on food confiscated in the city for various offences such as giving shortweight, and on the daily alms basket carried on his back by a man who went about calling: 'Bread and meat for poor prisoners, bread and meat.' The contents of the basket were shared out among the poor prisoners, under the supervision of a keeper, as Fox shares out the

The Counter Scuffle. A stay in prison depended on how much one spent on 'garnish' for the gaolers, keepers and tipstaffs. 'But the time of munching being come, all the sport was to see, how the prisoners . . . ran up and down, to arm themselves against that battle of hunger.'

basketman Gatherscrap's haul in an anonymous comedy of 1614, *Greene's Tu Quoque*. Another character in the same play, the prodigal gallant Spendall, utters a soliloquy which makes these scraps sound, to say the least, unappetizing:

> . . . unsavoury scraps
> That come from unknown hands, perhaps unwashed:
> As either by the weather has been tainted,
> Or children, nay sometimes full-paunched dogs
> Have overlicked . . . .

With such haphazard feeding arrangements (which came to a virtual halt in times of crisis such as plague) it is amazing that more poor prisoners did not starve to death in London's gaols. Nor were the living conditions calculated to improve their chances of survival. If a prisoner could afford it, he shared a bed with two or three others, with blanket, sheets and coverlet, for twopence a night; if he brought his own bedding the charge was fourpence a week. But if he was one of the unfortunates condemned to live in the Hole, he was likely to echo the sentiments of the prisoner Luke Hutton in *The Black Dog of Newgate* (1596):

> I lie me down on boards as hard as chennell [hard coal]
> No bed, nor boulster, may afford relief,
> For worse than dogs we lie in that foul kennel.

According to the keeper's own testimony the Hole in the Poultry Counter was not twenty feet square and yet forty or more prisoners regularly slept there; not was it possible to provide separate sleeping quarters for men and women. The inconvenience of snoring bedfellows was the least of the discomforts. There were also, in Dekker's words, 'jailors hoarsely and harshly bawling for prisoners to their bed, and prisoners reviling and cursing jailers for making such a hellish din. Then to hear some in their chambers singing and dancing, being half drunk; others breaking open doors to get more drink to be whole drunk. Some roaring for tobacco; others raging and bidding hell's plague on all tobacco. . . .'

Once again, those at the top end of the prison hierarchy could not only leave their cells on payment of tenpence for half a day or twenty for a full day, but even stay out overnight. And the amenities included not only drinking and gambling parlours but, at least at the Fleet prison, a bowling alley, if we are to believe John Taylor the Water Poet and the anonymous author of a play called *Look About You* (1600) where in one scene set in the Fleet the characters play a game of bowls.

Of the fourteen or so London prisons, nine were of special importance. The two Counters (there was a third across the river in Southwark) were Sheriff's prisons for all offenders against the city's laws. Newgate was of course the chief criminal prison and Ludgate was reserved for freemen and freewomen of the city. All four of these prisons came under the direct control of the city council. The Clink, as we have seen, was chiefly for religious offenders. The Fleet contained many prisoners committed by the monarch's decree and was particularly associated with the Court of Star Chamber till this was abolished in 1641. (John Lilburne the Leveller was whipped from the Fleet to the pillory at Westminster for refusing to incriminate himself.) The Marshalsea was also connected with religious prisoners as well as with those charged with maritime offences. Of the remaining two important prisons, the Gatehouse at Westminster (where there may have been two prisons) was mainly for political prisoners and was controlled by the Privy Council and the Bishop of London, and the King's Bench prison was mainly for debtors and was also ultimately controlled by the Privy Council.

If we include Bridewell and the Tower of London, which were not only prisons though they housed prisoners, as well as a couple of very minor prisons in Finsbury and Whitechapel, there were not fourteen but eighteen prisons in the London area in Elizabethan and Jacobean times. An annotated list of these in verse is provided by John Taylor in a pamphlet published in 1623 called *The Praise and Virtue of a Jail and Jailers*, a fitting bird's-eye view with which to conclude this survey of the underworld within London's underworld:

> In London, and within a mile I ween
> There are of jails or prisons full eighteen,
> And sixty whipping-posts, and stocks and cages,
> Where sin with shame and sorrow hath due wages.
> For though the Tower be a castle royal,
> Yet there's a prison in't for men disloyal . . .
> And last it is a prison unto those
> That do their sovereign or his laws oppose.
> The Gatehouse for a prison was ordained
> When in this land the third King Edward reigned:
> Good lodging-rooms and diet it affords . . . .
> Since Richard's reign the First the Fleet hath been
> A prison, as upon records is seen,
> For lodgings and for bowling, there's large space. . . .
> Old Newgate I perceive a thievish den,
> But yet there's lodging for good honest men . . .
> . . . No jail for thieves, though some perhaps as bad,
> That break in policy, may there be had.
> The Counter in the Poultry is so old
> That it in history is not enrolled.
> And Wood Street Counter's age we may derive
> Since Anno Fifteen Hundred Fifty Five. . . .
> Bridewell unto my memory comes next,
> Where idleness and lechery is vext:
>   . . . for vagabonds and runagates,
> For whores and idle knaves and suchlike mates,
> 'Tis little better than a jail to those,
> Where they chop chalk for meat and drink and blows. . . .
> Five jails or prisons are in Southwark place,
> The Counter (once St Margaret's Church defaced),
> The Marshalsea, the King's Bench and White Lion,
> Where some like Tantalus or like Ixion
> The pinching pain of hunger daily feel. . . .
> And some do willingly make their abode
> Because they cannot live so well abroad.

Then there's the Clink, where handsome lodgings be . . . .
Cross but the Thames unto St Katherine's then,
There is another hole or den for men
Another in East Smithfield little better,
Will serve to hold a thief or paltry debtor.
Then near Three Cranes a jail for heretics,
For Brownists, Familists and Schismatics.
Lord Wentworth's jail within Whitechapel stands,
And Finsbury, God bless me from their hands!
These eighteen jails so near the city bounded
Are founded and maintained by men confounded:
As one man's meat may be another's bane,
The keeper's full springs from the prisoner's wane.

CHAPTER TEN

Bridewell and Bedlam

John Taylor's casual comment on Bridewell that "'tis little better than a jail' does less than justice to what was in many ways a pioneering institution in its day, even if his words referred to those who were sent there for punishment. For 'the house of correction and occupation' at Bridewell embodies in its history many of the changes in attitudes to the causes and cure of poverty which took place from the middle of the sixteenth century onwards.

The medieval Christian attitude to poverty was simple and straightforward, in theory at least. Poverty was ordained by God. For the poor man it was a punishment which, if borne patiently, would prove his ultimate blessing. For the rich man it was a challenge to Christian charity. Like riches 'so likewise poverty is thy gift, O Lord; and as thou has made some rich to despise the worldly goods, so hast thou appointed some to be poor, that they may receive thy benefits at the rich man's hands'. In other words the solution to poverty was private charity, the individual relieving the needy for the good of the latter's body and his own soul. As Christ suffered penury and degradation, so should the poor man bear his cross of poverty and hardship with patient humility. As Robert Crowley put it in the 1550s:

> . . . though thou shouldest perish for food,
> Yet bear thy cross patiently;
> For the end shall turn thee to good,
> Though thou lie in the streets and die.

In a society where most people lived perilously close to starvation, where poverty was the familiar face of everyday life, made grimmer by bad harvests and plague, this fatalistic attitude was easier to understand than it would have been in the bustling, complicated and rapidly changing economic conditions of the later sixteenth century. As we have seen, the causes of poverty then seemed not inscrutably hidden in the mysterious workings of God, but were all too plainly the result of man's unrestrained avarice. The enclosure of common lands for sheep pasturage (because there were quick profits to be made in wool), the sudden way in

The familiar face of everyday life. Most people lived perilously close to starvation and abject
poverty, often made worse by bad harvests and plague

which employers who paid poor cottagers to do light industrial work at home
withdrew employment, the disappearance of monastic charity, the rocketing
inflation of the 1540s and 1550s—these were some of the causes to which
contemporary interpreters of society attributed the widespread poverty in Tudor
England. Which, if any, of these factors were really important in the growth of
poverty is still a matter of dispute among twentieth-century historians of the
period; many believe that the rapid expansion of population in England was

probably the single most decisive element. But for our purposes what men of power and influence believed at the time is even more important than the objective truth of the situation. And among the convictions rapidly gaining ground were, first, that poverty was not a God-ordained mystery but a human problem with roots in human society, secondly, that poverty was of different kinds demanding different responses, and thirdly, that individual charity was no longer adequate to make any real impact on the problem of poverty; it needed action from society as a whole.

It is against the background of this changing attitude to the problem of the poor—which, it hardly needs saying, did not take place overnight, but gradually over a period of decades—that we should see the foundation of Bridewell as a hospital and house of correction. Originally a royal palace, Bridewell stood on a site west of Ludgate Hill bounded by Fleet Street to the north, and the Thames to the south. In 1553, a few months before his death at the age of seventeen, Edward VI granted his royal palace of Bridewell to the city of London 'for to be a workhouse for the poor and idle persons of the city of London'. In January the previous year Nicholas Ridley, Bishop of London, had preached a sermon before the young King at Whitehall in which he had stressed the need to succour the sick and the needy. Later that year Ridley wrote to Sir William Cecil specifically mentioning Bridewell:

> Good Mr Cecil. I must be a suitor unto you in our good Master Christ's cause; I beseech you be good to him. The matter is, sir, alas! he hath lain too long abroad (as you do know) without lodging in the streets of London, both hungry, naked and cold. Now, thanks be to Almighty God! the citizens are willing to refresh him, and to give him both meat and drink, clothing and firing: but alas, sir, they lack lodging for him. For in some one house I dare say they are fain to lodge three families under one roof. Sir, there is a wide, large, empty house of the King's Majesty's, called Bridewell, that would wonderfully well serve to lodge Christ in, if he might find such good friends in the court to procure his cause.

In the good Bishop's identification of the poor with Christ we see the medieval idea of charity, while the grant of the royal palace to the civic authorities was symbolic of the recognition of poverty as a problem to be faced by society as a whole. The letter which the citizens of London addressed to the Privy Council requesting the grant of Bridewell showed a clear understanding of the different kinds of poverty. It recognized that, apart from the familiar categories of the sick or disabled poor on the one hand and able-bodied idlers on the other, there were those who, through no fault of their own, were unable to work even though they were willing to: 'And we considered also that the greatest number of beggars fallen into misery by lewd and evil service, by wars, by sickness, or other adverse fortune, have so utterly lost their credit, that though they would show themselves willing to labour, yet are they so suspected and feared of all men, that few or none dare, or will receive them to work.' Faced with this situation, the worthy citizens of London took upon themselves the responsibility of providing work for those who were genuinely seeking it. They had already done something to help the aged and the sick by taking on the administration of St Bartholomew's Hospital, while poor orphan children were cared for at Christ's Hospital, also run by the civic authorities. Now they sought to turn able-bodied vagrants and criminals into useful citizens by setting them to work at various tasks under regular supervision; and so Bridewell was born.

From the beginning Bridewell was intended as a training centre for three classes of poor; the children of the poor who did not show themselves apt for anything other than manual work, invalids who were sufficiently recovered to undertake light employment, and sturdy rogues and loose women convicted in the courts. For the latter groups, however, Bridewell was not conceived of as part of their punishment but as part of their cure. Their punishment would consist of being put in the pillory or stocks, whipping at the cart's tail or whatever; it was only after their punishment that their reformatory detention at Bridewell was to begin.

The citizens, in their declaration to the Privy Council, went into a good deal of detail as to how the new institution was to be funded and managed. They had already amassed more than £300 a year for St Bartholomew's Hospital and also had enough in hand for the day-to-day management of Christ's and St Thomas' Hospitals. They were sure that if the King granted them the building they would be able to find the money to run it. They proposed to organize 'sundry occupations, wherein shall be trained all the former sorts of people, and those occupations shall be such as may be profitable to all the king's majesty's subjects, and hurtful to none.' Among those first suggested were the making of caps (then mostly imported from France) and, especially for the halt and maimed who still had the use of their hands, the making of ticking for feather-beds, wool-carding, wire-drawing, silk-winding and similar occupations. 'The stubborn and fouler sort' were to be put to rougher tasks such as nail-making. The raw material for all these trades had already been promised by certain substantial citizens who also undertook to purchase the finished articles at a fair price. The day-to-day supervision of the house would be in the hands of paid craftsmen, called taskmasters (and taskmistresses) and there would also be a paid staff of porters, cooks, stewards and the like. We may see in this blueprint the resolve of the citizens of London to prevent Bridewell from degenerating into the conditions of squalid misery and corruption which characterized the common gaols of the city.

Bridewell was given to the city of London by Edward VI in 1553 'for to be a workhouse for the poor and idle persons of the city of London'. It was the first real remedial institution for rogues and vagrants in England

The King not only bestowed on the Corporation his palace of Bridewell but granted to the city the lands and rents of the Savoy Hospital to the value of £450 a year. In addition the citizens were authorized to enact regulations for the good government of the poor and the governors of Bridewell were given wide powers—which, in the late seventeenth century were to be challenged as violating the basic legal rights of the individual. These powers included the right of appointed officers to search any suspicious places of assembly such as alehouses, bowling alleys, gambling dens and cock-pits, and to convey to Bridewell not only any undesirable characters found there but also the keepers of such disorderly establishments. The governors were also given power to inflict punishment on offenders at Bridewell without fear of reprisal from the Sovereign or his successors. In their turn, the city authorities undertook to redeem the debts of the Savoy Hospital and to provide for its former officials and for those who had been cared for there as well as to run Bridewell efficiently and to provide apprenticeship schemes for the orphan children from Christ's Hospital.

Edward VI died just ten days after he had granted the letters patent concerning Bridewell to the city. His successor, the Catholic Queen Mary, did not share his enthusiasm for organized secular charity and it was three years before she confirmed the Charter. During the last year or so of Mary's reign Bridewell was not able to fulfil its original ambitious design but was merely a penal institution where whores and vagrants were punished.

When Bridewell finally got under way, a levy was made on the richer guilds to finance it, perhaps the earliest example in England of a compulsory poor rate. A treadmill was installed on which convicted vagrants were set to grind corn and there were stocks and a pillory as well as a block on which prostitutes beat out hemp with heavy wooden mallets. On 31 July 1556, Henry Machyn, funeral undertaker and diarist, records that there 'stood in the pillory at Cheapside a man and a woman, who were officers of Bridewell, who favoured sundry harlots and conveyed them away'. Machyn also tells us that a building labourer employed at Bridewell who was found guilty of breaking open a chest was hanged there and then without further ado. Evidently therefore, though corruption and theft took place in Bridewell from the very beginning, the city fathers seemed to have been honestly determined to deal with it as promptly and ruthlessly as they could.

By the end of 1556 Bridewell was fully operational as a house of punishment, if not yet of correction. In November that year the city council ordered that all monies owing to the institution from city guilds should be paid in without delay and in December a woman named Morton, convicted of having abandoned her infant in Southwark, was whipped on her bare back at Bridewell, after which she was dragged through the streets and put in the pillory at Cheapside with an inscription on her head announcing her crime:

WHIPPED AT BRIDEWELL FOR HAVING FORSAKEN HER CHILD IN THE STREETS.

In the following year the city beadles were instructed to patrol the streets as well as well-known places such as Paul's Cross in search of vagrants who were to be conveyed, if necessary, to Bridewell.

In the closing months of Mary's reign there was a definite possibility that Bridewell would be closed down. According to a contemporary chronicler, John Howes, the reason why Mary was hostile to Bridewell was that immoral women, under examination or whipping, would reveal too many scandalous truths about the sexual misdemeanours of Catholic priests. This, if we are to believe Howes, is also the reason why these cases were tried before ecclesiastical courts: 'The governors were never in quiet, but every term process came out against them for one cause or another, for some of the priests, having accusing consciences, feared that some foul matters should come to light by examination.' Howes may have been in a position to known as he was collector of rents to the royal hospitals at the time. He goes on to say that since there was an antipathy to Bridewell in high places, adventurous gallants made this an excuse for raiding the place in order to rescue streetwalkers who had been put there. However this practice originated, it continued throughout Elizabeth's reign; Machyn tells us that in the first year of the new queen's reign 'divers gentlemen and rufflers and serving men' stormed Bridewell in order to rescue certain women and the constables had much ado to keep the peace for the intruders 'drew their swords and began much business'. It is a pity that disinclination or near-illiteracy prevented Machyn from giving any further details regarding the incident.

Although Elizabeth herself did not seem particularly interested in Bridewell, it played an important part in the social ordering of the city in her reign. No less an authority than Sir Francis Bacon claimed that the powers exercised by Bridewell were contrary to the Magna Carta, but this did not prevent them being exercised and even extended. Bridewell even became an important recruiting centre for the Elizabethan military campaigns in Ireland and the Netherlands. Thomas Dekker, whose civic pride is evident in everything he writes, even when he writes of being imprisoned, gives an idealized picture of Bridewell both as a house of correction and as recruiting centre in the second part of his comedy *The Honest Whore*. The play is ostensibly set in Milan but that does not prevent Dekker from setting one scene in Bridewell; one of the masters of the establishment speaks:

> . . . when the iron doors
> Of war burst open, from this house are sent
> Men furnished in all martial complement. . . .
> Here providence and charity play such parts
> The house is very like a school of arts;
> For when our soldiers, like ships driven from the sea,
> With ribs all broken, and with tattered sides,
> Cast anchor here again, their ragged backs
> How often do we cover! that, like men,
> They may be sent to their own homes again. . . .
> The sturdy beggar, and the lazy loon,
> Gets here hard hands, or laced correction.
> The vagabond grows staid and learns t'obey,
> The drone is beaten well and sent away.
> As other prisons are, some for the thief,
> Some, by which undone credit get relief
> From bridled debtors; others for the poor,
> So this is for the bawd, the rogue, the whore.

Bridewell also served in Elizabethan times as a prison for captives from the Spanish

Portions from Wenceslaus Hollar's 'Long View' of London, 1647, showing some of the better-known buildings in Elizabethan London, including the Savoy Hospital which Edward VI gave to the city with his palace of Bridewell

Armada as well as for Catholic and Puritan religious prisoners. But we are chiefly concerned here with its function as a collection and correction centre for the Elizabethan underworld.

In spite of regular levies and later a general poor rate Bridewell's major income during Elizabeth's reign came from the sale of its products and from the collection of rags and bones. In 1562 the aldermen took away the endowment of the Savoy Hospital from Bridewell and transferred it to St Thomas' Hospital, which evidently put the financial state of Bridewell in some disarray for several years; when the Queen was carried in a litter across Fleet Bridge during a state procession after the Armada had been scattered, the boys and girls of Bridewell who lined the bridge had to depend on the charity of the other London hospitals for their new clothes.

In 1590, with debts of several hundred pounds, Bridewell was again in serious danger of closure, and the aldermen ordered an audit of the accounts, which brought to light the familiar story of crooked dealing. The treasurer Roger Warfield had been helping himself to the funds by not paying bills and rents. Matters improved under Warfield's successors, helped along by a bequest of £200 from William Whitmore, haberdasher and ex-mayor of London. But at the turn of the century Thomas Box, another crooked treasurer, paid bills twice over (not entirely through absent-mindedness), favoured some tradesmen over others for a consideration and diverted cloth belonging to the hospital to his own use. The treasurer who replaced him, however, was an honest man who at last managed to straighten the books and bring some order into the hospital itself. For instance, he ordered the removal of pigs and poultry from the yards and forbade the drying of clothes on the roofs, prompted no doubt by a distinguished neighbour, Lord Treasurer Buckhurst. Chapel attendance and catechism for children were made compulsory, though it is difficult to estimate how much this contributed to the spiritual edification of the inmates as the minister, according to a female witness 'abused his wife mightily' and had thrown a stool and a candlestick at her and knocked her down the stairs. But at least their material welfare was better provided for than that of the wretched prisoners, for they had meat, beer, bread, cheese and porridge as part of their regular diet.

As we have seen, it was the usual practice to lease the management and victualling of the prisons to the highest bidder. A variation on this custom took place as regards Bridewell in 1602, with not altogether happy results. A quartet of plausible Londoners persuaded the aldermen to pay them £300 per year to take over the entire management of Bridewell. Thomas Brownlow, draper, Nicholas Bywater, tanner, Thomas Daniel, weaver and Thomas Stanley, gentleman, solemnly undertook, in return, to see that all idle vagrants were usefully employed and that the workshops were kept busy. For a couple of months all seemed to go well and the aldermen doubtless felt well pleased with the arrangement they had come to with the four 'undertakers'. But soon it began to be noised abroad that Bridewell had become not so much a house of correction as a house of pleasure. The whores who had been whipped for their 'lewd and light behaviour' had exchanged the blue uniform of the house for their usual gaudy finery and regularly entertained their clients in Thomas Stanley's quarters. It also turned out that the number of vagrants had been reduced and many of the rooms let at a profit. Whereas Bridewell officially accommodated some 200 people, the total number of inmates under the regime of Stanley and his cronies was sixty-three; the rest had been discharged with no authority except that of the supervisors' greed. Of those left, twenty-five were boys and thirty-eight were women, of whom only eighteen of the poorest were at work. The others were entertaining and being entertained; crabs, lobsters, artichoke pies and gallons of wine were mentioned in the report of the committee of inquiry which looked into the scandal. No such dainty diet came the way of the rest of the inmates, some of whom were so badly starved that they had to be sent to St Thomas' Hospital. To make matters worse, the ladies of pleasure refused to come before the committee when summoned and the sheriffs had to break down the doors of their rooms and heave them out by main force. When charged with their misdemeanours, the conspirators at first accused each other of running a disorderly house but later confessed and appear to have got off scot-free on surrendering their lease to the city; even the debts they had accumulated were paid for them.

In spite of these and other difficulties, the Bridewell experience was notably successful in alleviating the problem of metropolitan vagrancy and in the next few years several other towns, such as Ipswich and Exeter, followed London's example in establishing houses of correction. Bridewell was the first remedial institution for rogues and vagabonds in England, though the principles behind it—notably the need to abolish beggary, corporate responsibility for vagrancy and relief in return for work—came from continental thought and experiment, particularly from the ideas of the great Spanish humanist Vives who spent some time at the court of Henry VIII and wrote a treatise on poor relief. The year 1572 saw the establishment of a new Poor Law under which responsibility for the care of vagrants was transferred from the Church to the local authorities. Three years earlier Burleigh himself had suggested that 'a Bridewell should be set up in every town, every tippler in the country to yield a shilling towards its maintenance.' The Poor Law of 1572 also gave each county power to levy a poor rate and four years later they were further authorized to build houses of correction where there would be a 'stock of wool, hemp, flax or other stuff, to the intent that youth may be brought up to labour, and not grow into rogues, and that idle rogues may not have any just excuse for saying that they cannot get any service or work'. In the wake of the 1572 Act, houses of correction 'after the manner of Bridewell' were established throughout the country and even in Scotland and Ireland. A document issued by the Justices of the Peace for Suffolk gives us a clear picture of how a provincial house of correction was organized. An officer (rather quaintly called the Foreign Officer) was to be appointed for each of several specified areas, whose duty would be to travel up and down in that area looking for vagrants, paying particular attention to fairs, markets and other assemblies. Any such person was to be taken, with the help of the local constable if necessary, to the nearest Justice of the Peace, to be committed by him to the house of correction. The responsibility of conveying the vagrant to the house was the constable's and he was to be reimbursed for his expenses up to a halfpenny per mile.

On arrival, every adult vagrant was to receive twelve strokes of the whip and every young one six strokes 'and the party that shall receive this punishment shall have his or their clothes turned of their shoulders to the bare skin down to the waist'. It was specified that the whips used should be made of two cords without knots. After whipping, the vagrant was to have a clog, chain, manacle or collar put on him, at the keeper's discretion. Particularly recalcitrant offenders were to have heavier shackles and a thinner diet. Those who disobeyed the keeper's instructions to work were to receive four and then six strokes of the whip and, at the third time of refusal, were to be committed by a Justice to the nearest gaol. As for diet, on meat days inmates were to receive four ounces of meat and eight ounces of bread as well as a pint of porridge and a pint of beer; on fish days, milk, cheese, pease pudding and fish as available. Those who laboured especially diligently were to have extra food and drink, again at the keeper's discretion. Slackers were to be put on a diet of bread and beer only. Children of vagrants were to be accommodated at the house and no charge was to be levied for any of this.

Bridewell and its provincial counterparts continued to flourish in England until the nineteenth century. Although their efficiency varied from institution to institution, there is no doubt that they helped to contain the problem of vagrancy. In London Bridewell was particularly efficient, despite such lapses as we have noted. In 1581, William Fleetwood, Recorder of the city, imprisoned 146 vagrants in a single week. Two years earlier the Privy Council had congratulated the Bishop and Justices of Norwich on their success in establishing 'a form for the punishment of loiterers, stubborn servants, and the setting of vagabonds, rogues, and other idle people to work, after the manner of Bridewell'. In the early years of James I's reign the system seems to have suffered some neglect and in 1609 we find legislation requiring the immediate building of houses of correction in every county 'with a convenient backside thereunto adjoining, together with mills, turns, cards and suchlike necessary implements to set the rogues or other such idle persons on work'. If the buildings were not erected within a year, each Justice in the county was to be fined £5. Many counties, though not all, did establish such institutions.

Thus for sturdy beggars, vagrants and dissolute women unfortunate enough to be convicted, there was an alternative somewhat less grim than branding or imprisonment. The very longevity of Bridewell is an indication that it answered a pressing social need. Of its function as a training centre for young apprentices we have said little, though it is worth remembering that not only trades but even music was taught there. Those responsible for Bridewell also helped its inmates to obtain employment by advertising their skills at St Paul's and elsewhere. But towards the end of Elizabeth's reign it became a prison not only for Spanish captives and religious prisoners but more and more for all types of offenders arrested in the locality. In 1613, the sheriffs of the city heard that some apprentices were putting on a clandestine performance of a play called *The Hog hath lost his Pearl*, an attack on the Lord Mayor. They arrested some of the performers 'and carried some six or seven of them to perform the last act at Bridewell; the rest are fled'.

An aspect of the Elizabethan underworld which was both spectacular and sinister is also one that we would perhaps hardly think of as belonging to it at all. This was the notorious asylum for the insane at Bethlehem Hospital, far better known as Bedlam, where watching the lunatics was a regular Elizabethan pastime, as much a part of their recreation as bear-baiting or play-going, or as a visit to the zoo would be for us today.

The hospital of St Mary of Bethlehem was housed in the buildings of an old priory outside Bishopsgate. It was founded in 1274 and began to admit lunatics just over a hundred years later. It was the first asylum for the insane in England and, except for one in Spain, the first in Europe. It had six lunatics and three sick persons to begin with, all transferred from Charing Cross hospital, possibly because that was too close to the royal palace. In 1546, on a petition from the city, Bethlehem Hospital was handed over to the civic authorities and for ten years it was controlled directly by a court of aldermen through a resident keeper. After a short period when it was administered by Christ's Hospital it came under the control of Bridewell in 1557. A 'brief' from the first year of Elizabeth's reign confirms its status as an asylum for the insane:

> Be it known to all devout and faithful people that there have been erected in the city of London four hospitals for the people that be stricken by the hand of God. Some be distraught from their wits and these be kept and maintained in the Hospital of Our Lady of Bedlam, until God call them to his mercy, or to their wits again.

The treatment of lunatics in the sixteenth century was as brutal as it was ineffective. Society was not prepared to put up with a poor man who was insane and so he was treated in much the same way as witches, whores, vagrants and others whose conduct was likely to be socially nonconformist. Where these vagabonds were sent to the pillory or Bridewell, the madman was confined in Bedlam.

All that a pauper lunatic could expect there was regular beating. In Sir Thomas More's *A Dialogue of Comfort against Tribulation* (1553), one of the many handbooks for the solace of the mentally distressed published in the sixteenth and seventeenth centuries, he tells of one who had fallen into 'frantic heresies' and then 'into plain open frenzy beside'. Although he had apparently been cured at Bedlam 'by beating and correction' he relapsed into madness and would come into church 'and there make many mad toys and trifles, to the trouble of good people in the divine service'. He was particularly prone to creating a disturbance while the priest was celebrating the Mass and try to lift women's skirts over their heads while they knelt in prayer. When the people complained to Sir Thomas, the Chancellor had the man arrested by the constable as he passed by his door, bound to a tree in the street before the whole town and beaten with rods 'till he waxed weary and somewhat longer'. Apparently the treatment appears to have been efficacious (though on the evidence the man is just as likely to have been an anti-papist fanatic as a certifiable lunatic) because Sir Thomas ends the story 'And verily God be thanked I hear none harm of him now'.

Confinement in a dark room, undergone by Malvolio in *Twelfth Night*, was one of the more civilized remedies prescribed for those whose wits were afflicted. This was an extension of the notion that the patient should have nothing to distract him. In *The Second Book of the Breviary of Health* (1552), Andrew Boorde, whom we have already met as one of the earliest English commentators on gypsies and their language, prescribed the following treatment for 'mania' which he distinguished from 'frenzy' because the former was not accompanied by fever, unlike the latter:

> First, in the chamber where the patient is kept in, let there be no pictures nor painted cloths about the bed nor chamber, then use in the chamber all things that is redolent and of sweet savours, and keep the patient from musing and studying, and use mirth and merry communication, and use the patient so that he do not hurt himself nor no other man, and he must be kept in fear of one man or another, and if need require he must be punished and beaten, and give him three times a day warm meat, and use to eat cassia fistula, and epithyme used is very good.

When Boorde wrote these words Bethlehem Hospital could accommodate some twenty persons; it is doubtful if any of them had chambers with pictures and

Dr Andrew Boorde, who prescribed a variety of questionable treatments for 'mania' and 'frenzy'

painted cloths but certainly they were punished and beaten and kept in fear of 'one man or another'.

In passing we may cast a shuddering glance at some of the other 'remedies' inflicted on the poor unfortunates who were judged insane. A book by Pope John XXI, originally published in the thirteenth century and translated into English in the middle of the sixteenth, gave the following recipe for insanity in its *Treasury of Medicines*: 'Take a frog and cut her through the midst of the back with a knife and take the liver and fold it in a colewort leaf and burn it in a new earthen pot which is closed and give the ashes thereof unto the sick person in his sickness to drink with good wine.' If this remedy had no immediate effect, we are asked to 'do so by another frog, and to do still [i.e. again] and without doubt it will heal him'. The same compendium asserted that a certain red stone found inside a swallow, wrapped in linen and carried under the patient's left arm was effective in certain cases and also that 'a roasted mouse eaten whole doth heal frantic persons'.

It seems that the governors of Bridewell devoted far more attention to the running of the house of correction than to the madhouse which was also their responsibility. Bedlam was situated between two sewers which were exceptionally noisome even by the standards of Elizabethan London. In the words of the report made after a visitation in 1598: 'It was so loathsomely filthily kept that it was not fit for any man to come into.' Needless to say, a keeper had taken over the concession from the city authorities at this time.

Committal proceedings were also informal to the point of non-existence. One of the sinister aspects of Bedlam in this period was that it was possible for unscrupulous operators to obtain the guardianship of feeble-minded but wealthy young persons whom they then delivered into the asylum. 'Hark, is there not one incurable fool that might be begged?' inquires Alibius the madhouse-keeper in Middleton's tragedy *The Changeling* (to beg a fool was to seek guardianship of him and thus control of his estate). Poorer folk could be committed by anyone in authority. Occasionally there was a faint murmur of protest from within the walls. Thus in 1574 a man was accused at Bridewell of committing his wife to Bedlam without any justification. The woman complained that for six weeks she was strapped to her bed by her husband and another woman till she was 'well nigh famished'.

At the beginning of the seventeenth century Bedlam held some twenty patients supported by parishes. The rest were private patients maintained at a weekly charge which varied between sixteen and sixty pence. Attempts at classifying the inmates did not in practice go much beyond the broad division into fools and madmen, that is the feeble-minded and the certifiably insane. Those who were harmless were allowed to wander freely about the building and yards, while the more dangerous were chained on beds of straw and beaten or humoured in turns. The keeper in the first part of Dekker's *The Honest Whore* explains:

> They must be used like children, pleased with toys,
> And anon whipped for their unruliness.

Earlier in the same scene he explains to a group of private visitors why they must leave their weapons behind:

> There are of madmen, as there are of tame,
> All humoured not alike: we have here some,
> So apish and, fantastic, play with a feather,
> And, 'though 'twould grieve a soul to see God's image
> So blemish'd and defac'd, yet do they act
> Such antics and such pretty lunacies,
> That, spite of sorrow, they will make you smile.
> Others again we have like hungry lions,
> Fierce as wild bulls, untameable as flies,
> And these have oftentimes from strangers' sides
> Snatch'd rapiers suddenly and done much harm,
> Whom, if you'll see, you must be weaponless.

Both the harmless and the violent were available for important visitors to amuse themselves with. The general public had to pay for admission. Amenities included a bowling alley within the precincts, if we can credit Henry Chettle's *Kind-Heart's Dream* (1592). The entertainment regularly provided included the beating of the inmates with wire whips and the opportunity to harass those who were chained from a safe distance. Visitors and lunatics were both easily amused, on the evidence offered by Nicholas Breton in his *Fort of Fancy* (1584): 'Think not that everything is pleasant that men for madness laugh at. For thou shalt in Bedlam see one laughing at the knocking of his head against a post, and yet there is little pleasure therein.' In the nature of things we can only conjecture what the unfortunate residents of Bedlam thought of being put on display (they were occasionally even hired out as a floorshow for weddings and similar festivities) though sometimes one of them spoke out. This happened in May 1619 for instance, while King James was walking in Theobald's Park, Essex. He was denounced in these terms by a Bedlamite: 'Stand, O King! I have a message to deliver thee from God. I brought thee out of a land of famine and hunger into a land of abundance. Oughtest thou not therefore to have judged my people with a righteous judgment? But thou hast perverted justice, and therefore God hath rent the kingdom from thee.' Alas we do not have James's answer on record.

It is heartening to record that unthinking amusement was not the only prevalent attitude towards the insane in Elizabethan times. 'Alack, alack, 'tis too full of pity to be laughed at' is the reaction of the madhouse-keeper's wife in *The Changeling* and Donald Lupton commenting on Bedlam shows that this humanitarian attitude was not confined to characters on the stage: 'It seems strange that anyone should recover here: the cryings, screechings, roarings, howlings, shaking of chains, swearing, fretting, are so many, and so hideous.'

To be inside Bedlam was a grim enough fate, but those who had been inside, or pretended to have been inside, found that it led to a fairly widespread and lucrative form of vagrancy; so much so that there was a thriving trade in forged Bedlam licences. At the sign of the Griffin at Waltham Cross one could be obtained for half-a-crown. These real or assumed ex-Bedlamites wandered up and down the land begging a living, sometimes playing the fool at fairs and markets but more often offering a fearsome aspect at a cottage or farmhouse door. Awdeley's description of one in his *The Fraternity of Vagabonds* (1561) seems to contain nothing to frighten the beholder: 'An Abraham man is he that walketh bare armed and bare legged and feigneth himself mad, and carrieth a pack of wool, or a stick with bacon on it, or suchlike toy, and nameth himself Poor Tom.' But when Edgar, in Shakespeare's *King Lear* is about to put on the disguise of 'Tom O'Bedlam' the picture he paints is far more menacing:

> My face I'll grime with filth,
> Blanket my loins, elf all my hair in knots,
> And with presented nakedness out-face
> The winds and persecutions of the sky.
> The country gives me proof and precedent
> Of Bedlam beggars, who, with roaring voices,
> Strike in their numb'd and mortified bare arms
> Pins, wooden pricks, nails, sprigs of rosemary;
> And with this horrible object, from low farms,
> Poor pelting villages, sheep-cotes, and mills,
> Sometime with lunatic bans, sometime with prayers,
> Enforce their charity. Poor Turlygood! Poor Tom!

And later in the play after he has assumed his new role he gives the demented king an even more frightening picture of the way of life that goes with it:

Poor Tom; that eats the swimming frog, the toad, the tadpole, the wall-newt, and the water; that in the fury of his heart, when the foul fiend rages, eats

☙The Fraternitye of Uacabondes.

As wel of ruflyng Vacabondes, as of beg-
gerly, of women as of men, of Gyrles as
of Boyes, with their proper names and qualities.
With a defcription of the crafty company of Coufoners and Shifters.

¶ wherunto alfo is adioyned the .xxb. Orders of Knaues, otherwyfe called a Quartern of Kuaues,
Confirmed for euer by Cocke Lorell.

(*)

¶ The Vprightman fpeaketh,
¶ Our Brotherhood of Uacabondes,
If you would know where dwell:
In graues end Barge which fyldome ftandes,
The talke wyll fhew ryght well.

¶ Cocke Lorell aunfwereth.
¶ Some orders of my knaues alfo
In that Barge fhall ye fynde:
For no where fhall ye walke I trow,
But ye fhall fee their kynde.

¶ Imprinted at London by Iohn Awdeley, dwellyng in little Britayne
ftreete without Alderfgate.
1575.

The title-page to Awdeley's *The Fraternitye of Vacabondes* (1561), in which he describes an ex-Bedlamite as, 'he that walketh bare armed and bare legged and feigneth himself mad, . . .'

cow-dung for sallets; swallows the old rat and the ditch-dog, drinks the green mantle of the standing pool; who is whipped from tithing to tithing, and stocked, punished and imprisoned; who hath had three suits to his back, six shirts to his body, horse to ride, and weapon to wear—

> But mice and rats, and such small deer,
> Have been Tom's food for seven long year.

Stocking and whipping were not the only hazards which Tom O'Bedlam (or his female counterpart Bess or Maudlin) faced in his wanderings. In Cornwall, the Abraham beggar was pushed into a river and ducked repeatedly until he was exhausted. For all that, the Bedlamite was a familiar if frightening figure in the English countryside for several centuries and survived in the northern areas into the middle of the eighteenth century. It is not clear whether released inmates of Bedlam were ever authorized to go begging about the country. What is evident is that many people believed there were such 'genuine' beggars and that an army of imposters took advantage of this belief. 'Some of these abrams', says Thomas Dekker in *O Per Se O* (1612):

> have the letters E and R upon their arms; some have crosses and some other mark, all of them carrying a blue colour. Some wear an iron ring, etc. Which marks are printed upon their flesh by tying their arm hard with two strings three or four inches asunder, and then with a sharp awl pricking or razing the skin to such a figure or print as they best fancy. They rub that place with burnt paper, piss and gunpowder, which being hard rubbed in and suffered to dry, sticks in the flesh a long time after. When those marks fail, they renew them at pleasure. If you examine them how these letters or figures are printed upon their arms, they will tell you it is the mark of Bedlam. But the truth is, they are made as I have reported.

Late into the seventeenth century the authorities were still trying to cope with the problem of sham lunatics. This announcement by the governors of Bethlehem Hospital appeared in the *London Gazette* in June 1675:

> Whereas several vagrant persons do wander about the city of London, and Countries, pretending themselves to be lunatics under cure in the Hospital of Bethlem commonly called Bedlam, with brass plates about their arms and inscriptions thereon: These are to give notice that there is no such liberty given to any patients kept in the said Hospital for their cure, neither is any such plate as a distinction or mark put upon any lunatic during their being

there, or when discharged thence. And that the same is a false pretence, to colour their wandering and begging, and to deceive the people, to the dishonour of the government of that Hospital.

But however dishonoured the governors felt, the sham Tom O'Bedlam continued to haunt the roads of England for nearly a century more; an inn sign in the village of Redbourne in Hertfordshire preserves his memory to this day, and he finally disappeared only when the institution from which he allegedly came transformed its nature and methods so radically that such a fearsome figure was no longer plausible as an ex-inmate.

* * * * *

After a brief interlude of Draconian savagery (1547–50) when branding and reduction to slavery were considered suitable deterrents to vagrancy, the sixteenth century saw a growing recognition of the principle of communal responsibility for the less fortunate members of society. This showed itself in the introduction of a parish poor rate, first in the form of a voluntary contribution and then, in 1563, as a compulsory tax. The parish was the administrative unit of Elizabethan life and parochial responsibility the governing rule of social organization. Concern that his parish would have to bear the financial burden of looking after a pregnant bawdy basket's illegitimate child led the constable of Ardleigh in Essex in 1605 forcibly to transport the woman while she was in travail to the neighbouring parish of Langham; it is sad to record that his zeal was unavailing for the Justices decided that the woman's child was properly a charge on the parish of Ardleigh.

Although there was a substantial gap between what went into the statute book and what actually happened, and although it was a long time before practice conformed to intention, the poor laws of the sixteenth century laid the foundation of a system of care and relief. This heightened responsibility marked the passing of the heyday of the Elizabethan underworld and it was centuries before an 'anti-society' emerged on a scale to rival the colour, diversity and elaborateness of the Elizabethan demi-monde.

Glossary of Underworld Terms

This glossary of Elizabethan underworld terms includes words that do not appear in the text. For words still in use, only the common Elizabethan meaning is given. An asterisk denotes a word in thieves' cant.

Abram or Abraham man   real or pretended ex-inmate of Bedlam
abroad   out of doors
adversary   opponent in a lawsuit
advise   observe
alate   of late
alehouse   lowest variety of drinking place, usually part of a private dwelling
angel   gold coin worth about fifty pence
**angler*   see curber
appall   make pale
apparitor   servant of ecclesiastical court
**apple-squire*   pimp, servant in brothel
artificially   artfully, skilfully
augmentation   see multiplication
**autem*   church
**autem-mort*   female vagrant married in a church
avoid   empty, bring out

bale (of dice)   set required for a game
**barnacle*   cony-catcher who comes in, apparently by chance, when game is already in progress
barrator   cheat, agent provocateur
Bartholomew babies   gingerbread dolls sold at Bartholomew Fair
**bawdy basket*   itinerant female pedlar and whore
**bawker*   bowler practising fraud at play
**beak*   magistrate
beg a fool   seek guardianship of feeble-minded person

207

bellman   watchman

*belly-cheat   apron

*bene   good

*bene faker of gibes   skilled forger of licences, etc.

*beneship   very good; goodness

beray   befoul

Bess o'Bedlam (Maudlin)   name given to female ex-inmate of Bedlam

*bird   cheater's victim

bitchery   whoredom

*bit, bite   coin, money

*black art   picking locks

Black Book   prison register

black crow   alchemical symbol for putrefying matter

blackjack   leather beer-jug coated with tar on outside

*bleating-cheat   calf or sheep

blessing witch   see cunning man

blind   obscure, remote

booty   dishonest play at bowls

*booze   drink

*boozing ken   alehouse

*bord   shilling

brabble   quarrel

brewis   bread soaked in salt-beef stock

*bring a waste!   Get out of here!

bristle dice   dice with short bristle attached to one edge

broker (or brogger)   middle man; receiver of stolen goods

Brownist   member of puritan sect

*budge a beak   flee from the law

budget   bag, wallet

*bung   purse, pocket

*cackling-cheat   poultry

cajoux (French)   undesirables; epithet applied to gypsies

calcination   one of the first six stages of alchemical experiment

callet   whore

candlemas   2 February, Feast of the Virgin

*cant   beggar's language—(verb) to beg

cap-case   travelling bag

*cassan   cheese

cassia fistula   variety of senna pods

GLOSSARY OF UNDERWORLD TERMS

caster   cloak
catchpole   arresting officer, sergeant
chapman   pedlar
charm   lock-picker
chats, cheats   gallows
cheapen   bargain for
Chapmans   Cheapside Market
cheat   thing
cheating, cheating law   art of cheating at dice
chennell   hard coal
chop a card   to change secretly the place of a card in a pack
clapperdudgeon   see palliard
cleym   sham sore
cloy   steal
Clubs!   rallying cry of London prentices
cly the jerk   be whipped
cog   cheat, especially at dice or cards
cokes   simpleton; name of chief dupe in Jonson's *Bartholomew Fair*
colour   pretence, appearance
committer   prostitute's client
conjunction   coming together of planets; one of the first six stages of alchemical
    experiment
constable   parish law officer
cony   dupe, victim (literally 'rabbit')
cony-catching   trickery, especially at cards
copesmate   comrade
couch a hogshead   lie down to sleep
counterfeit crank   pretended epileptic
country   county
cousin   dupe
cove   fellow
cozen   cheat
cozenage   cheating
cozener   cheater
crackmans   hedge
cramp-rings   fetters
crank   epilepsy
crashing-cheats   teeth
cross   coin
cuffin   fellow

crossbiting, crossbiting law   swindling, blackmail, etc., associated with prostitution

cross-lay   a bet intended to mislead hearer as to better's real intentions

cunning (wise) man or woman   person practising beneficent magic ('blessing witch')

curb   hook used to steal from open windows

curber   one who uses hooks to steal from windows

curbing   stealing through open windows

curbing law   art of stealing from open windows

cursitor   tramp

cut   speak

cut benely   speak gently

cut bene whids   speak truly

cuttle   knife

cuttle-bung   cutpurse's knife

cypress   black fabric or ribbon

darkmans   night

dearling   darling

dell   sexually unitiated female vagrant

demander for glimmer   female beggar pretending to have lost goods through fire

dewse-a-vill   the country

dissolution   alchemical process

diver   one who steals by employing a small boy to wriggle into rooms through small spaces

doxy   sexually initiated female vagrant

dragon   alchemical symbol for imperfect matter

draw   pick a pocket

duds   clothes, lag o'duds: bundle of washing

dummerer   mute (real or pretended)

Egyptian   gypsy

elections   astrological indications of auspicious moments for important actions or decisions

elf (verb)   twist, tie

engrossing   see forestalling

ephemeris (pl ephemerides)   almanac(s)

epithyme   plant parasitic on thyme used as medicine

eyne   eyes

210

fact   deed, crime
factor   collecting agent
fain   be inclined, compelled
fairy   spirit, often evil
falling sickness   epilepsy
*famblers   gloves
*fambling-cheat   ring
Familist   member of the Family of Love, a religious sect
familiar   spirit, often in animal form, supposed to assist witches
*ferret, ferret-beat   cheat
fet   fetch, fetched
*figging law   cutpurse's art
figure caster   astrologer
*filchman   truncheon
firing   firewood
flamen   (pagan) priest
*flick   thief
fly   witch's familiar spirit
*foin   pickpocket
*foist   pickpocket; the act of picking pockets
Foreign Officer   (after 1572) parish official with special responsibility for seeking
   out vagrants
forestalling (engrossing)   buying up a particular commodity before it comes to
   market in order to resell at an exorbitant price
forspoken   bewitched
frantic   insane
*frater   see proctor
French crown, pox, welcome, etc.   venereal disease
frenzy   madness
frieze   cheap woollen cloth
*fullams   weighted dice

*gage of booze   quart of ale
garnish   bribe given by prisoners to prison officers
*gentry cove   upper-class man
*gentry mort   upper-class woman
*gilks   skeleton keys
*glaziers   eyes
*Gracemans   Gracechurch Street Market
*grannam   corn

greenmans   fields
gripe   griffin
groat   coin worth twopence
grunting-cheat   pig
gybe   false licence; any document

'halek'   Simon Forman's code-word for sexual intercourse
harman beck   parish constable
harvest ale, Whitsun ale, etc.   annual festivals
headborough   parish constable or his assistant
hearing-cheats   ears
high law   highway robbery
high lawyer   footpad
high men, low men   dice wrongly numbered on one face
high-pad   highway
Hole   lowest grade of prison accommodation
honest (applied to women)   chaste, virgin
hooker (angler)   see curber
horary questions   method of determining answers to questions based on planetary
    positions at time of questioning
horn-book   board with letters of alphabet or Lord's prayer with transparent horn
    covering
horn-thumb   thumb with sliver of sharpened horn attached to it to make cutting
    purses easier
horse-courser   dealer in trained horses
hoyting   masculine behaviour

inkle   tape
intelligencer   spy, secret agent
interlude   short play, usually with allegorical characters
instrument   sexual organ
Irish toyle   Irish pedlar

jade   old horse
jakes   privy
jark   seal
jarkman, jackman   forger of licences
jet   strut about
jingler   horse-courser (dealer in trained horses)

GLOSSARY OF UNDERWORLD TERMS

ken house
kennel gutter
kern Irish foot-soldier
kinchin co vagrant boy
kinchin mort vagrant girl
Kit Callot traditional English rogue's name
knight of the post hired witness to person's respectability; perjurer
Knight's Ward middle grade of prison accommodation

langrets dice which are not exact cubes, being longer on one axis
la peine forte et dure (French) pressing to death
law branch of roguery
let prevent
lewd common, of no account, low
lib sleep
libbeg bed
libken sleeping place
lift rob a shop; one who robs shops
lifts stolen goods
lifting law art of stealing from shops
light-heeled wanton
lowing-cheat cow
lurch get more than one's fair share
lurcher cheater at bowls
lute (verb) in alchemy, to enclose in clay as protection against heat

margery-prater hen
mark sum of money worth about sixty-five pence
marker accomplice of one who robs shops
Master's Side highest grade of prison accommodation
Maudlin see Bess O'Bedlam
maunder(er) beggar
maunding begging
merripen gypsy word for 'life', and 'death'
minstrel any singer or musical entertainer
mistress jack, or smaller bowl in bowls
mistress o'the game prostitute
mittimus letter from Justice of the Peace or other authorized official committing a
   person into custody
moon-men gypsies

mort   woman
motion   puppet show
multiplication (augmentation)   in alchemy, the process of increasing the quantity of a given substance

nab   head
nab-cheat   hat, cap
nativity   prediction based on planetary positions at time of birth
neeze   sneeze
Newmans   Newgate Market
nip   cutpurse
nip a bung   cut a purse

occupy   have sexual relations with
ordinary   eating house
ought   owed

pad   road
padder   highway robber
paled   fenced
palliard (clapperdudgeon)   vagrant in patched cloak, often with sham sores
pannam   bread
Paper-house   Office of Counter prison
pardoner   licensed vendor of religious pardons (indulgences)
patriarco (patrico)   hedge priest
peck, peckage   food
pelting   low, mean
peradventure   perhaps
philosophers' stone   see red stone
pick-hatch   brothel
picking   picking pockets
Pie-Powder Court   court with jurisdiction over commercial activities of a fair
pigeon-holes   stocks
pippin-pie   apple-pie
piss-prophets   contemptuous term for those claiming to practise divination by examination of urine
pizzle   penis
pluck a rose   urinate
plumps   groups
poking-stick   ironing-rod

Glossary of Underworld Terms

prancer horse
prattling-cheat tongue
presently immediately
prig ride
prigger of prancers horse thief
proctor (frater) authorized collector for charity
profitable beneficial (not necessarily in material terms)
projection twelfth and final stage of alchemical process, the transmutation of base metal into gold
provant provisions
puckrel witch's familiar spirit
punk prostitute
putrefaction alchemical process

quacking-cheat duck
quaint elaborate, ingenious, intricately wrought
quarroms body, back, arms
quean slut
queer paltry, bad
queer-bird jail-bird
Queer-cuffin Justice of the Peace
queer-ken prison
quetch stir
quillets quibbles, sophistries
quoif head scarf

rakehell thorough scoundrel
red stone final object of alchemical experiment, the philosophers' stone that would transmute base metals into gold
regrating see forestalling
rich-guarded richly embroidered
rivel shrivel, wrinkle
roarer habitual user of fashionable oaths
rogue originally a vagrant with forged papers
Roman, Romany gypsy
rome great, good
Romeville London
ruffler able-bodied rogue claiming to be ex-soldier
ruffmans hedges
ruff-peck bacon

Rules, The   area near Fleet Prison where privileged prisoners were lodged
rumpscuttle   tomboy
runagate   vagabond

*sacking, sacking law   prostitution
sallet   salad
*santar   outside accomplice of one who robs shops
*sapient   itinerant quack
scot   bill, or share thereof
*scruff   scraps of food
scryer   crystal-gazer
*setter (or taker up)   first of a group of tricksters to strike acquaintance with a
    prospective victim
several   separate, individual
shamefast   modest
*shave   to steal cloaks, sword and similar smallish articles
shore   ? curving throw in bowls
*shrap   wine
*simpler   victim of swindle or blackmail associated with prostitution (cross-
    biting)
sinciput   part of skull
si quis   Latin 'if anyone'; first words of advertisement for employment posted
    inside St Paul's
skene   long knife used by gypsies
*slates   sheets
*smeller, smelling-cheat   garden
*snap (noun)   share
snout-fair   handsome
spital house   hospital
spurring   sexual prowess
St Bartle   St Bartholomew
stale   whore
*stall   decoy
*stalled to the rogue   formally initiated as a beggar
*stamps   legs
*stampers, stamping cheats   shoes
stew   brothel; originally those at Bankside in Southwark
*stow you!   shut up!
streightly   strictly
styptic   harsh, bitter

surfling water   sulphur water or similar cosmetic lotion
*swadder   see swigman
*swigman   pedlar

tables   backgammon
*taker up   see setter
term   period when London courts were in session
*tib   goose
*tip   give
tipstaff   prison official
*togmans   coat, cloak
Tom O'Bedlam   name given to alleged ex-inmate of Bedlam
toy   trifle, small object
trace   tread
traded up   brought up
*traffic   whore
*trining-cheats   gallows
'tronco'   Simon Forman's code-name for Mrs Forman
trug   slut, whore
trugging-house   brothel
turnkey   gaoler

unguentem aureum   'golden ointment', i.e. bribe money
*upright man   head of the hierarchy of vagrants

*vantage   general tendency of a die
*vaulting-house   brothel
venery   lechery
*verser   cony-catcher who begins game
videlicet   viz., namely
*Vincent   victim of bowling-alley trickery
*Vincent's law   cheating at bowling alleys

*walking mort   unmarried female vagrant, often pretending to be soldier's wife or
   widow
*warp   curber's look-out man
weasand-pipe   throat, windpipe
*whid   word; to speak
while   during, throughout
*whipjack   vagrant pretending to have suffered losses at sea

white money silver coins
white stone end product of first six stages of alchemical experiment
*wild dell female born into vagrancy
*wild rogue one born to roguery or vagrancy
Winchester goose prostitute
witch person male or female, claiming, or believed to possess, magical powers, celestial or diabolical

*yarrum milk

A Note on Books

As I have not distracted the reader with footnotes or elaborate references, it is particularly necessary to make as full an acknowledgement as I can of my debts. But since the subject is one that has interested me for a long time, I apologize in advance if I have inadvertently omitted to mention a book or article I have used.

The date of publication and the title of most of the primary works used is given when these are first cited. The most important among these are the cony-catching pamphlets of Robert Greene, Dekker's *Lanthorn and Candlelight*, Harman's *Caveat for Common Cursitors* and Awdeley's *Fraternity of Vagabonds*. All these and much other relevant material are assembled in *The Elizabethan Underworld* edited by A. V. Judges (1930) which also has a stimulating introduction and many helpful notes. Other important collections of primary material are *Tudor Economic Documents* edited by R.H. Tawney and Eileen Power (3 vols, 1924), a very useful collection of Elizabethan letters assembled by Thomas Wright under the title *Queen Elizabeth and Her Times* (2 vols, 1838) and *A History of Vagrancy and Vagrants* by C.J. Ribton Turner (1887) which reprints many Elizabethan statutes regarding rogues and vagabonds. A smaller but still very useful collection of documents is J. Pound's *Poverty and Vagrancy in Tudor England* (1973) which also lists several recent articles and theses on the subject. William Harrison's *Description of England* has been invaluable throughout.

The other chief source of information about Elizabethan low life which I have used is of course the drama of the period, particularly the plays of Jonson, Dekker and Middleton. Wherever possible I have tried to substantiate illustrations drawn from the drama (or from semi-fictional material such as the 'rogue' pamphlets) with examples from more formal documentary sources—court records, official letters and the like. Normand Berlin's *The Base String* (New Jersey, 1968) is a moderately useful guide to the use made of the underworld by three Elizabethan playwrights; he does not discuss Middleton.

The following secondary works have been helpful in varying degrees (the place of publication is London, unless stated otherwise):

Elizabethan Rogues and Vagabonds by F. Aydelotte (Oxford, 1913) one of the earliest and still one of the best studies of the subject, *Elizabethan Life in Town and Country*, an informal but scholarly study by M. St Clare Byrne (rev. edn 1961), *The Literature of Roguery* by F.W. Chandler (1907), *Philanthropy in England* by W.K. Jordan (1959), *The Early History of English Poor Relief* by E.M. Leonard (Cambridge, 1960), *Tudor Economic Problems* by P. Ramsey (1963) and the two volumes of *Shakespeare's England* by various authors (Oxford 1916). An earlier work with the same title by G.W. Thornbury also in 2 volumes (1856) is interesting and often informative, though not always reliable or scrupulous about citing the evidence for various statements.

For individual chapters I have used, in addition to the works mentioned above, the following:

For London life, Stow's *Survey* edited by C.L. Kingsford (2 vols, 1908), *Shakespeare's London* by T.F. Ordish (1904), *Bygone London Life* by G.L. Apperson (1903), the six volumes of *London* edited by Charles Knight (1843), *A History of London Life* by R.J. Mitchell and M.D.R. Leys (Harmondsworth, 1963), and *Stuart London* by Malpas Pearse (1969).

Much of the illustrative material in the chapter on prostitution in the suburbs is derived from two books by E.J. Burford, *The Orrible Synne* (1972) and *Bawds and Lodgings* (1976). Wherever I could I have tried to verify Mr Burford's references. I have also consulted *Southwark and the City* by David J. Johnson (Oxford, 1969).

The chapter on fairs is of course chiefly indebted to Ben Jonson's great comedy and to the notes and commentary on it in the great edition of Jonson's *Complete Works* by Hereford and Simpson (Oxford, 1925). The notes were particularly useful in indicating real life characters and events which Jonson dramatized. I have also used Henry Morley's *Memoirs of St Bartholomew Fair* (1859), E.A. Webb's *Records of St Bartholomew's, Smithfield* (1921) and *Popular Entertainment through the Ages* by S.F. McKechnie (n.d.). Most of the information regarding fairs other than St Bartholomew's comes from *Elizabethan Life: Disorder* by F.G. Emmison (Chelmsford, 1970).

I am conscious of my heaviest indebtedness to a secondary work where the chapters on witchcraft and astrology and alchemy are concerned. This is to Keith Thomas' brilliant survey *Religion and the Decline of Magic* (1971), from which I have taken not only numerous examples but also the framework of interpretation. I can only plead in mitigation that I find Dr Thomas' account wholly persuasive, notwithstanding some critical comment on it which I have also read. I have also found much useful information in *Witchcraft in Tudor and Stuart England* by Alan MacFarlane (1970) and in an earlier study, *Witchcraft and Demonianism* by C.L. Ewen (1933). Reginald Scot's great work on *The Discovery of Witchcraft* (1584) was of course my chief primary source for the evidence regarding contemporary witchcraft and alchemy. On the latter I also found *The Alchemists* by F. Sherwood Taylor (1952) very rewarding. *Witchcraft* edited by Barbara Rosen (1969) is a fascinating anthology of contemporary documents, skilfully arranged and introduced. For the account of Simon Forman's career I have used Dr A.L. Rowse's biography (1974) with a caution which doubtless the distinguished author would not approve of. Much of the information about Dr Dee comes from his Diary published by the Camden Society and the biography of P.J. French (1972).

For knowledge about alehouses used in the chapter on vagrants I am indebted to the book by F.G. Emmison already mentioned, to *Vexed and Troubled Englishmen* by Carl Bridenbaugh (New York, 1969) and to a lecture delivered to the Sussex University Renaissance Seminar by Dr Peter Clarke.

I have used no secondary sources, other than those cited in the general section for the chapter entitled 'Autolycus and His Tribe'. On gypsies and their early history in England, various articles in *The Journal of the Gypsy Lore Society* have been very informative especially, 'Supplementary Annals of the Gypsies in England before 1700' by H.T. Crofton.

An article entitled 'London's Prisons' by Clifford Dobb in *Shakespeare Survey 17* (Cambridge, 1964) gave me much information and told me where to look for more. An article on 'Constables, Fictional and Historical' by C. Evans in *Shakespeare Quarterly XX* (1969) was both enjoyable and informative. On Bedlam and Bridewell the two books by E.G. Donoghue (1914 and 1923 respectively) were invaluable. *Three Hundred Years of Psychiatry* by I. Macalpine and R. Hunter (1963) provided much useful information on the early treatment of mental illness.

Index

Page numbers in parenthesis refer to illustrations in the text. † indicates titles and authors in the list of sources.

222

INDEX